ENDORSEMENT OF UNVEILING JOY

This riveting memoir took me through the range of all my emotions.

I laughed, I cried, I raged, I sobbed. I have never been so emotionally engaged, motivated, and inspired all at the same time.

Above all, my main takeaway was that no matter what we go through in life, if we don't give up, we will see the light at the end of the tunnel. We can come through our struggles, and walk out with grace, and become even stronger than we ever could have imagined.

Through Unveiling Joy, you too can unveil your own joy.

Thank you Joy Iweka, for taking me and all your readers on this extraordinary journey.

Dr. Shola Ezeokoli
Physician, Bestselling Author, Speaker, Professional Coach.

Unveiling Joy

a memoir

Joy Iweka

Contents

Foreword...ix

Dedication xi

Acknowledgments...xiii

Prologue.. xv

Chapter 1 1

MY SOURCE, MY ROOTS

That Little Corner of Africa – Obosi

Chapter 2 6

NEW TOWN, NEW TERROR

My New Life Begins

Chapter 3 26

SECONDARY SCHOOL

Another Life, A Little Escape

Chapter 4 47

FROM LAGOS TO JOS

A New Phase of My Life

Chapter 5 70

FINDING AND LOSING A FATHER

Chapter 6 82
GRADUATION AND RETURN TO LAGOS

Chapter 7 100
MARRIAGE
New family; New Drama

Chapter 8 137
AMERICA BECKONS

Chapter 9 159
FLIGHT OR FIGHT

Chapter 10 187
FORGING NEW PATHS

Chapter 11 238
DIAMOND OF BIAFRA

Blurb/About 265
About the Author 267

Foreword

There is a rare treat in store for the reader of Unveiling Joy.

This memoir reads, not as the expected arc of the average Nigerian girl's life, but a remarkably eye-popping journey of a woman who is admirably grounded in her self-assessment and unrestrained vulnerability. Joy Iweka masterfully takes us with her on a ride marked with her fears, hopes, bliss.

I know Joy - as a friend.

We've broken bread in each other's living rooms, hung out on a girls' spa day, called on each other just to chat. Yet, it took reading Unveiling Joy for me to be truly immersed in Joy's life.

I truly connected with her experiences as it relates to growing up in Nigeria, becoming a mom of two gifted children; being a woman who strives to leave the world better than she found it - same as Joy.

I know Joy - as a leader.

She often tells me that sharing the harrowing story of her escape and her abuser's pursuit, in the Facebook community I founded and lead, Female IN (FIN), was one of the most freeing experiences she's had. Her leap of faith helped set free hundreds of women who were struggling to move on from abusive people, communities and an enabling system which historically devalues and diminishes women. And that's just a single story from her incredibly thrilling journey as written in Unveiling Joy.

I know Joy - as a winner.

This is a woman the world applauded when her children went viral for their academic excellence. The energy in her laughter, her deep love for her daughters, family and friends; the determination in her countenance as she tells of her visions for herself, and her service to others endeared me to her even more. In this book, she paints an unforgettable picture of it all.

I know Joy and knowing joy did not sufficiently prepare me for Unveiling Joy.

This book, Unveiling Joy, reveals in its entirety, the highs and lows of the life of a woman who lived through heart wrenching helplessness, grief and loss. Marked by tough decisions and inspiring victories, her story is so shocking, that just when you think you see a clear path of where Joy is headed, life throws her a twist that might blow your mind.

Unveiling Joy is a reminder that while many of us had no control over the life that was handed to us, we certainly have the ability to create a new path and to define the story we tell about it.

Lola Omolola
Founder, Female IN (FIN), Community Engagement Strategist.

Dedication

To everyone who grew up feeling un-
loved. This is for you. You matter.

Acknowledgments

Writing this memoir was one of the bravest things I've had to do. It forced me to relive some of my most difficult memories. It forced me to confront demons that I thought were best left buried.

It all started when I would write short snippets on social media, when my daughters would sit beside me with keen interest as I narrated to them, some parts of my peculiar journey, and it all culminated when I shared a chunk of my life on a large all-female social media platform.

I would like to thank my daughters, Ketandu and Amara, my biggest fans and my first audience. My big cousin, Chukwudum Ikeazor, who stood by me like a rock, encouraging me that I had a story to tell the world. My cheerleaders; Ifeoma Egbuna, Terwase Ogbonnaya, Doo Obileye, Bunmi Ajai, Elizabeth Nomwhange, Mernan Oluyede, Ugonna Menakaya, Catherine Okpiabhele, Philipine Ishak, Chioma Ngaikedi, Chioma Okoye and Andrea Mbanefo. Not forgetting, Ayo Mathews who did not live to see this memoir in print.

Thank you Lola Omolola, for giving me the large platform to share my story, an experience that made me realize that my story was worth telling.

To my indefatigable editor – Ifeoluwa Watson, thank you for your patience and your professionalism. Thank you Shola Ezeokoli, for your support and author coaching services.

Prologue

"Why did you have me?" I yelled at her in rage.

"If you knew you wouldn't love me, why did you have me?"

Staring me in the face, my mother replied, "I wasn't trying to. I tried to get rid of you but you wouldn't go. That Enugu doctor told me to leave the pregnancy alone after my third attempt…"

It felt like I had just been hit with a ton of bricks. I stumbled out of my mother's house for what would be the last time for many years. I was 19 years old, a first-year student at the University of Jos, and on the brink of suicide.

The seven-mile bus ride home to my grandparents' felt much longer. But it was time that I had to reflect upon what had transpired in the last hour. I placed my head on the window of the weather-beaten jalopy, struggling to grasp what had just happened. The rainy season was well underway, so the potholes had expanded exponentially, making it hard to put my thoughts in motion as the bus jostled in and out of them on the rough, worn roads.

I stared at the bus conductor as he collected the fares, harsh lines etched across his dark oily face. I wondered what pain each of those lines represented, and if he had to beg for his mother's love like I did. I knew in my heart that it was time to stop pleading for my mother's acceptance. I had tried in the past to understand the many unanswered questions about my past, but this only led me to more questions. I shut my eyes for a brief second and thought about the words she had so carelessly flung at me. They were cold words that would linger in my mind for a long time. But I didn't have to dwell on them – not right now. It was too painful. Suppressing the lump that rose in my throat, I surrendered my mind to the awkward waltz of the rickety bus and the repetitive pounding of the potholes.

Chapter 1

MY SOURCE, MY ROOTS
That Little Corner of Africa – Obosi

I CAME INTO A FRAGMENTED WORLD. ON THE CUSP OF A PAINFUL history; of lives lost in a relentless bloodbath. They called it a war, but in action, it was a genocide.

It had all started in January 1966, barely five years after independence, a group of disenfranchised army officers staged a coup to overthrow the civilian government and rid the country of corruption. This group of coup plotters was led by two officers of the Southern Igbo ethnic group. The prime minister, who was from the Northern Hausa ethnic group, was killed alongside twenty-one others, the majority of whom were also northerners. A southern Igbo military officer was then named the military head of state, a gesture that confirmed to the northerners that this coup staged by Igbos, targeted northern civilian leaders.

Six months later, a counter-coup was launched by northern military officers. This time the Igbo head of state, as well as other

Igbo officers, were assassinated. The die was cast for a rampage of revenge.

I was born shortly after this civil war by an Igbo mother and fathered by a non-Igbo Nigerian soldier. Growing up, I was a dichotomy of some sort; a painful reminder of the war that ripped Igbo families apart and changed their lives forever. It was not uncommon to find children like me in many homes across Igboland. It was regular knowledge that during the war, Nigerian soldiers abducted and even raped many young Igbo girls, leaving them with children. Many of those children would grow up and go in search of their fathers. Some families chose not to reveal the true identity to some of these children, sweeping those details under the carpet as part of the many casualties of the Biafran war.

Though I wasn't born during the war, I lived it through the sadness stamped on the faces of the Igbos that recounted the stories. They spoke of the uprising starting in Kano, a major city in the North with a large presence of Igbos who held sway in the commerce of the city. Their places of business and homes were burnt. They did not escape the flames themselves.

The Igbos fled the North to the Southeast in droves.They were hunted like prey and vehicles were ransacked to pick out the "yan-mirins" – the derogatory term, used by the Northerners to identify the Igbos. It was gotten from the thirsty fleeing Igbos' plea for water, "Nye'm miri" (Give me water). They were singled out for their fair skin and distinct inflections and beheaded in the light of day.

When the road trail proved too dangerous, they turned to the rail. I could imagine the stuffiness and putrid air from the over-crowded trains, and the fear in their eyes from the shadows of grief cast in the eyes of the storytellers.

I tasted the lack that the war brought in the stiff curve of my grandmother's mouth when she talked about the quest for salt. Salt, one of the commonest cooking condiments, became gold as the Nigerian Army continued to push the Biafran Army deep into their villages. Mama's eyelids fluttered as she remembered the horror of salt hunting. The women, afraid of being abducted, smeared their faces with coal and mud as camouflage. As young children, we shared stories of the war in hushed whispers, comparing notes. One of my friends recounted how children, swollen-bellied from kwashiorkor, fell like flies each day. The tales were grim but paled in comparison to the actual terror and hardship the Igbos had suffered.

After over two years of harrowing distress, Biafra surrendered and the documents were signed on January 15, 1970. The Nigerian Head of State, Gen. Yakubu Gowon gave his famed speech titled, "The Dawn of National Reconciliation," extolling the eagerness of the government to embark on the task of healing the nation's wounds.

Igbos slowly but cautiously began to make their way back to their hometowns; towns that they had abandoned as they escaped the vicious attacks of Nigerian soldiers. They also began the agonizing process of burying their fallen soldiers. Heart-wrenching cries of widows could be heard across communities as they lowered their loved ones into the graves. Some families received the bodies of their dear sons, and for others who never received the bodies, funeral rites were performed in absentia and empty coffins lowered into the graves. There were the desperate optimists who remained hopeful that their sons would return home one day.

The defeated Biafrans, survivors of the cauldron, resumed citizenship in a country they had fought so desperately to leave. They began an uncertain and excruciatingly difficult future as Nigerians.

The war was over but its travails were forever engraved in the minds of the Igbos. This was the Nigeria I was born into.

Soon after the war, Igbos began the painstaking journey of rebuilding their communities and businesses. They had received the paltry aid of twenty pounds per family from the Nigerian government. This was a slap in the face for many Igbos considering the fact that the vast majority owned flourishing businesses across many regions of the country. Properties owned by Igbos in many of these regions were declared "Abandoned Property", and shared out among the indigenes of the area, mostly well-connected bureaucrats and political figures who had cooperated with the Federal Military Government during the war. It was a long hard road to recovery.

My grandfather, Dr. Jonas Emenanjo Iweka, a U.K. trained medical doctor and his family, had fled to Nnobi, a neighboring town during the war. As the war wound down, he relocated his family to his hometown of Obosi and returned to Onitsha, a southeastern city, to begin the journey of rebuilding his medical practice. Papa was instrumental in saving the lives of many Biafran soldiers during the war. He extracted many bullets from wounded soldiers, saving many limbs from amputation. He tended to the civilian population in Nnobi and its environs, treating kwashiorkor ravaged children along with other healthcare workers from the area who also fled the war as their hometowns fell to the federal military.

My earliest recollection of my childhood is living in Obosi with my grandmother. Obosi, a town southeast of Onitsha, was relatively untouched by the war. Many indigenes of Obosi who had bolted during the war slowly returned home. Almost every week, we would hear a cry of jubilation in the distance. They were cries of families whom their sons presumed dead, returned home from the war. This kind of celebration carried on into the mid-seventies.

My grandparents were the only parents I knew. They doted on me. I was loved by them, but I was also aware that they were my grandparents and not my parents.

My mother was the fifth of ten children. I didn't see much of her, but she came home to visit on some weekends. I didn't know much about her, except that she was a lady who always looked unhappy and was a teacher in Nnobi, the town her family had fled to during the war.

I was a curious child with a quick mind and a love for books. Surrounded by books, and loving nannies, I was oblivious to my mother's absence and lack of open affection.

One of the weekends my mother visited, she came with a tall dark bearded man. I approached him cautiously as he handed me a book. It was an Enid Blyton storybook. I stared intently at the colorful cover of the book, flipping it open to peruse its content. I liked the book but I decided that I didn't like the man. As a little girl, I didn't like men who wore beards for some reason.

Later that evening, I asked my mother, "Mummy, does my dad wear a beard?'

"No," she answered curtly.

Satisfied, I retorted, "Good, because beards are ugly."

This became the only vision I had of my father – the man who didn't wear a beard. This was also one of the few times I asked about him as I was afraid of upsetting my mother. I sensed that it was not a topic she wished to broach. I turned to my nannies for answers, but I was often left with a stiff uncomfortable silence or a change of topic.

That marked the beginning of my search for an identity. The only certainty on my plane of existence was my name – Joy Nnenne Iweka.

Chapter 2

NEW TOWN, NEW TERROR
My New Life Begins

I WAS A HAPPY-GO-LUCKY CHILD LIVING MY BEST LIFE, TRAVERS-ing through the three cycles of – eat, play, sleep, and press repeat. I was the apple of my grandparents' eyes. I feasted on my select food choices that comprised corn flakes, custard, and Quaker oats. I shunned the regular staple meals of rice, beans, garri and fufu. I wore imported designer clothes, St. Michael's from England. They were bought in Leventis, a trendy popular store in the 70s.

I loved to read my storybooks but I disliked going to school. Every morning, when I was woken up to prepare for school, I began a crying fest that was only quietened at the sight of my grandmother's cane, which she never used on me. I just wanted to play.

Playing house with my cousins was the best pastime during my childhood at Obosi. Empty sardine cans served as pots, sand as rice, stones as meat, and grass as vegetables.

Behind my aversion to school was a reason unknown to my grandparents. My cousins and I were driven to school together. I was in the nursery section while they were in the primary school. We had to follow a bushy path to cross from one side to the other, so we could leave school together. Toby, my mischievous cousin, would start to run and tease me that "ndi ntor" (kidnappers) would catch me. In a flurry of tears and fear, I would chase after him, trying to keep up with his longer strides. I didn't quite understand what the kidnappers were capable of, but the mere thought of being captured and being without the comfort of my family sent shivers of dread down my spine. I was a sheltered child, well catered for and babied, so much that I was still being piggybacked on a regular basis by my nanny, a position mostly reserved for growing infants. My simple life had yet to take its unexpected turn.

A few months after my seventh birthday in 1978, Aunty Stella, my mother's younger sister, arrived to take me to live with her family. Aunty Stella was married to a doctor whom she met during his housemanship at my grandfather's hospital. They were moving to Makurdi, a city in the Middle Belt of Nigeria, to start a new life. That morning as we loaded my suitcase into the car's trunk, I could hear animated voices from the neighboring compound.

"What's that noise?" I asked Nwakego, my nanny.

She waved her hand in dismissal, and said, "Their son has just returned from the war. They thought him dead and had 'buried' him many years ago."

Over the years, I had become familiar with that noise – the joyous screams of families whose sons returned from war. My mind drifted as I wondered if my father was one of the sons who were presumed dead at war. I wondered if he would also go home one day like the rest. Shaking off the nagging thought, I jumped into the car, waving goodbye to my wonderful nannies and grandmother who had all been an integral part of my early childhood.

Aunty Stella's husband, Uncle Nicholas, drove us. He was a dark, stocky man who wore an Afro. I had met him a few times when he visited Obosi with my aunt. He didn't smile much and something about him made me a little uneasy. I sat stiffly behind him, his thick afro hair blocking my view of the road as we journeyed north. The roads were mostly deserted except for a few cars that passed us occasionally. Mirages glistened across the tarred roads, teasing the shiny black tires of our automobile. It was a long tedious journey that seemed to last forever. My impatience grew as the trip progressed.

The sun had begun its slow descent when we arrived at Makurdi. I pressed my face to the window, taking in the view as the clouds slowly gobbled up what was left of the sun. I was glad that we had finally arrived.

Aunty Stella's house was a cream-colored three-bedroom bungalow with a detached boys' quarters (servants' accommodation). The walls were faded and in need of a fresh coat of paint. It sat on a vast piece of land surrounded by luscious green grass. Two gigantic mango trees stood in front of the house waiting for the season when they would yield their fruit. The derelict, water-logged boys' quarters sat at the back of the compound, and beside it was a big barren cashew tree. I walked around, taking in the view.

Suddenly, I heard my name in the distance, "Joy, come inside." I briskly made for the front door, stopping in the middle of the almost bare living room as I was introduced to the two maids who lived with Aunty Stella. They were both teenagers and couldn't have been older than seventeen.

"Hello, my name is Nwadinma," the taller one said, perusing me from head to toe.

I smiled nervously as I mumbled a weak, "Good evening."

"Come with me," she said, "let me show you the room."

I followed her to one of the rooms, and pointing to my suitcase, she said, "Here are your things, you can take a bath when you're ready."

I thanked her shyly and proceeded to soak in the sight of the room. It was sparsely furnished, almost bare except for a chest of drawers, a bunk bed, and a queen-size bed. The window overlooked the mango trees, and I could see the branches swaying softly to the gentle nudge of the evening breeze.

That night after dinner and a warm bath, I lay on the bunk bed listening to the sound of rustling dry leaves on the nearby trees. I hugged my pillow, the distant chirps of crickets in the waterlogged grass serenading my mind like a sweet lullaby. I fell asleep.

As I settled into my new home, I began to miss Obosi. I missed my grandmother and my nannies. It was the rainy season, and I hardly saw the sun as the clouds were often dark with rain. I longed for the sunshine in Obosi. I yearned for the sound of my grandmother's voice as she laughed in conversation with her best friend, Nne Azu.

I didn't like Makurdi after all, and so one day when I couldn't bear it any longer, I said to Aunty Stella, "I want to go home." She didn't look surprised or impressed by my demand. She simply glanced at me and said, "You're homesick. You will get used to being here soon."

Days became weeks and weeks turned to months but I still felt that ache in my heart that Aunty Stella called "homesick." I begged her many times to take me home to Obosi but it fell on deaf ears. It was soon clear to me that this was my new life and I had to adjust. I had to learn to live with that ever-present pain in my heart that refused to go away. With the twists and turns that came with navigating my new life, it gradually became a dull ache.

At the beginning of September, I was enrolled in an elementary school about one mile away from the house. Demonstration Primary School was different from the school I had attended. I was driven to my nursery and primary school at Onitsha every day when I lived in Obosi. In Makurdi, I had to trek to school alone and it was a good distance. I came home many afternoons exhausted. I was aware that children from less privileged homes walked to school, unaccompanied, but until then, I had neither the experience nor the stamina that it required.

One afternoon, I returned from school and heard noises from the room I shared with Nwadinma and Nwanyiuka. Uncle Nicholas was in the room with both girls. Aunty Stella stood by the door as if to bar me from going in.

"Please brother, please!" they both begged. Their loud shrieks of pain were terrifying as Uncle Nicholas' leather belt scourged their skin. I stood glued to the spot, confused as to what they had done to incur such venomous wrath from Uncle Nicholas. Later that night, Nwadinma said, "He flogged us because he said we were bad girls." I didn't understand what she meant and she tried to explain more. "He made us undress so he could peer down our private parts to check if we were still virgins." These conversations were all in Igbo, our native tongue. But the familiarity of the language didn't lessen the awkwardness of that dialogue.

I wondered if that had anything to do with what happened most nights when we turned off the lights to go to sleep. I often heard strange noises and giggles coming from their bed along with what seemed like a wrestling match. Many nights, I could only fall asleep after I muffled those sounds with my hands over my ears.

Two weeks later, I came home from school, and Nwadinma and Nwanyiuka were gone. I didn't even get a chance to say goodbye. The following week, they were replaced by a houseboy, Mmadu, and a house-girl, Adora. I had just turned eight when they arrived. Aunty Stella was expecting her second son that October, and so we needed more help in the house. Mmadu took an instant dislike to me, and I had no idea why. I soon realized how much Nwadinma had pampered me. I felt as though I was thrown in a lion's den after being coddled in a kangaroo's pouch. Within a few weeks my chores became heavy in volume and intensity. It was my duty to serve Uncle Nicholas his dinner when he came home late from the hospital. Every morning when I woke up, I swept the courtyard and washed the baby napkins (diapers) which had been soaking overnight. While everyone was in bed, I sat in the kitchen, exhausted from my long day, nodding off between swiping at mosquitoes that fed on my flesh as I waited to serve Uncle Nicholas his dinner. I woke up tired every morning, and I was late to school every day. I slowly began to unravel. I was the granddaughter of a wealthy medical doctor who was once overindulged at every turn. Now, I was a laborer, worse than a domestic helper. It was a rude awakening, one that I struggled to come to grips with.

Then, it started – the bedwetting. The first time it happened I was shocked and embarrassed. I never wet the bed when I lived with my grandparents. I didn't know what to make of it or how to handle it, so I threw clothes over the wet bed and pretended it didn't happen. It occurred the following night and the night after. By the end of the week, the room I shared with Adora developed the putrid stench of urine which attracted Aunty Stella's attention.

"So you wet the bed Joy! You should be ashamed of yourself." She made me take the wet mattress out in the sun to dry which brought about massive humiliation as Mmadu took it upon himself to mock me and call me "dirty pig," and "bed-wetter."

Aunty Stella's patience with my bedwetting wore thin, and one day she announced to me, "You will no longer sleep on a bed in this house. I will buy you a mat and you will sleep on the floor from now on."

The first few nights of sleeping on the mat were unpleasant. I lay on the cold hard floor listening to the crickets and frogs chime their symphony. It was soothing and it helped distract me from the discomfort. I wet the mat the next morning and had to take it out into the sun to dry. At least it was better than ruining Aunty Stella's mattress. As the weeks wore on, I learned to deal with Mmadu's cruel jokes about my bedwetting. It was clear that the jokes were not going away anytime soon.

My condition continued to decline. Adora and I were soon moved from the main house to the boys' quarters; that dilapidated structure that was detached from the main house and surrounded by water-logged grass. Frogs croaked in the wet grass every night. The trash from the house was dumped behind our window, and the stench pre-vented us from opening the window to let in fresh air. The room was hot and stuffy. We looked forward to every other week when Mmadu would burn the refuse dump, handing us the respite of opening our window until the garbage and the stench returned. Aside from the stuffiness of the room, there were also mosquitoes to contend with: Enormous insects that bred in the wet grass surrounding our abode, unleashed terror on us every night. Many times when Adora and I couldn't get any sleep from the unrelenting creatures, we would get up and start to kill them. Our already murky walls were soon covered with bloodstains from these mosquitoes. We would sometimes joke about these insects draining every last drop of blood out of our bodies.

I was exhausted at the end of every day, but I dreaded going to sleep. I hated being at the mercy of mosquitoes and the bedwetting that had taken what was left of my dignity. Uncle Nicholas began to weigh in on my bedwetting situation. He decided that the antidote to my malady was spanking; as if the humiliation I felt each morning was not enough punishment. So, flog me he did.

From then on, the floodgates of corporal punishment were thrown open. I was flogged for every little error, no matter how mundane. I was scourged for accidentally breaking a dish or forgetting to relay a phone call. Uncle Nicholas' whip was no benign one. It was made from an old telephone cable. This improvised source of terror hung on the wall above Uncle Nichola's dining chair where it was handy after a hearty meal which happened to be when he liked to flog me. It seemed that whipping me was his dessert, perhaps something that aided his digestion. I lived in constant dread of Uncle Nicholas.

Aunty Stella and Uncle Nicholas welcomed their second son in late October 1979. He was a chubby light-skinned baby who looked nothing like his parents. Three months after his birth, they had his baptismal ceremony. Friends gathered in their living room chatting and having a good time. I peered through the crack of the kitchen door, marveling at how much they seemed to be enjoying themselves. I was about to settle into my routine daydreaming when Uncle Nicholas poked his head in the kitchen and said, "Bring me the baby's cup." I knew exactly what cup he was asking for. I got up briskly, found the cup, and made for the door with it. As I opened the door that led to the living room, my heart began to race. I suddenly felt self-conscious. I couldn't walk into that room full of important-looking people while I was dressed in scruffy clothes.

Every now and then, a quiet voice would remind me that I was the beloved granddaughter of a very important man. But I no longer carried myself with confidence. I seldom remembered who I was. On an evening like this, with all these elegantly dressed people, I was reminded of who I once was and who I had become. I froze in the corridor, clutching the white cup nervously.

Uncle Nicholas got tired of waiting for the cup so he marched towards the kitchen, and found me by the door. He snatched the cup from my hand and slapped me hard across the face. Deep waves of pain rocked my slight frame as I staggered backward. I had read a comic about someone seeing stars when they got slapped hard. I found out on this day that those stars were literal ones! His palm etched deep marks across my face. I deserved the slap, I thought to myself as I rubbed my numb cheek. I had wasted his time.

With each passing day, I grew distant from my Aunt. She was no longer "My Aunty Stella" from Obosi. She had become a cold stranger. The one who sat and watched her husband rip my flesh with a wire and did nothing to stop him. She never hit me, but she did not protect me either. She would occupy herself with some chore or sit back and watch him ravage my delicate frame.

I missed Obosi desperately. I longed for the mother I barely knew and the father I never knew. My 8-year old mind sought to understand why I didn't have a father. Didn't he love me? Didn't he want me? Did he die at war? I wondered if he was tall and thin with deep-set eyes or if he was thickset. I no longer cared if he was bearded. I wished he would come and rescue me. I willed him to show up, tell me how much he loved me, tell me he was sorry for being away for so long, and take me away.

I was lucky if I had lunch before 6 p.m. on many days. Uncle Nicholas' day was highly regimented. He turned in for a two-hour siesta every day after lunch. Aunty Stella would retire to the bedroom with him and sometimes forget to dish my lunch. The giant mango trees in front of the house served me on many days. I would munch on the fruit, oblivious to the unripe tangy taste. Sometimes, I would steal a bottle of coke from the crate or even a few scoops of the baby's Cerelac (infant cereal), and powdered formula. It brought me deep shame and guilt that I had to resort to stealing baby food to assuage my hunger. I loved my little cousins and even though I was maltreated by their parents, I never did anything to hurt them. They were both much younger than I was and the only people close to siblings that I had.

We went to church every Sunday. My aunt and her husband were very religious. Uncle Nicholas was a lay pastor in the Anglican Cathedral Church where we worshipped. I hated going to church because I wore the same dress almost every Sunday. I felt the kids in church noticed, and it caused me great shame and distress. On the days that Uncle Nicholas preached, I would sit in the back pew and watch him read and expound scripture. It left me confused as I assumed preachers were usually kind. The whip-wielding Uncle Nicholas at home was totally different from the Bible-toting Uncle Nicholas in church.

Christmas approached that year and I heard we might travel to Obosi. I was beside myself with joy. It had been two years, and I saw that as my opportunity to leave for good. The thought kept me sane through October and November. I made a calendar on the back of my school notebook counting down to the D-day.

We finally traveled to Obosi for Christmas. It felt as though I had been away for many years. Everything and everyone looked different. My grandmother had a few age lines on her face, and my grandfather looked a little older too. I shared my ordeal with my nannies who still lived with my grandmother.

"Aunty Stella's husband is a really wicked man," I said to them. "He flogs me with a wire and Aunty Stella starves me. She gives me two thin slices of bread for breakfast, and I don't get to eat lunch until 5:00 pm on most days."

I don't think they believed my story. It was dismissed as the fantastic tales of an imaginative child.

That Christmas, my mother came to Obosi to take me to spend some time with her new family. She was married to that same bearded man whom I had disliked at first sight. I felt she had betrayed me by marrying him. My mother had not changed much. She was still emotionally withdrawn, but I was happy that she at least took me to her new home.

The next day was a Saturday. I accompanied my mother to the market to shop for Christmas. Onitsha Main Market was one of the biggest markets in West Africa. The Igbos were great merchants. Bouncing back from the ravages of the Biafran war was no easy feat, but the Igbos made it seem effortless. Barely ten years after the war that crippled their lives, their businesses were thriving once again, not only in the southeast but also in northern Nigeria where they had suffered the devastating loss of life and property. Little wonder they were nicknamed the Jews of Africa; their grit was second to none.

Main Market was busy on this last Saturday before Christmas. Hundreds of shoppers bumped against one another as they hurried to conclude their shopping. Christmas carols blasted loudly from the makeshift speakers hanging on poles above stalls.

I locked my tiny fingers with my mother's as we meandered through the large crowds, carefully avoiding the piles of merchandise on the ground. As we went from store to store, we ran into a tall thin woman who was a colleague of my mother's in the school where she taught.

"Good afternoon ma," she greeted my mother warmly.

"Happy Christmas!" my mother replied.

They chit-chatted a bit, and glancing down at me she asked, "Who is the little girl?" My mother still clutching on to my hand and never breaking eye contact with this woman said,

"She is my sister."

I started to say, "No, I'm not your sister. I'm your daughter," but something held me back. From that moment, I started to think that maybe she really wasn't my mother, that maybe my real mother and father were together somewhere, and someday soon, they would come and get me. I started to believe that just like the soldiers that went to war and were still returning home after many years, my real mother and my father would return home one day.

With the festivities in the air, I hardly had time to mope. The fun of going from house to house with my cousins, eating Christmas rice and chicken, dulled the sharp reality of the anguish that awaited me.

With January came the trepidation of returning to Makurdi with Uncle Nicholas and Aunty Stella.

"I won't go back with them," I repeated incessantly.

"I will die before I get in that car with them."

No one seemed to pay me any attention.

On the day we were to leave, I was bundled into the car screaming and kicking. "They beat me with wire." I protested.

"They starve me. I don't want to go back there," I continued to cry and plead to no one in particular. I buried my face in the sleeve of my pink blouse in a desperate attempt to muffle the painful sob that rocked my entire body. My heart broke into pieces. I felt betrayed by all those grownups in Obosi who I begged to rescue me from the cruel clutches of Uncle Nicholas and Aunty Stella. I wasn't sure I would survive another bout of the Makurdi experience: the incessant bullying from Mmadu, the starvation, the mosquitoes, and Uncle Nicholas's vicious wire. I planned to kill myself - it appeared to be a far easier option than what awaited me.

An unusually hot city, Makurdi ushered in Harmattan winds in full blast, the cool dry January air shriveling up the mango and guava trees. I sat beneath the barren trees staring into the distance. I felt empty. Pain spread across my chest and down my stomach. This was worse than the pain Aunty Stella called "homesick." That night, the man with the deep-set eyes came to rescue me. I was crying and asking what took him so long. He held me tenderly, wiping my tears with both hands. "It's okay. I'm here now and they're never going to hurt you again."

I woke up. My cheeks were damp. I had wet the bed.

Uncle Nicholas' wire left bruises on my skin. Wounds that would heal only to be ripped open with a new bout of flogging. The rainy season approached. The mango and guava trees bloomed, so did the plush carpet grass that surrounded the compound. But the change in seasons didn't result in any changes to my plight.

One morning, as Uncle Nicholas left for work, he asked us to cut the grass. The section apportioned to me was the thick carpet grass in the waterlogged area.

"Cut this before I get back from work today," Uncle Nicholas instructed us as he made his way to the front door. Mmadu being older and quite dextrous with the cutlass finished his portion in record time. He went on to help Adora with her portion. Then, he taunted me, saying there was no way I would finish my portion before Uncle Nicholas got home. He was right – I struggled with the unrelenting carpet grass, my fingers burning with blisters from the bare machete's handle.

The sun made its way west, casting shadows on the stubborn unyielding grass. My body ached from hours of being hunched over. I heard the sounds of children laughing in the distance. I reminisced about the little girl who once lived in Obosi with her grandmother and who didn't have a care in the world. Uncle Nicholas' white Peugeot 504 made its way into the driveway as I made one last futile swipe at the grass.

"Why did you not finish cutting that grass?"

I had no answer except that my 9-year old body could not handle the task of cutting thick carpet grass buried in the water and surrounded by crickets, frogs, and grasshoppers. He grabbed the wire off the wall, lifted it high above his head, and brought it down on my already bruised hand. He took turns on each hand. Each stroke sent waves of excruciating pain through my hands and down my spine.

I tried to maneuver from the wire so that it wouldn't touch the blisters on my hands, but I didn't have much success with that. By the time he was on the fourth round, my hands and wrists were numb.

That night, I lay down, nursing the blisters from the cutlass and Uncle Nicholas' wire. It was another rainy night. The cacophony of rain on the zinc roof above me and the sound of croaking frogs soothed me into a fitful sleep. I dreamed about my father again.

One evening, Uncle Nicholas' older sister, Mama Ify, and her daughter, Ify came to visit. I had heard about them but had never met them. Ify was a pretty gangly teenager with a toothy smile and a foreign accent. She rolled her tongue every time she spoke and pronounced certain words like I heard people do on television. They lived in East Africa where her father was a diplomat; that might have been why she sounded different. Her mother was tall, buxom, and looked just like Uncle Nicholas. As I set the dinner table that evening, Aunty Stella reminded me to include an extra place setting for Ify. She was an only child and was obviously beloved. I could also tell that she was indulged. I served her at the table, brought her an extra dessert spoon when she needed one, and made the bed in the room where she slept. It appeared that I was going to be her maid for the duration of their visit. While Ify lounged on the brown cushion that padded the wooden chairs in the living room, I sat on the floor next to her. I was not allowed to sit on the chairs.

On this certain morning, the whiff of her breakfast plate of bacon and omelet teased my nostrils as I struggled to gulp down the yam and palm oil that was mine. I forced down the lump that rose in my throat, willing myself to believe that this lump had everything to do with the dryness of the yam and nothing to do with the fact that I longed for my life in Obosi. I missed sitting on the mahogany dining table each morning, staring down in delight at my bowl of Kellogg's corn flakes coated in sugar and doused in rich Peak milk. I missed my Sunday morning breakfast of bacon, eggs, and baked beans; that rich English breakfast that was preceded by a trip to the St. Andrew's Anglican Church. The loud chimes of the rusty church bells were often a reminder that it was time to don a pretty Sunday dress and trudge up the hill to the old cathedral clutching my grandmother's hand. I would sit beside her in the front pew, her large flamboyant "ichafu" head-tie blocking the view of everyone who sat behind us.

I decided I didn't like Ify. She reminded me of who I once was; of everything I had that was stolen from me. I was jealous of her, envious that she was treated so nicely and I, so shabbily. I rolled my eyes at her when she wasn't looking, and I stamped my foot in defiance every time I was asked to run an errand for her. I felt guilty for disliking her so much. Even though she treated me with slight condescension, in retrospect, that could be interpreted as how most teenagers treated those younger than them. At the end of their visit, I was glad to see her leave.

Although I couldn't justify my dislike for Ify, I had every reason to dislike Mmadu who continued to taunt me day and night.

"Bastard!"

"What is bastard?" I asked Mmadu. This was a new word in the list of names he called me.

"You are a bastard. Bastard of Biafra," he snarled. "You have no father."

That was the first time anyone referred to my father.

"Well… everyone has a father," I stuttered.

"You don't have one. You are a bastard!" Mmadu retorted, in full glee.

My body began to shake. My voice quivered as I tried to come up with something to say to him. I couldn't think of anything. Was that why nobody would tell me about my father? Because I didn't have one? The man with the deep-set eyes did not exist after all. My hopes of him ever coming to get me had just been dashed, annihilated by the cruelty of Mmadu's revelation.

I ran to Aunty Stella. "Mmadu said I'm a bastard, is it true that I don't have a father?" I asked, wiping the tears that escaped the corners of my eyelids.

"That word must never be mentioned in this house," Aunty Stella said to Mmadu who of course denied saying it.

My dislike for Mmadu intensified. He had found a new weapon to taunt me with. He called me that word at least once every week, and every time he did, something died in me a little. He pummeled me with that word until one day I decided I would stick up for myself.

"You may have a father Mmadu but you smell really bad," I hurled back at him. He raised his left arm to his face, sniffing at his soaked armpit as if to dispel my claim. I was enjoying the person I had become, one who was no longer afraid to stand up for herself.

Aunty Stella overheard us many times. I was always the one whose voice was audible. Mmadu was clever enough to jab at me in hushed tones. One Saturday morning, Mmadu and I were bickering again and Aunty Stella called us to the courtyard.

"Joy, I hear you insulting Mmadu all the time. He is a boy and he is older than you. You are going to learn a lesson today."

"But Aunty, don't you hear him call me bastard all the time?" I replied.

"I told you people already, I don't want to hear that word in this house."

Turning to Mmadu she said, "I want you to beat her so that she will know you're a man and give you respect."

Aunty Stella grabbed a small wooden stool and sat, signaling Mmadu to beat me. Mmadu was a strong teenage boy. He didn't need a second invitation to do what he had always wanted to do. Aunty Stella sat and watched as Mmadu threw me to the ground. He sat on my stomach, punching my face. I will never forget the look of sheer pleasure on Mmadu's face as he had his way with me or the amusement of Aunty Stella. Her facial expression could have easily passed for that of an eager spectator watching a gladiator fight in an ancient Roman Colosseum.

I never talked back to Mmadu another day after that. "Bastard," he would say, his upper lip curled in that ugly twist that I hated so much. He claimed that the day he beat me, he also farted in my face. That became his latest taunt.

Later that year, my grandmother's great-niece, Oby, came from

Obosi to visit. Oby was in her final year of high school. She was beautiful and had a larger-than-life personality, lighting up every room she walked into. I once overheard Aunty Stella saying that she was grooming her to marry Uncle Nicholas' little brother. I felt safe in Oby's presence. She was quick to notice that Mmadu bullied me nonstop. One day when she couldn't take it anymore, they had a shouting match.

"She is Aunty Chari's daughter," she shouted at Mmadu. "God forbid that I will stand back and watch you treat her like trash."

"Go and sit down," Mmadu screamed.

"Why don't you make me," Oby yelled back, approaching him fiercely. They were both teenagers. Oby was fearless and matched him toe to toe.

Mmadu retreated. He did not bully me as long as Oby was in the house. It felt good to have someone protecting me from Mmadu. I had forgotten that I was Aunty Chari's daughter. I had forgotten that I was Aunty Stella's niece. I had forgotten who I was. Oby's presence started to remind me again.

My anxiety heightened as Oby's departure date drew close. I knew what awaited me when she left.

True to my expectation, Mmadu's constant bullying returned. As Oby waved at me from the back seat of Aunty Stella's white Honda Civic, I wished more than anything that I could go with her. For many hours after she left, I wandered around the compound feeling lost and empty. Thick black clouds of despair began to follow me everywhere. They were there in the morning and when I went to sleep at night. I could see them, almost touch them. Sometimes I heard voices in the clouds, telling me to end the pain; to kill myself.

One morning, while I sat beneath the guava tree staring into the far distance, I saw a movement in the compound next to ours. The house had been vacant for many years; the wild green grass so tall, the faded white bungalow was barely visible. That house scared me. I was always afraid to look at it while I stared through the kitchen window at midnight waiting for Uncle Nicholas to return home. It looked like a haunted house. I got up and walked gingerly towards the bushes. I saw her. Long bristle grass covered part of her face, giving her the look of an apparition. I waded through the lawn until we were barely inches apart. She was beautiful. A long pointed nose sat on a perfectly symmetrical face. She brushed off the green bristles that caught in her rich black curls and smiled, exposing a perfect set of ivory-colored teeth. She looked about my age and was the same height as I was.

"Do you live here?" I asked, pointing at the bungalow buried in the grass.

"Yes," She answered. "We moved in last night."

"My name is Joy."

"Janice."

Janice and I hit it off immediately. Her father was a professor. He found a teaching job at the University of Agriculture, Makurdi, and moved from Ghana with his family. Janice had a tall lanky twin brother, Japhet, and a big sister, La Verne. She also had a little brother, Isaac. Their mother was gorgeous. I could tell from her skin tone that she was of mixed race. They were a beautiful family. It wasn't long before I discovered Janice loved books. It had been so long since I had read a new book. Having outgrown those colorful Enid Blyton storybooks my grandparents bought me, I was in search of new stories and new adventures. Janice came into my life with the right combination of both. She began to ply me with books. Every few days, we would meet across the lawn. I would hand her the bundle I had finished reading and she would hand me a fresh pile.

We would sit on the lawn and talk about the characters in the books. Their once rundown bungalow now sparkled with fresh white paint and a nicely mowed lawn. It also housed the only pleasant memory of my life with Aunty Stella.

The dark clouds began to disappear - the ones that followed me everywhere telling me to kill myself. I became immune to Mmadu's cruelty, no longer caring that he called me unpleasant names. Burying myself in books, I would transport myself into the lives of a character that I really liked. Books became my safe haven. They were the balm that bound my broken heart. They were my happy place and my addiction.

It didn't take long to devour every book in Janice's library. One day, I came up with a plan – we could ask Olivia for books. Olivia lived across the street and was much older than us. I always saw her sashaying down the street clutching a book in her hand. I would peer closely to get a glimpse of the book cover. "Tell La Verne to ask her for books." I tried to convince a hesitant Janice. One week later, Janice ran across the lawn waving a thick book at me. "I got a book from Olivia," she said, grinning from ear to ear. She handed me Danielle Steel's *Coming Home*.

"This book was very sad," I complained to Janice a few days later.

"Maybe, I should ask for books with happy endings," she said.

My quest for finding happiness in my imaginary world of books didn't stop me from reading the next Danielle Steel and the one after that until I exhausted Olivia's library.

Those books saved my life.

Chapter 3

SECONDARY SCHOOL
Another Life, A Little Escape

Ⓣ WAS TIME FOR A NEW BEGINNING. LIKE A BIRD MIGRATING from the Sahara Desert to the luminous greenery of the Serengeti, I flapped my wings in readiness for my freedom flight. The year was 1982 when I turned eleven. In August, I received news that I passed the state common entrance exam into secondary (high) school. I was going to attend the Queen of the Rosary Secondary School, a catholic boarding school located in a small quiet town called Gboko. It was a decent school run by nuns in conjunction with the state. I was excited at the prospect of going off to boarding school, but sitting on the crest of my excitement was the anxiety of moving to a new town and meeting new people. I struggled with the growing anticipation that gnawed at my insides as the day approached. Surely, nothing could be worse than Mmadu's merciless taunts or the torture from Uncle Nicholas's wire.

Attached to my acceptance letter was a list of required items for boarding school life. Aunty Stella was not one to waste resources on frivolities like clothes, and so I got new clothes only at Christmas. Those came in the form of dowdy gowns all of which I absolutely detested. But I looked forward to shopping for school and eagerly accompanied my aunt to the market when the day came.

Aunty Stella scowled at the long checklist as we headed towards the entrance of Modern Market.

"You don't need this," she said, crossing off yet another item. My eyes narrowed as I glanced at the once robust list, now stripped of more than half its contents. I walked behind her, as we went from shop to shop looking for the best bargain on a suitcase. It was a blistering sunny day, so hot that eggs could fry on our skins. I wiped my damp forehead, cringing as she haggled over the price of another suitcase. Aunty Stella finally settled for a grey metal box. It was the cheapest she could find. I dragged the metallic contraption to the car, the sharp edge of the suitcase scraping my calf as I hurried to keep up with her pace.

I began the countdown to September, the time of my emancipation. I didn't allow the dismal shopping experience with Aunty Stella to dampen my elation. My chores didn't seem so unbearable anymore. It was only a matter of time before I left them all behind.

The first Saturday in September, Mr. Chris dropped by. He was a good friend of Uncle Nicholas who lived in Gboko. His sonorous voice boomed in the living room as he chatted with Uncle Nicholas.

"Joy quickly, go and pack your things. Chris is taking them to Gboko," Aunty Stella said.

There wasn't much to pack. The metal box we bought already contained most of my necessities. I threw in the packet of St. Louis sugar, Cabin biscuits, and the small tin of Peak powdered milk and carried the box to Mr. Chris' car.

Early Monday morning, Aunty Stella drove me to the bus station.

"When you get to Gboko, walk straight to your school, and don't talk to anybody. Your school is next to the motor park. Chris will bring your box later today or tomorrow."

I had spent weeks dreaming of that moment, but in that instant, the child in me craved for a little succor. My insides quivered at the thought of embarking on that new sojourn without the trusted guidance of an adult. I had a million things I wanted to say to Aunty Stella. I wanted to tell her I was scared. I also wished to tell her I didn't want to travel to Gboko alone, but my dry mouth and parched tongue betrayed me when I needed them to intercede for me. I settled into my seat in the bus, wedged between two burly men. Everything happened very quickly.

It was a ninety-minute ride to Gboko. The weather-beaten bus made its sluggish descent down the deserted road, passing small obscure villages. There wasn't much to see as we traveled along. I drifted in and out of sleep and in between, I thought about Janice. I didn't get a chance to say goodbye to her. I tried to focus on my new life, what my new school would look like, and if I would make new friends easily.

We pulled into the bus station around noon, and as I got out of the bus, I took in the sight of my new surroundings. It was a small, developing town. The blazing sun illuminated the dusty brown untarred roads, lending the town a shabby look. I sighed nervously. Queen's was supposed to be close by.

"You can't miss it," I remembered Aunty Stella reiterating.

Glancing around in expectation, I instinctively picked a random direction, hoping, somehow, to stumble across the school.

A hundred brisk steps later, it was clear that my adventitious sojourn only led me farther and farther away from my desired destination. Scared and disoriented, I turned around, a ploy that only seemed to worsen my predicament. Shoulders slouched from exhaustion, I began to walk in what seemed like circles. My head hurt from the hot dry weather, and my dry throat begged for hydration. After several futile attempts, I did what a scared 11-year old would do – I burst into tears.

"Why are you crying, small girl?" A short hairy man stopped to ask.

"I can't find my school," I said, lips quivering.

"Which school is that?" he enquired with a scowl. Aunty Stella had warned me about speaking to strangers but if I was to find respite from the scorching sun, I realized I needed to speak up.

"Queen's," I muttered.

"Oh, Queen's. Come with me."

He took me by the hand and led me through some back roads until we got to the front of a gigantic compound with a signboard that read – "Queen of the Rosary Secondary School." I thanked this kind stranger profusely and made my way into the compound.

Red and green Ixora flowers lined either side of the entrance and tapered into a roundabout. A gentle breeze flapped the Nigerian flag that stood tall at the center of the roundabout. A sigh of relief escaped my dry lips as I beheld what would be my abode for the next five years. It was beginning to feel like home already. Leaving behind the horrific adventure of the past hour, I matched towards the administrative block, my dry throat suddenly self-lubricating.

Later that evening, Mr. Chris arrived with my grey metal box.

Settling into my new life and new school was seamless. I made friends quickly. One of my first friends was Shirley, a precocious child who had passed the entrance exam and gotten into secondary at the age of eight. She was three years younger than the rest of us. The first few weeks were tough for Shirley. She cried every day.

One day, I asked her, "Does being away from your mom make you sad?"

She said, "Yes."

"Do you get this terrible pain in your chest when you think about home?"

She nodded.

I said, "You must be homesick."

I knew that pain. I understood it all too well. It was that painful ache I felt in my chest every time I thought about Obosi. Aunty Stella called it homesickness.

I had my share of struggles. I was assigned the top of the bunk bed in my dormitory. I was terrified that I might wet the bed and it would trickle down to my bunkmate. This fear kept me awake many nights in my first week. But it never happened, not once in all of my five years in boarding school. I left bedwetting in Makurdi. It was part of a very painful past.

Like a caterpillar waiting to blossom into a butterfly, I was spinning my silky cocoon, and leaving behind the ugliness of my recent past. But there was a certain awkwardness that arose from being different from the others. It crept up like hives on my skin when the other girls spoke of their families with longing. It hung like a shadowy presence when I saw the abundance the other students enjoyed. I tried not to draw much attention to myself but my lack stuck out like a sore thumb.

"Is that all you came with?" A senior student enquired, staring at the scanty contents of my metal box.

I nodded awkwardly.

"This won't last you three days."

I discovered that this senior was right. I tried to stretch my provisions but by the end of the first week, they were gone. The food rations supplied by the school were small, and terribly bland. Students depended on their provisions from home to tide them over. I had no provisions to fall back on. I looked forward to the chime of the dining bell. I didn't care what the food tasted like; I was usually just too hungry.

Many of the seniors were bullies. But no bullying compared to that of Mmadu's. I was grateful they didn't know the details of my life like Mmadu did, and so they couldn't call me any horrible names. The seniors sent us on errands all the time. They called us "Injukas." I'm not sure what it meant but I knew it was derogatory. First-year students were seen as little minions who hung around after school to heed to seniors' every command. Sometimes in the middle of siesta, they would rouse us from sleep, "Injuka! Form one!"

"Form one," was another way they referred to us and it simply signified our grade in the school. On hearing the seniors' beckoning, we would all leap off our beds and rush to the bedsides of the seniors. The seniors would pick a random "injuka" to send on an errand. The errand could be anything from fetching them water to drink, to washing their clothes, or even fanning them while they slept.

Boarding school was tough but I was tougher. The bathrooms were disgusting so we would wait till late evening when it got dark and early morning before sunrise to shower in the open space outside.

In the stillness of the night, after lights-out, there were alleged strange occurrences that buzzed on every student's lips in the daytime. They were paranormal tales of strange beings sharing our living space. "Bush babies" believed to be spirits of aborted babies who cried all night for their unjust deaths. There was also the mysterious "Madam Koikoi," whose notorious clicking heels' sounds, ruled the night. Almost every boarder could swear that these experiences were real. I am not certain if I ever heard those sounds or imagined them but with the rationality that comes with adulthood, I would like to believe they were noises from wild cats.

Four weeks into the school year, we had our very first visiting Sunday. We trooped to the front of the school where parents of nearly every new student had converged, waiting to hear all the exciting and not-so-exciting stories about boarding school life. A blend of sadness and fascination belabored my fragile mind as I watched parents come and go. The young boarders unveiled brown boxes handed to them, squealing in delight at the abundant supplies of provisions and the delicious home-cooked foods. I sat and waited patiently, hoping that perhaps someone would come to visit me.

The sun cast its final shadows as the rusty old bell chimed its dinner call. If there was a silver lining to that day, it was the fact that I could have multiple rations of the bland, soggy palm oil rice, since my fellow young boarders shunned the disgusting school food that day for their mothers' gourmet meals.

I hadn't dreamed about him in a long time, but that night I dreamed about the man with the deep-set eyes.

Visiting Sundays were pretty much the same each time, except that I stopped going to the front of the school with my friends. I saved myself the shame and embarrassment of repeatedly showing up only to find that no one visited me.

The boarding school regimen was not a struggle for me. We had classes in the morning, lunch, siesta, afternoon prep, evening prep, and lights were out by 10 p.m. I discovered I was a good student and that perhaps what I lacked in Aunty Stella's house was structure.

Once this structure was established, I was in the top four of my class for the entire five years of boarding school.

My love for books never waned. I had a renewed source of supply from my classmates. Within one month of boarding school, I was introduced to books by Pacesetters Publishers. I would spend many prep nights buried in Helen Obviageli's *Evbu My Love* or Jide Oguntoye's *Too Cold for Comfort*.

One visiting Sunday several weeks later, I was summoned to the school's front yard. I had a visitor. I had no idea who it might be. I walked slowly as I approached the building, and parked in front of the principal's office was Uncle Nicholas' white Peugeot 504. I broke into a sprint. There, seated in the car were Aunty Stella, Uncle Nicholas, and their three children. They had a third child earlier in the year, a little girl this time who again, looked nothing like either of her parents. They brought me home-cooked food and some provisions. Uncle Nicholas smiled at me and this felt weird and almost sinister, as the only time he ever looked my way was when he flogged me with the wire. I had finally earned the bragging rights that someone visited me on visiting Sunday. I also ate home-cooked food from a shiny metallic bowl like my friends, never minding that I wasn't allowed to eat from that dish back at home. But it didn't matter. All that truly mattered was life in that moment. They never visited again.

Apart from the regimented life at boarding school, I was exposed to new principles that formed the building blocks to my character as an adult. Being a catholic school, we were taught by nuns. There was a particular nun who stood out in her bearing and expectations from the students: Sister Kathleen, our Home Economics teacher. She was tall and handsome with a deadpan expression. Classes with Sister Kathleen were like attending a finishing school. She had a fit if you dropped something and you bent over to pick it up. Instead, she insisted we bent from the knees. Such was the depth of these ingrained teachings, that I still practice many of the ethics I picked up from those catholic nuns many years ago.

I placed those nuns on a high pedestal. They represented a certain dignity that appealed to my sense of decency. Their convent was a block away from our hostels. The immaculate walls and the polished floors beckoned me to join the convent. I wasn't Catholic but I was drawn to the religion and its propensity for order. The grounds of the convent were just as pristine. The statue of the Virgin Mary, surrounded by rose bushes, captured its age-old sanctity. I always looked forward to the weekends when the reverend sisters invited us to the convent to wash the statue of Mary. I also loved to attend Mass and watch the priests in their immaculate white robes administer the sacraments. My young mind didn't quite grasp the novelty of the Catholic Church, but I was intrigued by it all.

One weekend, Shirley went to the Convent to wash the statue of Mary and she was stung by a swarm of bees. We were horrified by her puffy face as she sat in the principal's office bawling profusely from excruciating pain. Her parents showed up soon after to take her home. She was away from school for a week. The evening she returned, we were in class for prep and she tapped me on the shoulder and asked, "Can I borrow your Agricultural Science notebook?"

"Sure," I said, opening my desk to hand her the thin notebook. Leaning back on my desk, I shifted my focus back to my novel. The class was usually quiet during prep, but all of a sudden everyone was giggling uncontrollably. I looked up, wanting to be a part of the joke. My heart stopped momentarily, mortified by Shirley's actions. She had passed my notebook around the class, and they were sniggering at the thin forty-leaf notebook that I used for three subjects.

A notebook of this kind was usually used for just one subject, but Aunty Stella had bought me only four notebooks for 12 subjects. She said I didn't need a separate notebook for each class. So, here I was, the joke of the class. Snatching back my notebook I vowed never to let it out of my sight another day. If there was something I learned in my first term at secondary school, it was that you couldn't rely on anyone.

At the end of the school term, I returned to Makurdi for the Christmas holiday. All the students were excited to go home but I was indifferent. I was no longer afraid of Aunty Stella's house because I knew that I was only there for a short time until school resumed. It was with the same indifference I met Aunty Stella's announcement that we would be traveling to Obosi for Christmas. Makurdi or Obosi, it no longer mattered either way. Boarding school was my new safe place, one where I didn't expect too much. The adults in Obosi had failed me, leaving me to suffer cruelty in the hands of Mmadu and Uncle Nicholas. I no longer cared and I no longer missed Obosi. However, beneath my apathy, was a furtive excitement that rested on the threshold of caution.

It was Christmas Eve and I was home in Obosi. The aroma of chin-chin frying in vegetable oil permeated the air. Christmas carols boomed on loudspeakers in the neighborhood, and firecrackers could be heard in the distance. Glittering red and green decorations hung precariously on the living room walls. Our compound buzzed with activity. Igbo families typically return to spend Christmas in their hometowns, and my cousins were home from every region of Nigeria.

On Christmas Day, we trooped to the dusty red streets to watch "mmuo agwo," the traditional masquerades that showed up during festive periods to entertain and harass young indigenes. These masquerades, dressed in costumes and masks made from raffia palm leaves, took to the streets chasing and flogging young boys and girls. The belief that these masquerades were spirits or deities made it all the more thrilling and spectacular. We camped at the entrance of St. Andrews Anglican Church waiting for the masquerades. We didn't wait long as one tumbled out of nowhere, running towards us, waving his bamboo cane. Shrill sounds of fear and excitement erupted as we ran into the church premises. Masquerades were not allowed past the church's entrance so the church was our refuge. This carried on until sunset when we dragged our dusty tired feet home. We would be back on the streets again on New Year's Day. Christmas in Obosi was magical. It came with the trappings that mattered; family, food, and the communal love that made everyone forget the squabblings of the past year.

January came and with it, the apprehension of returning to boarding school. My fear of Uncle Nicholas and Mmadu suddenly paled in comparison to the starvation that awaited me in school. I needed more provisions than Aunty Stella bought me the last time, and I also wanted a nice fancy suitcase. I informed my grandmother and she asked me to make a list of everything I needed. Oby, my erstwhile protector from Mmadu's taunts, helped me make a list. It comprised every item Aunty Stella had crossed off my earlier school list and more. Early the next morning, we made our way to Onitsha Main Market.

"You said your classmates laughed at you for using one thin notebook for three subjects right?" Oby asked as she grabbed two-dozen notebooks off the shelf of a bookstore.

"Yes," I whispered, cringing as I recalled that evening. It was a day I wished to delete from my memory.

I thought I had taken care of my major problem, to avoid being ridiculed amongst my mates. But while I celebrated my abundant stock of provisions for school, Aunty Stella seethed in the background until we left Obosi.

"How dare you humiliate me like this," she yelled when we got home to Makurdi.

"People will think we bought nothing for you," she railed. "What are you doing with this box? It's too expensive! And this flask?" pointing at the toffee-colored thermos flask I clutched nervously.

"This is such a waste of money!"

The thermos flask slipped from my hands and shattered. Oby had taken great care to select the flask, and I didn't even get to use it.

I saw Janice briefly before I left for school. We sat on the lawn like old times and caught up on the latest books we had read. My classmates had introduced me to romance novels. I told Janice all about the tall dark handsome men I read about in the Mills & Boon paperbacks.

"Isn't it funny that they all have chiseled faces and square jaws?" I asked, giggling bashfully.

Aunty Stella's annoyance did not dampen the excitement I felt about going back to school with nice things and generous provisions. It would be a while before I started to starve again. She dropped me at Mimi's house the morning I left. Mimi was one of my good friends from school. She had offered me a ride when she found out that I traveled unaccompanied to school. I was grateful I didn't have to get on public transport to Gboko. I still shuddered every time I remembered my first experience, how I got lost.

"My dad will be happy to have you ride with us," she had said on the last day of school. Her dad was a retired army officer with a large heart and a great love for his family.

Aunty Stella watched as Mimi grabbed one end of my fancy new suitcase. I was past caring if she was still upset about my shopping spree. I was just glad I would no longer be the odd one out amongst my mates.

Apart from the classroom routines, extracurricular activities were also a big deal at Queen's. I wasn't much of an athlete but I was happy to cheer on my more athletic friends and dormitory mates as they took up major roles in the Inter-House Sports event. Inter-House Sports were yearly competitive sporting events between "School Houses". Upon becoming a student of the school, everyone was assigned to a "House", represented by a different color. I belonged to "Iveren House", which was pink. We sometimes won the first prizes in Relay Race and High Jump. The events were colorful, with each house dressed in their assigned colors of pink, blue, green, and yellow. Parents often graced the occasion to support their children as they participated in the competitive sports. I was content to watch from the sidelines because I didn't want to be the center of any attention. I fared better with short story competitions where my words instead of my person took center stage. My only attempt at a performance was the make-believe concerts Mimi and I had, singing Abba's songs after many days of memorizing the lyrics. School life was fun and engaging. I didn't really look forward to the holidays.

When I went home to Makurdi for the Easter Break, Janice was gone. Her father got a new job in Swaziland. I stood under the guava tree where I first saw her, fighting back the tears that welled up in my eyes. The grass that once covered the white bungalow had slowly begun to grow back. A few days later, Mmadu saw a green snake crawling into the room I shared with Adaora in the Boys' Quarters. Adora always left the door ajar, letting in mosquitoes that feasted on our blood all night. But a poisonous green snake was by far more dangerous. I stood inches away from the door terrified out of my mind as Mmadu rummaged through the room looking for the snake. I heaved a big sigh of relief when I heard the clank of the machete as Mmadu chopped at the snake. I lay in bed that night, wondering what might have happened had he not seen the snake as it crawled into the room, and for the first time, I was grateful for Mmadu.

The Easter Break was over quickly and I was happy to return to school. Janice was gone and Makurdi felt empty again.

The period from Form One to Form Five flew by quite fast. Nothing much changed except that from being an "injuka", I became a senior, one very much unlike my predecessors. I had experienced first hand the painful effects of bullying, and I wasn't about to mete out the same treatment to my juniors.

Hunger was no longer a stranger to me. I had learned to manage the measly supplies of provisions I got from my aunt. In Form Four, my fate took an unexpected turn for the better. Nne Azu's daughter moved with her family to the neighboring town of Yandev. Nne Azu and my grandmother were best friends, so it was natural for her daughter, Azu to consider me her kin. She visited me in school often bearing gifts of money, provisions, and home-cooked food. Azu's gentle brown eyes and her kind disposition were a true portrayal of her deep devotion to the Christian faith. My trips to Makurdi became less frequent as I began to spend my short breaks in her home. She lived in a beautiful estate in Yandev with her husband, an engineer at the famous Benue Cement Company (BCC). Visiting her was a delight and a respite from the dreariness of my aunt's somber home.

I visited Makurdi during the midterm break before my graduation. Aunty Stella and Uncle Nicholas had moved to Hudco

Quarters, a prestigious part of Makurdi. Their new home was a four-bedroom duplex with a semi-detached servants' quarters. I was relieved that the new servants' quarters was not surrounded by water, an indication that I wouldn't be up half of the night swiping at mosquitoes. The smell of fresh paint bounced off the immaculate walls as I strolled around the new house. Mmadu and Adora were gone and Aunty Stella had a new housemaid, Mary, a seventeen-year-old girl with bloodshot eyes and dark brown skin. As I made my way to the detached apartment with my bags, Mary said to me, "Your things are in the main house upstairs." Taken aback by the news, I turned around and made my way back to the house and up the stairs to a room she showed me, wondering why I was moved into the main house. Did that also mean I could now eat at the dining table and sit on the couch? I tucked my bags away in an obscure corner of the room, afraid that I might smudge the fresh pink paint. I sat gingerly on the edge of the narrow bed made of brown hardwood, scared that it was all a mistake, and that soon Uncle Nicholas would peek his head into the room and ask me to take my things down to the servants' quarters. I was left to ponder on my new living situation, wondering if Mmadu's leaving had anything to do with it.

My graduation was a quiet affair. No one showed up, not Aunty Stella or my mother. Not that I expected my mother, since she never visited or sent anything for the duration of my time in secondary school. However, a tiny part of me still hoped she would attend. As I gathered my belongings for the last time, it dawned on me that this phase of my life was over for good. I stared at the empty bunk beds and the vacant lockers; suddenly I wasn't sure I wanted it to be over. I began to cry, gut-wrenching sobs that rocked my body. Mimi stood beside me, her face wet with tears. Gradually, our other friends gathered and we hugged each other as the tears flowed, cascading like torrents of rain. I had come to love these girls who shared their provisions with me when I was hungry; these girls who took me home to their mothers on days we had short passes to leave the school premises; these incredibly generous Tiv girls with hearts as warm as fuzzy bears.

"Why are we crying so much?" Caro asked, wiping her face with the back of her hand.

"We will see one another in Makurdi." Caro and her sister, Bibiana lived close to my new house in Makurdi.

"That is true. Why are we even crying at all?" Doo asked. She was a petite beauty with a great love for romance novels. She lived even closer to me in Makurdi. But I knew I wouldn't be seeing much of them after we left school. I was returning to Obosi, and then I was going to my mother in Onitsha to ask her about my father and go in search of him.

The month after graduation, I wrote my mother a letter, demanding information about my father. I did not get a reply. I however wasn't going to let her stone silence discourage me. I would ask again and again until I got an answer. I deserved to know who he was. I deserved a father. I had spent all these years dreaming about him, wondering if he was dead or if he did something outrageous that made them hide his identity from me. I was tired of wondering. I was going to find him.

My restlessness grew and so did my anxiety. The father figure I had known for nine years was a man who looked my way only when he flogged me mercilessly. Even though Uncle Nicholas had stopped flogging me as that phase of my life seemed to have gone with the old house, I was still morbidly terrified of him. I broke into a cold sweat each time I saw him. I was on edge every time he was home.

I shared a room with their only daughter, Nne, who was a typical daddy's girl. I developed attitude problems and started to talk back at Aunty Stella. One could blame it on my raging sixteen-year-old hormones, but all I wanted to do was to leave and go in search of the father I desperately wanted to know.

Three weeks later, I was on the bus headed southeast. My sole mission was to see my mother and get the information I needed. My mother, never much of an expressive person, was cold and detached. When I knocked on the door of the three-bedroom apartment that she shared with her husband and children, it didn't surprise me that her eyes were expressionless as she let me in. Her family had grown; she now had four children. I made my way into the living room, and the children glanced at me with indifference. They retreated to their room and didn't reappear for the duration of my visit. I wasn't sure they knew I was their sister. I sat across the room from my mother, nervously tapping my foot on the chair leg, as she started to speak. This was the first time I heard his name and I thought my heart would stop. I could finally put a name to the face with those deep-set eyes that I constantly dreamed about. "Austin Abraham," I muttered gingerly, afraid that if I spoke too loudly the precious moment would vanish. My mother reiterated what I already suspected. They had met during the Biafran war. "We were in love," she said, "but the war ended and he was recalled to the north."

"Where is he from originally? I can't tell from his name,"

"He is from Makurdi," she whispered.

"Makurdi?! You mean Makurdi…."

"Yes," she replied.

Staring at her in utter shock, I willed my mouth to speak but no sound escaped.

I had lived in my father's hometown for nine years and I did not know it. I had dined with his people, sung with them, laughed with them, mourned with them, not knowing that I was one of theirs. It now began to make sense why I was so drawn to these people; faded patches of grey began to look bright. I was sad and I was happy all at once. Sad that I had been denied a life of love and laughter with him, and happy that I now had the opportunity to know him.

"I'm going back to Makurdi. I'm going to look for him," I blurted out.

"Wait… I'm not sure where he is. I heard he left the country after the war."

"But he must have relatives, people who can tell me where he is."

I got up to leave, and as I walked towards the door my mother said, "I will come with you."

Exactly two weeks later, on a Wednesday morning, I embarked on an adventure with my mother. I sat beside her buried in my private thoughts. What would I say to him? Was he going to be happy to meet me? Several thoughts raced through my mind as the bus sped down the Enugu expressway. I had plied this route many times, but this time, it felt like a sacred journey of pilgrimage. I glanced at my mother, her eyes were closed. I wanted to tap her arm and ask her if she was nervous like I was. I wondered how she was with her other children. I wondered if she was cold and detached from them as she was with me. A gush of pain swept through my heart for a fleeting second as I relived the horrors of the past nine years. The pain intensified with the knowledge that she didn't care that I was being maltreated in her sister's house. I hoped that she loved her other children and that they made her proud and happy.

Our journey to find my father proved fruitless. No one we asked had ever seen or heard of him.

"Does he not have a native last name?" I asked my mother. "Abraham is a Bible name, it won't tell much about the family he's from."

By the end of one week in Makurdi, it was clear that we were not going to find him. I had recruited all my friends from school to help. They asked their parents and grandparents, uncles and aunties, friends and foes, neighbors and priests but no one had heard of him. I didn't tell them that this mystery man was my father. I told them he was a friend of my uncle's during the Biafran war. Had I told them the truth, they might have intensified the search.

I lost all hope and began to wonder if this man even existed; if he was a figment of my mother's imagination. But imaginations don't make babies. I was proof that he existed.

"Maybe he's dead. Maybe he died just after the war," I said to my mother.

We went back to the southeast. I was emotionally spent and even though my mother seemed calm on our way back to Onitsha, I could tell that the journey had rattled her in many ways. As we approached Onitsha, I asked to be dropped off at Nkpor junction. I got on another bus home to Obosi, and my mother journeyed home to her husband and children.

Back home in Obosi, it would have been just like the old times but a lot had changed. I was no longer the carefree happy child that I used to be. Life had touched me in deep ways and left its scars. But there was one bright spot on my pale horizon - Papa, my grandfather.

That year, my grandfather turned seventy. He retired from his medical practice and moved home to Obosi. Papa was a great man. He had dedicated his life to this noble profession. Much of his success could be attributed to his father, my great grandfather, His Royal Highness Igwe Israel Elebo Iweka. He was a pioneer in many aspects and made sure his six children, including my grandfather, received sound education. He was known for many great feats, including receiving Christian missionaries into Obosi in the 1800s. He was also the author of one of the first Igbo history books and was the King of Obosi until he died in 1934. His first son and my grandfather's only brother, Igwe Isaac Iweka, was the first Igbo engineer and was also later crowned the King of Obosi. His oldest daughter was a midwife, and another daughter the first female Igbo pharmacist. My great-grandpa, Igwe Israel Iweka, was an accomplished man in every sense. In fact, the very popular street, Iweka road in Onitsha, which he constructed, was named after him. Pa Israel Iweka left a great legacy for his children.

My grandfather shared a close bond with his only brother. Nobody could come between them, not even their sometimes feuding wives. The brothers built their homes on the property their father left them. They continued to share this property until their deaths. After Papa retired, he spent time visiting with his brother when he wasn't treating patients for free at the annex he built behind the house. I had his ear now that he was retired. He listened attentively as I narrated my nine-year ordeal with Aunty Stella. Shaking his head with horror, he kept saying, "Why didn't you tell me? Why didn't you tell anyone?"

"I did. I cried out for many years but no one listened."

"You won't go back there Joy-jor," he said. It had been so long since I heard him call me that pet name. I managed a half-smile at the memory it evoked, recalling the times I was sick and was taken to the hospital. His plump staff nurse would chase me down the hall with a huge syringe in hand. I got so disruptive that Papa would suspend his consultation with his patient to administer the injection himself. There was no negotiating with my five-year-old self, it was Papa or nobody. The shots seemed less painful with him.

I was relieved that that horrifying part of my life with Aunty

Stella was over. But a certain feeling of restlessness pervaded as I spent my days awaiting my West African Senior Secondary Examination (WASSCE) results and worrying about my future. This was one set of exams that would determine whether I would get a spot in a University. During this period, something happened that triggered a truckload of awful memories. I got into an argument with Uncle Godi, my mother's younger brother.

"Bastard!" he cursed at me. It hit me like a dead weight, its impact like Hiroshima's atomic bomb. All the pain of my past anguish at the hands of Mmadu came flooding back. It hurt more because I was older and understood the meaning of the word on a deeper level. Papa chastised my uncle strongly, but that offered very little comfort. The floodgates of pain were thrown open, rekindling the burning desire to find my father.

While leaving Makurdi had marked the end of a protracted physical ordeal, the psychological trauma was only beginning. The incident with my uncle proved that my experience at Aunty Stella's had shaped my life in more ways than I would ever understand.

Days crept by slowly as I waited to begin another phase of my life. My WASSCE results finally came from Aunty Stella. I failed. I was disappointed but not altogether surprised. Many students failed at their first attempt, and attending coaching classes to prepare for a retake was quite the fad. I was uncertain of the next steps to take. I thought of enrolling for a retake class in Onitsha. It would be just like old times: living in Obosi and schooling at Onitsha.

I was eager to begin a new phase of life, but I grappled with feelings of isolation and abandonment, and the ever present voices of despair that whispered at night, telling me I was a worthless loser whose life would not amount to any good. But I vowed to prove those voices wrong or die trying.

Chapter 4

FROM LAGOS TO JOS
A New Phase of My Life

IT WAS DECEMBER OF 1987. THE POMP OF THE FESTIVE SEASON was a soothing distraction from my existential worries, but as the celebrations wound down, my anxiety grew worse.

Aunty Irene, my mother's sister, came to Obosi to visit. She was the oldest of my grandparents' children and lived in Lagos. Her voice echoed in the hallway as her petite frame bounced up the stairs to the suite I shared with my grandmother.

"Oh God, not now," I muttered beneath my breath. I could only take this woman in small doses. Her knack for talking nonstop and her penchant for finding faults in everyone had me avoiding her like the Bubonic Plague. I was happy to vacate my bedroom for her and even happier to avoid her throughout her stay until she cornered me in the dining room one afternoon.

"So, Joy, how were your WASSCE results?" she asked.

"They were okay, Aunty," I replied, shuffling my feet uncomfortably. I didn't want to continue the conversation. I knew what would follow. But Aunty Irene was not one to back down.

"Go and bring it, let me see."

Resigned to my fate, I went upstairs, grabbed the wrinkled statement of results, and handed it to her.

Scowling at the paper, she spat, "I thought they said you were smart. This is not a good result."

"I just need to retake my physics…" I started to explain.

"No university will admit you for medicine with this result," she interjected, waving my result as if it were some worthless piece of paper. I wasn't sure why she thought I wanted to be a doctor, but I was in no mood to argue with her.

"You will come to Lagos with me so that you can retake the exam." It was a command, not a suggestion.

My heart sank at the thought of going to live with another aunt. I could tell that my grandfather sensed my worry. The night before our departure, he summoned me.

"Joy-jor, your grandmother and I are old. Your aunty will do a better job than we will."

I nodded at him, struggling to keep the dam of tears at bay. Deep down, I knew that moving to Lagos was in my best interest. Queen's (my alma mater) was decent, but it didn't prepare me enough for the West African Senior Secondary Certificate Examination or any standardized test for that matter. Weighing my options for success helped quell the fear of my past from rearing its ugly head in the present. I struggled to find the peace I needed to leave with Aunty Irene. It was me against the world once again, but I was going to be alright.

We were up at the crack of dawn the following morning. Aunty

Irene could not resist one last jab at my Uncle Godi as we rolled our suitcases down the stairs.

"You are a ne'er-do-well, living off your father at your age!" she lashed out. "Shame on you."

I suppressed a chuckle at Aunty Irene's cruel words, my eyes searching Uncle Godi's face. I willed him to talk back, knowing that a response from him would elicit further vitriol from Aunty Irene. My last wish before my departure was to get my pound of flesh even if it came vicariously through my aunt. I never forgave him for taking over from where Mmadu left off. I never forgot that he called me that horrible name.

The bus terminal at Iweka Road, Onitsha, bustled with activity. Young hawkers patrolled the dirt littered streets, with trays of freshly baked "Our Lady's Bread" perched on their heads. Touts tugged at our bags as we approached the fleet of buses.

"Enter this bus, it's almost full," each one chanted in Igbo, desperate to convince us to board their assigned vehicle. We finally settled into the comfortably padded seats of an olive-colored "The Young Shall Grow" bus. The touts were aggressive in their pursuit of passengers. They had to be as they were paid a commission by the drivers for each passenger they successfully convinced to board their vehicle. I rubbed my sore hands, relieved that the tug of war with the touts was finally over. I leaned on the thick glass, feigning sleep in a bid to ward off Aunty Irene's endless chit-chatting. While I didn't care to be entertained by my aunt, the rest of the bus was held spellbound by the shenanigans of the young ambitious salesman who stood beside the driver. His body swayed to the motion of the bus as he reached for the tattered leather bag wedged between his skinny legs.

"You see this one," he said, flapping a small transparent packet that contained two red capsules, "You need only one tablet and you will fire all night. Your wife will give testimony in the morning." The bus roared with laughter and applause.

Aunty Irene looked away uncomfortably as the man seated beside her demanded for four packets of the aphrodisiac. The salesman alighted at a junction in Benin, beaming satisfactorily. I was baffled by the number of junk remedies he offloaded on the travelers, including a suspicious-looking brown tablet he claimed could cure every disease known to man.

We pulled into Lagos three hours later. I gasped at the huge blue signboard that read, "Welcome to Eko." Eko is the native name for Lagos. The River Niger Bridge connecting Onitsha with the neighboring city of Asaba was impressive, but it paled in comparison with the Eko Bridge. This gorgeous edifice towered above the Lagos lagoon, its silvery reflection bouncing off the aqua blue river. My eyes feasted on the beauty of my new city. Magnificent skyscrapers graced the paved streets. I willed the bus to go slower so I could take in this vision of sheer elegance. The sun seemed to defy nature as it beamed at this breathlessly gorgeous city at 7 p.m. This was in contrast to Makurdi or Obosi where it would have already begun to set. I smiled at the imaginary cupid's arrow that seemed to have struck my heart. I was in love with this city.

Aunty Irene lived in a quiet estate in Victoria Island called Transit Village. Her wooden cabin was a mile away from the Bar Beach, and late at night, I heard the rustling sound of sea waves as they pounded the coarse sands. I dreamed of visiting Bar Beach. It was as much of a tourist attraction as the New York Statue of Liberty or the London Trafalgar Square.

At first, I wasn't sure of what to expect from Aunty Irene - the servants' quarters treatment or the main house treatment? I started to relax after she found me sitting on her pastel-colored Persian rug and asked me to sit on the chair instead. It took getting used to, but I was relieved that Aunty Irene was nothing like Aunty Stella. Her gesture was a kind reminder that I was her niece and not a servant.

The week after we arrived, I enrolled in the remedial program at the Federal School of Arts and Science, Victoria Island, where I would write my General Certificate Exams and prepare for university. This was my opportunity to prove to myself and Aunty Irene that I was as smart as she had heard.

It was the dawn of a new era, and I was in a better place emotionally and physiologically. I hoped my newly found tranquility would reflect in my upcoming results. I threw myself into my studies, the passion to ace my exams consuming every waking moment. I still thought about my father, but finding him became a frivolity in the face of the monumental task that lay before me.

It was on one of my many trips to the school library that I met Andrea. I sat on the metallic grey chair beside her, watching the bangles on her left wrist jiggling against her butter light skin as she flipped the pages of an oversized textbook. Matching in drive and ambition, we hit it off almost immediately. Passing our exams and getting into the university of our choice was all we cared about, and from then on, we were together every day.

We struggled with the jitters as our exams approached and one day I said to Andrea, "Let's attend fellowship."

'Why?' she asked, searching my face to see if I was serious.

"Our exams are coming up and I know you're nervous like me. Let's go and pray."

We joined a Christian fellowship group in school. We met every Friday evening in the garage of a house in Victoria Island. The pastor was a dark-skinned middle-aged man. His fake American accent rattled the loudspeakers each week as he chided us to answer the "sinners' call". One Friday evening, after much persuasion by the flamboyant pastor, Andrea and I walked gingerly up the altar and recited "the sinner's prayer". The pastor laid hands on us, and we began to "speak in tongues." My Pentecostal experience was different from the Catholic experience; while the latter was more restrained and regimented, the former had an abundance of razzmatazz. We looked forward to Friday evenings and all the charisma that accompanied the meetings. As the congregation grew so did the pastor's copious display of weekly miracles.

The day Aunty Irene came home with my results, I stood in the middle of the living room wringing my hands nervously, waiting as she put on her reading glasses.

"You failed all the subjects," she said, her glasses perched precariously above her fleshy nose. I knew instinctively that she was joking. My diligent studying and the dutiful attendance at those Friday meetings could not have been in vain.

"Congratulations," she said, her face breaking into a wide smile. "Now I know you're as smart as I heard."

The future began to look bright. I could now dream of attending university. Andrea and I began to look at schools. Coming from a family of lawyers, she wanted to pursue a law degree and was interested in Obafemi Awolowo University, one of the prestigious colleges in the west. I liked the University of Jos but knew absolutely nothing about it except that it was located in a cold hilly city in northern Nigeria. We had one last hurdle to overcome before securing seats in these universities. The Joint Admissions Matriculation Board exam otherwise known as JAMB was the other test that had to be taken to gain admission into any Nigerian University. It was a tricky multiple choice exam. Students enrolled in special classes to help boost their scores. Even with high scores, there were no guarantees that you would land a spot in your top choice. More often than not, you had to know someone influential to be able to hold down a spot in your chosen university. Many excellent students made the cut-off mark for their school of choice but were denied admission for the mere fact that they were either not influential enough or did not know a prominent person. There were rumors of university registrars accepting bribes to enroll students in their universities.

I was at another crossroad, deliberating on the best path to lead me to my desired destination. I didn't dwell long on my dilemma as my new friend came to my aid. Andrea's parents lived in Enugu, an southeastern Igbo city. They found her a good JAMB prep class and she was going to return home to enroll in it.

"Come to Enugu with me," she said. "Nobody attends this class and fails JAMB."

I didn't need further persuasion. We shared many ideals and I knew that I could trust her judgment. My grandmother's younger brother, Great Uncle Maurel, lived in Enugu. I knew I had a home in their house. Two weeks later, I reunited with Andrea.

Enugu, seventy miles north of Onitsha, was known as the "Coal City." Coal was discovered in this region in the early 1900s by British colonialists, and by 1914, the shipment of coal to Britain began. As mining activities increased in the area, foreign companies began to move into the region and soon an urban city emerged. It was a beautiful city, set on a hill, for which it was named – Enugu; which literally means "on top of a hill" in the Igbo language.

One of the major attractions of this city was the famous Milliken Hill Road, a dangerously steep and narrow road that wound to the foot of the hill where coal was mined. Navigating the bends of this eerily tapered road brought on a wave of adrenaline even for the most courageous daredevils. As the city developed and alternative roads were built, Milliken Hill Road became merely a point of interest for thrill chasers.

My Great Uncle Maurel and his wife were great hosts. He was a retired chief magistrate and his wife was a nurse. They were mostly empty-nesters except for their youngest son, Nnamdi, who was a first-year student at Enugu State University.

Nnamdi and I hit it off immediately. He regaled me with stories of his campus life. There was a heavy fraternity presence in most of the campuses in the southeast. Rival fraternities clashed often and there were many incidents of shooting and bloodshed.

"I'm a Black Axe," Nnamdi boasted. "We are the *baddest confra* on campus."

I had heard too many bad stories about these fraternities and it made me a little uncomfortable to learn that my cousin was in one of them. If there was anything I learned from his stories, it was the tactics of keeping a low profile to ward off unwanted attention from fraternity members when I entered the university.

Andrea and I were excited to begin the JAMB lessons. Most afternoons after class, I went to her home for lunch. Her family lived in a nice bungalow in the Government Residential Area (GRA), a middle-class residential area. Andrea shared a special bond with her father. My eyes brimmed with tears every time he stepped out of his official white Peugeot 504 and enveloped her in a bear hug. I never lost hope of finding my father. I was going to try again when the time was right. Every time Andrea asked about my family, I changed the subject. I didn't know what to tell her; how to tell her that I was one of those children born out of wedlock, a Biafran bastard, and a product of the Civil War. It caused me too much shame. No one, not even my friends in secondary school, knew. I was afraid that once they found out, they would despise me and call me names like Mmadu did. It was my secret that I did not wish to share with anyone. I was relieved when Andrea finally stopped asking. Most days after lunch, I hitched a ride with her father's driver to the corner where I would get on the bus home.

One evening after class, I stood at my usual spot waiting for a bus. Several buses all full, drove past. Two hours later, frustrated and tired, I began to walk home. I hadn't taken five steps when a battered brown van pulled up beside me. I peeked into the van, and a repugnant smell of alcohol assaulted my nostrils. Staring into several pairs of smokey eyes, I stepped back cautiously.

"Are you going to Trans-Ekulu?" A voice asked.

I nodded nervously.

"Come in," he said, popping open the rusty door.

Hesitating for a few seconds, I got in, shutting the door very slowly. I was either going to take a risk with these suspicious-looking boys or walk ten miles. I tried to convince myself that they were harmless college boys from a nearby university. A muscular guy with large scary eyes sat beside me. I hugged myself a little too tightly, leaning against the door.

"Relax baby, I don't bite," he said, perusing my uptight frame.

I smiled tensely.

"My name is Uzo," he said, extending his hand.

"Joy," I mumbled, too afraid to shake his hand.

They ignored me for the rest of the journey, bantering in unfamiliar slang.

The van pulled up in front of my house twenty minutes later. Heaving a sigh of relief, I alighted, mumbled an incoherent "thank you," and rushed to the black gate, colliding with Nnamdi.

"What are you doing with those boys?" he asked sharply, the smoke from his cigarette forming a haze in my face.

"I don't know who they are. They were kind enough to drive me home. There were no commercial buses out there."

"Those are cult boys!" Nnamdi continued, "They are my rival fraternity. Stay away from them."

It was a scary experience, one that I did not think I would encounter so prematurely.

I wrote the JAMB examination a few months later and awaited my results with deep apprehension. I had applied to study economics, a competitive course at the University of Jos. Weeks later, I received my results with cautious optimism. Even though my score was high, I wouldn't know if I made the cut-off mark until much later. Andrea's score was also potentially good enough for her dream school, Obafemi Awolowo University.

My next assignment was finding a contact in my selected university. Aunty Stella sent word that she knew someone in Jos, a professor at the College of Botanical Science who could assist with my admission. I traveled to Makurdi to get the contact information from her. It felt like a lifetime since I had been in Aunty Stella's house.

As Aunty Stella dropped me off at the bus station, my stomach twisted in tight knots. I recalled that morning seven years earlier, when she had put me on the bus to Gboko, only that this time, her instructions were different.

"The professor has a reputation," she said. "Be careful around him."

I didn't understand what she meant and didn't pause to dwell on it. I had a new town to get to, and that was all that preoccupied my mind.

The lazy bus journeyed sluggishly along the narrow tarred roads. Vast farmlands sprawled across rural towns. Jos, the capital of Plateau state, is home to over forty ethnic groups in central northern Nigeria. Early European settlers discovered tin in Jos, so it was nicknamed "Tin City." As years passed, the booming tin business attracted foreigners and other ethnic groups such as Igbos, Yorubas, and Hausas to the city. It was arguably the coldest city in the country, another reason why many foreigners of Caucasian descent chose it as their primary place of abode. Surrounded by gorgeous mountains, it was home to Hillcrest, a prestigious American High School, and the top choice for children of expatriate Caucasians. Hillcrest was a rite of passage for children who were looking to attend university in the United States.

It was a grey day, the clouds moved in unison with the bus as it kissed the tips of the grass-covered mountains. The bus pulled into the terminal just after noon. Shivering slightly, I tugged at the cuffs of my long-sleeved blouse, grateful that I remembered to pack two cardigans for the trip.

On my arrival at the Professor's home, I was greeted warmly by his wife. She was a bespectacled petite woman in her late forties.

"How is your Aunty?" she inquired.

"She is fine, Ma," I replied.

"My husband is not home, and he is the one that will help you with your admissions. He is a lecturer in the university," she said, leading me to a bedroom down the hall.

"Okay, Ma," I answered politely. I was grateful for the chance to rest after the long journey and looked forward to a hitch-free process in securing my admission.

The professor came home late in the evening. He was a tall nerdy-looking man probably in his mid-fifties. His bushy afro reminded me of Uncle Nicholas. He didn't say much to me except that I would go with him to the University the next morning to begin my admission process.

I woke up early the next day, ready to start the next phase of my life. The professor was already up and in the living room reading the morning newspapers. I greeted him respectfully.

We set out after a delicious breakfast of yam and fried eggs. The university was less than four blocks from the staff quarters, where the Professor lived, but we drove past the gate. I glanced at the professor's face and as if reading my mind, he said, "I want to pick up a document first, and then we will go to the university."

The Professor drove to a building under construction in a deserted part of Jos. The road leading to the building was dusty and untarred. Several buildings, all of which were also under construction, lined the streets on either side. He pulled into a gated compound, and getting out of the car, he ushered me out. I hesitated but he signaled forcefully. I got out of the car and followed him into the house. It was a two-story building, complete except for window paneling and painting. He made his way upstairs and beckoned for me to follow.

I walked slowly behind him, an uneasy feeling creeping up in my chest.

"This is my latest project," he announced proudly. He unlocked a room and asked me to step inside. My heart began to pound.

"Come in my dear, don't be afraid."

It was a furnished room. The mattress on the floor was covered in faded floral sheets, and the pillows were bare. I stood with my back pressed to the door, struggling to shake off the eerie feeling that was beginning to stifle me.

"Sir, you said you were picking up a document. We really should get going," I blurted out.

He ignored my request to leave and approached me menacingly. "You're such a pretty girl. I laid my eyes on you last night and I knew you were mine."

"Please stop it, sir!" I cried, my blood running cold.

He shoved me away from the door and locked it. My heart began to race wildly. I knew I was in danger.

"Don't scream. No one will hear you." Pushing me violently to the mattress, he ripped open the button on my dark blue jeans.

"Please, don't do this to me. I've never done this… please sir!" I pleaded desperately. It was clear by now what he wanted to do.

"Oh a fresh virgin, so young and so fresh," he chanted excitedly.

I looked into his lust-filled eyes and there was something else I saw, something very dark and sinister. In that instant, I knew I wasn't going to win. But I fought back, clawing at his face and shoulders, an effort that proved futile as he forced his way into my young fragile frame. Excruciating pain like I had never known paralyzed my body. I screamed and begged for his mercy, but my pleas fell on deaf ears. I lay motionless for several minutes after he was spent, too afraid to move. But I eventually summoned courage and walked gingerly to the bathroom, wiping off the blood and liquid that trickled down my thighs.

The ride to the university was quiet. I didn't know what to do, who to talk to or where to go. A few minutes passed and he started to apologize.

"I didn't believe you when you said it was your first time. I'm sorry."

My face twitched, but I was determined to remain silent, my gaze fixed on the road ahead of us.

"Please, you must not tell anyone about this okay?"

I was stone silent.

The professor took me to the office of the registrar who was a personal friend of his. "This is the daughter of a family friend," he said. "UniJos is her first choice. Please help her with her admission."

I was gone before the professor and his wife returned home in the evening. I left word with their maid that I had returned to Makurdi. I had no idea where I would go after I left the professor's house, but I knew I wasn't leaving Jos. I was going to stay and fight for my admission. I reasoned that there must be somewhere I could stay, maybe the hostel. I could find a student willing to let me squat in her room until I completed my admission process.

I lugged my bags back to the campus, and as I made my way past the makeshift canteen, popularly known as "Bukka", I heard my name. I turned to see who it was but she didn't look familiar.

"Aren't you Joy Iweka?" she asked, in a matter-of-fact manner.

"I'm your sister from Obosi, Ndubuisi Family," she continued. "Our house is behind the palace."

She took me to her room in the hostel. That night as I lay on a mattress on the floor of Naraguta Hostel, I finally let the tears flow. I felt dirty, defiled, humiliated, but I was too scared and too ashamed to tell anyone. No stranger to pain, I shoved my latest trauma in Pandora's box where it rightfully belonged. I focused on the one thing that mattered – securing my admission into the University of Jos. I made many trips to the registrar's office to enquire about the status of my admission. I always left with the assurance that my name would be on the admitted list. But because of the many tales of woe I had heard from people who had been on the admission run for years, my mind did everything but stay at rest.

When the cut-off mark was announced and I was sitting six points above it, I knew that I stood a good chance of getting admitted. Some of my tensions subsided but I knew hitting the cut-off mark wasn't enough. The campus buzzed with rumors around the admission process.

"The governor has sent his list to the dean," a prospective student said. "They are removing names of qualified students and offering the spots to the students on the governor's list."

Such tales were in abundance and I started to lose hope with each passing day. All the admissions lists were released as the matriculation date approached: the dean's, the chancellor's, and the registrar's. Each time I walked to the announcement board in front of the registrar's office and found my name missing, my heart sank. Had I spent all this time and endured this trauma for nothing? Had all my hard work and perseverance come to naught? By this time I had depleted my money and sent many SOS messages to my grandfather.

Fighting to hold my tears back, I turned to the registrar for a much-needed reassurance.

"Be patient," he said. "You will be admitted."

"When sir? Nearly all the lists are out."

The Matriculation Ceremony was the next morning and there was just one final list left – the supplementary list. Prospective students huddled in front of the Admissions' Office. The tension in the air was palpable. The last list was supposed to be released at noon. It was 3 p.m. and yet it was nowhere in sight. I was beginning to lose hope. At 5 p.m. when the list finally made it out, I rushed to the board, my chest pounding so hard it made my head throb. I glanced at the board. My name was not there.

I was consumed by utter hopelessness, a feeling quickly replaced by anger; a rage so strong it rocked my body violently. Eyes brimming with tears, I stormed to the office of the registrar. Not bothering to knock, I barged in and said to him, "You lied to me. You told me I would make the last list."

The tears were now falling freely, drowning the hope that I had kept alive for the last few weeks.

"Your name is on the board," the registrar replied.

"No, it's not there," I insisted.

"Come with me," he said.

I followed him to the board and watched as he lifted his index finger and pointed at the fifth line. I peered closely and there it was, my name next to a matriculation number – UJS/17578/89. I stopped feeling anything at that point, just overwhelming numbness.

I matriculated the next morning without a gown. With the last-minute commotion, I couldn't get one. But I didn't care. My dream had come true, and the trauma leading to my admission, as painful as it was, had become my badge of honor.

Classes started soon after matriculation, giving me no time to travel home to Obosi to bring back adequate necessities. I sent word home to my grandfather, and the money I needed was sent to me. Finding accommodation on campus was not a problem as long as you could afford to pay extra to the students who sold their rooms and moved off-campus. I bought a room in Naraguta hostel from a final year architecture student.

I settled into the whims and caprices of university life. Music and fashion were important aspects of the culture on campus. Your tastes in these categories determined whether you belonged to the cool or boring cliques.

Anita Baker was one of the popular music artists on campus in the early nineties. Her rich deep voice echoed through the window of every room as you walked down the long hallways. Naraguta hostel had a unique vibe and always bubbled with activity. Every popular girl on campus lived in Babylon, a block of rooms within Naraguta.

At least once every week, students gathered to witness a fight on this block. These fights were usually about who stole someone's boyfriend or something equally mundane.

Shoulder pads were a huge fashion statement on campus. To wear a shirt without those protruding additions was to set oneself up to look like a fashion misfit. They were the fashion religion of our time. Parties were also a huge thing. Each weekend, cars lined up outside the hostels, waiting to take the latest students, also known as "Jambites," to parties in town. I loved the campus, the city, and how seamlessly I integrated into my new life.

As I navigated my new life in the university, news came that Papa was diagnosed with cancer. He had given up medical practice altogether. Upon receiving the news, I got on the next night-bus out of Jos to be by his side. Christmas break was only a week away and lectures were winding down already. Being a doctor, Papa understood that his prognosis was poor, so all attempts to convince him to fly abroad for treatment failed. He had lived a good life and embraced the inevitable. He was in good spirits when I got home, his gentle smile greeting me as I opened the door to his bedroom. I fought back the tears that welled up as I held his frail hand, shocked at how emaciated he looked.

My cousins were home from every corner of the country for Christmas. Nnamdi was also home from Enugu. I was excited to see him after such a long time. We were now young adults who had outgrown our favorite yuletide traditions of watching the Mmuo masquerades on Christmas Day. But we still fancied hanging out in large numbers, and on Christmas Eve, my cousins and I trooped to a popular pepper soup joint. Chief Osita Osadebe's *Osondi Owendi* boomed from the cheap loudspeakers, and the whiff of goat meat pepper soup teased my salivary glands as we settled into the rickety chairs in the dingy restaurant.

"Do you have congo meat?" Nnamdi asked, pointing to the jovial waitress who stood waiting to take our order.

"Which one is Congo meat?" I asked, chuckling at Nnamdi.

"Snail," Ebele, my other cousin shouted from across the table where she sat with a group of others.

"You must try it Joy girl if you haven't."

As we devoured the delicious peppered snail, I looked towards Ebele's table and I saw him. Our eyes locked and the earth stood still for a minute. He was the most stunning boy I ever saw. I couldn't take my eyes off him and neither could he stop staring at me. It felt like nobody else was in the room but us.

"Obi, that is Joy, my cousin. Joy, meet Obi," Ebele said, chuckling mischievously, and breaking the awkward silence.

From that night onwards, we were inseparable. Obi was the life of every party, his lanky 6'2 frame filled every room he walked into, and his deep love for life was evident in the manner he took to the dance floor, gyrating tirelessly to Fela Kuti's *Zombie*. I was hit by Cupid's arrow. We attended parties in Obosi and the neighboring cities and danced all night. On his last night in Obosi, under the dim light of a shabby kiosk next to my house, he asked me to be his girlfriend. I didn't want him to leave, didn't want the magic to end. He came to Obosi to spend Christmas with his maternal grandmother, and he had to return home to his family at Nkwere.

"I will come and see you in Jos, I promise," he whispered, pulling me close.

Long-distance relationships were no walk in the park but Obi made it work. He came to Jos as often as he could get away from a busy school schedule. He was attending the reputable University of Nigeria, Nsukka in the southeast. Obi was every girl's dream guy;

gorgeous, kind, loving, tender, generous, and attentive. He was too good to be true, and sometimes my insecurity got the best of me.

"What if he has another girlfriend in Nsukka?" I asked my friend, Mernan.

"Pay him a surprise visit and then you might catch him red-handed," she suggested. One Friday evening after lectures, I got on a night bus to Nsukka. I tapped on his door early the next morning, sleep-deprived from the long hours on the bus. A groggy Obi opened the door and swept me into a tight bear hug. He took me to every party on campus and showed me off to all his friends. I got on the night bus back to Jos on Sunday evening, confident in his love. We promised to be at Obosi for Christmas that year; we planned to dance all night and eat Nkwobi at our favorite local restaurant. That Christmas, I waited for Obi at Obosi. He never came. He was involved in a fatal car crash a few days before Christmas. Just like that, my Obi was gone. He left my life as swiftly as he entered it, taking a huge piece of me with him.

As I mourned my deceased heartthrob, I worried about my grandfather. The reality of the swiftness of death had hit me in the face, and I realized that if it could take someone as young and vibrant as Obi, my grandfather only had but a limited time left.

Papa's condition continued to deteriorate. Every morning when I blended Weetabix, the only food he could tolerate, I whispered a silent prayer for a miracle. His brother, Igwe Isaac Iweka, was a daily visitor. I looked forward to the rustle of his footsteps as he made that dutiful trudge up the staircase to sit by the bedside of his ailing brother. "Jo, Ke ka isi laru?" he would ask. "Jo, how was your night?"

"The pain was unbearable. If I could cross to the other side of the living, last night, I would have," Papa would reply, his voice hoarse from pain.

As I got on the bus back to Jos after the break, I wondered if I would see him again. I also worried about money for school, should he pass away before I graduated.

I was happy that my grandfather was still clinging to life when I returned months later, though it broke my heart to see him in so much pain. He embodied the father I didn't know and a mother I knew but who couldn't care less if I lived or died. That morning I decided to visit my mother. It had been many months since I had seen her. She did not know of the travails leading up to my acceptance into the university. She never asked or cared to reach out to me, laying eyes on me only when I showed up at her doorstep. Those visits were becoming fewer and farther apart.

It was a wet morning. Light rain splattered on the sand, filling the air with a familiar rich earthy scent. I stopped by Nkpor junction to buy roadside "Oka na Ube", corn and pear. They were my favorite rainy season snacks. I bit into the succulent flesh of the roast pear as I stood waiting to board the next bus.

Alighting from a rusty old bus forty minutes later, I walked down the narrow slope that led to my mother's apartment, wondering what reception I would receive this time. Indifference? Slight Irritation?

I was let in on the first knock, her deadpan expression dashing the minute hope I harbored that she might be happy to see me. I sat uncomfortably on the edge of the faded brown sofa, patiently awaiting the awkward silence that lingered to blow over.

"Look at what you're wearing," she finally said, scowling.

"What's wrong with what I'm wearing?" I asked, glancing down at my blue baggy jeans.

"You don't see anything wrong with what you're wearing?" she posed.

"No. This is how we dress in Jos," my voice trembled with emotion, hurt that the first thing she did was to criticize me.

"You're walking the streets of Obosi with those things," she continued. "Ndi fugi ya si na ife agwo mu ayali ito ogonogo."

"People that see you will say that a snake is sure to give birth to something long."

"What does that mean? Maybe you're a snake but I'm not a snake like you," I hurled back. I felt that she was projecting her insecurities onto me; that she resented me because I was proof of her indiscretion as a young girl.

She left the room and returned a short while later, brandishing a cane.

"Don't touch me. Don't you dare touch me with that cane!" I yelled.

"What have I ever done to you? Why do you hate me so much? If you knew you wouldn't love me, why did you bother having me?"

She dropped the shocker. "But I wasn't trying to. I tried to get rid of you but you wouldn't go, that Enugu Doctor told me to leave the pregnancy alone after my third attempt..." I had heard enough. Snatching the cane from her, I snapped it in two and stormed out of her house.

I was summoned to my grandfather's bedroom a few days later. My stern-faced relatives gathered around Papa's sickbed, waiting.

"Your mother sent word that you went to her house to beat her," Uncle Godi, the leader of the gang, said.

"I didn't beat her," I retorted.

They did not believe me, neither did they care to listen to my version of the story. They began to yell at the same time like a pack of wolves chasing down its prey. It was a nightmare playing out in slow motion. I willed it to stop but it spiraled.

"You horrible child, don't you dare lay hands on my sister again," yelled Ngozi, a light-skinned obese cousin who was nicknamed "udu awoh," fat frog.

"I didn't beat her. I didn't touch her," I screamed back.

At that moment, I understood what it felt like to be mobbed. I was being attacked by the people who were supposed to protect me. I looked at my grandfather, begging him with my eyes to stop them, but cancer had stolen his voice. I noticed that he was trying to speak amid the many animated voices but no one noticed. I sobbed, fought back, and begged to be heard. Twice I tried to blurt out the cruel words my mother flung at me on that day, and twice I couldn't.

"She said I was a snake like her. She said she tried to kill me," my mind screamed but the words wouldn't leave my lips. A sinking realization hit me. I was nothing but a piece of crap to my mother and all of those adults.

I whimpered softly, as their rage gradually abated.

"We love you Joy," Aunty Stella crooned. I felt laughter bubble up in my throat, the cynical kind you feel when someone says something utterly and ridiculously untrue. My subconscious made a fleeting trip to my nine-year abode in her home. Looking her in the eye, my voice hoarse from crying, I whispered, "Don't ever say that to me again."

The feeling of worthlessness that ruled my existence since my childhood was once again evident. I didn't belong to anyone or anywhere. It felt like I couldn't catch a real break from pain. It chased me down and had its way with me at every juncture, leaving me to wonder what I ever did to deserve its cruel visits. I wondered what the universe had in mind; if it derived special pleasure in watching me suffer.

The morning I was returning to Jos, I had a feeling I was seeing my grandfather for the last time.

"Joy-Jor," he murmured in a voice laden with pain. "Don't join students' unrest."

I nodded, fighting back tears. I had gotten so little affection in my lifetime, I wasn't ready to let go of the only fatherly love I had ever known. I had no other shield to cover me. I questioned if there was even truly a God and if there was, why he abandoned me and was so indifferent to my plight. I wondered why he allowed my one true love, Obi, to be snatched by the cold hands of death. I was angry at the world, angry at the mother who could not love me, and who did nothing to help me navigate the terrain of life. I was angry that in my quest for higher education, I was brutally violated, a tragedy that could have been avoided if there was one parent in my life who was willing to love me. I felt lost, empty and suicidal. But beneath the turmoil that threatened to drown me, was a zest for life, fueled by the desire to survive and prove all the naysayers wrong. I was going to live and achieve great success to shame them all. That single thought kept me going.

Against all odds, I was set on the track of becoming a conqueror.

Chapter 5

FINDING AND
LOSING A FATHER

BEAUTIFUL FRIENDSHIPS ARE LIKE BALMS, THEY SOOTHE THE putrid wounds left by the gaping absence of familial love. The love I lacked at the home-front, I found in friends I made at different stages of my life.

Fate brought about one of those cherished friendships towards the end of my first year when I met Florence, a light-skinned beauty with hazel eyes and a carefree personality. Florence was a victim of a rocky childhood, but that didn't take away from her warm and sunny disposition. She laughed at everything, including herself, a trait that thoroughly endeared me to her. One day, after class I tagged along with Florence to her professor's office, a decision that changed my life in ways I did not expect. We walked down the poorly lit corridor until we got to a dark wooden door. Turning the faded brass handle, Florence peeked her head into the office. I followed closely behind, taking in the view of the office as we both shuffled in. It was a big office, bigger than most I had visited, and books were sprawled across every space within the room. A short man sat behind a littered desk, swiveling his chair absent-mindedly as we leaped across several piles of books to get to his desk. Professor Hagher was the head of the Department of Theater Arts, and his love for drama was not in doubt as he spent the next half hour entertaining us with a variety of theatrical jargon. As he basked in his dramatic display, I began to pick out a familiar accent, one that I had heard for nine years and wouldn't miss anywhere.

"I take it that you're a Tiv man, Professor," I said.

"Yes I am," he replied with a smirk.

My next question was compulsive, one that I had asked a million times to a million Tiv people. I had all but given up hope that I would ever get an answer, but I asked anyway. It had become routine to ask.

"Do you know a Tiv man called Austin Abraham? He served in the army during the Biafran war and was in Enugu Cantonment."

"Oh yes, I know him," Professor Hagher replied. "He is Brigadier Malo's cousin."

My heart started to beat fast, beads of perspiration lacing my forehead.

"Do you happen to know where he is at the moment?" I prodded, trying my hardest to maintain composure.

"He lives in Makurdi and works at the Sports Council."

My heart raced. It was either going to stop beating or fall out of my chest. The man with the deep-set eyes was alive. He was not an apparition. Professor Hagher did not ask why I made those inquiries, neither did I feel compelled to explain why. I was still numb from shock as we left his office that evening. I knew exactly where the Sports Council was. I had passed it many times on my way to Makurdi Main Market. Who would have thought that my years of searching for my father would end on the night of a random visit to a professor's office?

The following Friday after classes, I hopped on a bus to Makurdi. I was filled with dread, afraid that my trip would be an illusion like the mirages that danced on the tarred roads. To think that all those years I lived with Aunty Stella, my father was within reach, and I did not know it. It felt surreal.

Aunty Stella's eyebrows curved in surprise as I walked into her living room later that evening.

"My classmate is sick so I brought her home," I said.

I hated that I lied over something I held so dearly, an occasion I had dreamed about all my life. But it was going to be my private moment with my father. I wasn't going to let anyone rain on that parade.

I tossed and turned all night, barely able to shut my eyes. What if he rejected me? What if he said he didn't know what I was talking about? What if he was the wrong man?

I was up at the crack of dawn the next morning. I dressed with care, donning my favorite blue jeans with a set of huge shoulder pads tucked underneath my turquoise shirt. I put on some makeup, careful not to make it too heavy. I was told many times that I looked exactly like my mother, so the more familiar I looked, the less awkward it was going to be for both of us.

I walked into his office at about ten o'clock, my stomach twisting in knots. "I'm looking for Mr. Abraham," I said to the bespectacled middle-aged woman I met at the front desk.

"He went to the post office, but will be back shortly," she replied, eyeing me suspiciously as she offered me a seat by the door.

Time lapsed, and there was no sign of him. Shifting my gaze to the silver clock on the beige wall, my heart synched with its second hand. I shuddered slightly, wondering for the umpteenth time if I had made the right choice.

Forty-five minutes later, he walked in. I was not sure at first if it was him as several men had come and gone.

"This young lady is here to see you," the woman at the front desk said, pointing in my direction. He turned around and looked at me, and for thirty seconds, I stopped breathing. I was staring into the most beautiful face I had ever seen. The man with the deep-set eyes, I had searched and yearned for him all my life. He was standing two meters from me, but his eyes were not deep-set after all. I couldn't stop gazing at the aquiline nose perched above his chiseled jaw or the beautiful thick brows that sat on either side of the perfectly symmetrical face. He looked like a figure carved by a master sculptor, a Roman god of some sort.

"What can I do for you?" he questioned, jolting me out of my trance.

"Can we go somewhere and talk privately?"

If he was curious about my request, his perfect features did not show it. Fifteen minutes later, he led me through the door, and we walked to a nearby canteen. I sat across from him, twisting my fingers nervously as he ordered drinks.

"Would you like a stout?" he asked.

"Malt is fine," I replied. Who offers their teenage daughter alcohol? I wondered. There was a long awkward silence while we waited for our drinks. He was not in a hurry to initiate conversation and wasn't curious to find out why a young girl decided to seek him out in the middle of a workday. Did he think I had come to hit on him? I wondered, suppressing a nervous chuckle.

Just as our drinks were set on the table, I looked him in the eye and asked, "Did you serve in the army during the Biafran war?"

He nodded in the affirmative.

"Were you based in Enugu during this time?"

Again, he nodded.

"Did you happen to meet a young woman called Charity?"

A muscle on his perfect face twitched gently. "Yes," he replied.

"I'm her daughter. I was born after the war."

He looked like he had seen a ghost, flinching almost violently.

For the next ten minutes, I couldn't make out what he was saying. All I remember was his lips moving and me sitting there, staring at him, and tears rolling down my face.

He knew I existed. He knew when I was born. He tried to come and see me but my grandfather would not have it. The war had just ended. The Igbos were massive casualties of this war, one that devastated them in every way. They wanted nothing to do with "Nigerians," least of all a Nigerian soldier, so he stayed away.

Our drinks hardly touched, we left the canteen and got into his car.

"We are going to see my mother," he said. "You look just like her. She will love you."

Daudu was three miles east of Makurdi. As we made the trip to see his mother, I couldn't help but wonder how often I passed this town and had not the faintest idea that I was tied to it in any way. It was a small village, different from anywhere I had ever been. Little thatch-roofed huts were scattered in no particular order. The villagers were subsistence farmers and seemed content with the simplicity of life as they knew it. My newly found grandmother spoke no English, and when her son explained who I was, she burst into chants of adulation. He started to interpret what she was saying but I interrupted him.

"I understand her," I said. "I lived in Makurdi for many years."

My father's mother gathered as many villagers as she could find to meet her granddaughter who had returned home. They converged around me like I was some sacred being, bare-chested women with breasts saggy from years of nursing multiple infants. I never felt more loved my whole life.

"Kumashe. Mngueshima," my grandmother said, looking at my father. Those were the names she chose for me. "Tall elegant being. Bold hearted."

I returned to Jos two days later, and every now and then, I would receive a letter from my father. We communicated through the post for a few months but slowly, the correspondence started to dwindle.

One cold evening, I heard a gentle tap on the window of my hostel room as I stirred the pot of beef stew on my small camping gas stove. I opened my door to a tall handsome woman I had met in Aunty Stella's house. She lived in Jos but I didn't expect to ever see her. She came bearing the news I dreaded most - Papa had passed away. I had spent many months thinking about that moment, yet nothing prepared me for the devastating grief that flooded my being. Everything came to a standstill as I left Jos to pay my final respects to my grandfather.

The compound in Obosi buzzed with activity on the eve of Papa's funeral. Relatives from all walks of life gathered for the occasion. Several cows purchased for the funeral mooed noisily in the backyard, and young men from the community set to work erecting white canopies around the compound. The next day, I watched as my larger-than-life grandfather was laid to rest. My one true anchor was finally gone, and I was left to wonder how I would survive and what I would do with my life. Obosi began to feel like less of a home moments after my grandfather's burial. My grandmother was ailing and had started to lose her short-term memory. She would ask the same question many times in a span of minutes.

"Nnenne ili gonni?" "Nnnene have you eaten?" she would ask repeatedly. She began to keep things in bizarre places; sometimes she would tie keys to the edge of her wrapper and we would spend hours looking for them. My grandfather left a will that listed me as a beneficiary of a solid education along with every need that would arise until I got married, but I feared I would be excluded from it. My grandmother, the only one who would have been my advocate, was out of the picture as she struggled to hold on to the cognitive abilities that were fast deserting her. My relationship with my mother had broken down irrevocably. I had not seen her since the last time I stumbled out of her house, and I didn't think that how I would survive in school was of any concern to her.

The morning I was leaving Obosi after my grandfather's funeral, I went to my uncle, the executor of my grandfather's estate, to ask for money to return to school. I was nervous about approaching him, I suspected from the get-go that it was going to be a tall order. He handed me a few notes and when I counted them, it was barely enough to cover my transport fare back to Jos.

"Oh, Uncle this is one thousand naira. My transport fare alone is eight hundred," I said, trying to negotiate for more money.

"I won't survive on two hundred naira. I still have to eat and transport myself to class and back each day...."

"Well this is all the money you're going to get," he interrupted, pointing to a notebook on the centerpiece. "Sign here that I gave you money."

I walked away, my new reality slowly sinking in. It was the beginning of another era of deprivation, uncannily similar to the one I suffered in Gboko and Makurdi.

The years ahead in school were tough. I was afraid that I might drop out because I couldn't afford the tuition. If I dropped out, what would I do with my life? I had no home to return to. Dropping out was not an option, I would stay and finish school no matter the odds piled against me. I started to spend a lot of time with Florence at her off-campus apartment. Many nights, her spaghetti tossed in egg stew kept me alive, but there were other nights we went to bed hungry, nights when we couldn't convince the man who sold provisions by the roadside to sell us some eggs on credit for our spaghetti concoction. I did not let hunger crush my spirit. I had faced it in the past and overcame it.

As I wrapped up my third year, news of the possibility of a nationwide strike of the Academic Staff Union of Universities (ASUU) and Non-Academic Staff Union (NASU) began to filter in. Within two weeks, classes were suspended and students began to trickle out of campus. Negotiations between the federal government and university staff had met a gridlock. The university staff wanted better pay and better working conditions, and the government, under the military dictatorship of Ibrahim Babangida, was not willing to meet those demands.

One month later, Naraguta Hostel was transformed into a ghost town. The busy hallway that once bubbled with pop music was reduced to hollow silence, my footsteps echoing as I walked past empty rooms to the bathroom. I was alone on the entire floor and scared. One morning, I bumped into Shola, a tall dark bubbly final year architecture student.

"You haven't left?" I asked, relieved that I had company.

"No, I'm still here. I went to town for a few days," she replied.

I wondered why Shola didn't go home. She was the daughter of a wealthy army general, so I was sure it wasn't for lack of a house to return to. But I didn't pry, I was happy to have company. That night, I lay on my narrow bed, no longer afraid of the howling wind beckoning in the dark, or the thuds of booted footsteps that stopped at my door. I felt safer with Shola next door. Going to Obosi was not an option, it was no longer home since Papa died. Nearly one year had gone by, and no one asked after me or checked to see how I fared.

One morning, I heard loud voices coming from Shola's room. Curious to see whose they were, I tiptoed to the window to get a view.

"No Dad, I'm not ready to go home," I heard Shola say.

"You will not stay here, this place is no longer safe. You're coming home with me," her dad chided gently.

Thirty minutes later, Shola walked past my room, clutching a duffel bag in one hand and a huge painting canvas in the other. Her dad followed closely behind, dragging an oversized suitcase. Shola's departure was a cruel reminder that I was all by myself in the world. My insides quivered at the emptiness of my life without a family that loved me. I craved for a home, not just a building, but people I could call family. Alone and at my wit's end, I was grateful when Florence offered me a lifeline.

"I'm going to Lagos on Friday. Come with me,"

I didn't have to be offered twice, not when I had nowhere to go, and she offered to pay my fare. We left for Lagos a few days later.

Florence's house was a two-bedroom apartment in Surulere, a Lagos suburb. It belonged to an older cousin of hers who was gone most of the time. We had the apartment to ourselves. While we lounged in the nicely furnished house, waiting impatiently for the strike to be called off, negotiation between the government and the association of university staff continued to stall. With hopes of our returning to school slowly dwindling, Florence and I found jobs in a Mortgage Finance Company on Lagos Island. The Mortgage Finance industry boomed under Babangida, the military head of state. Our pay was poor and the hours were long, but we were only too glad to have a means of income and somewhere to go each morning.

In June of 1993, Nigerians headed to the polls to elect a civilian president. The country had jostled between military and democratic leadership for most of its existence and corruption continued to eat away at the fabric of society. General Ibrahim Badamosi Babangida, had been in power for eight years. Nigerians, disgruntled and dis-enfranchised, were ready to embrace democracy once again. Hours after the elections, Chief M.K.O. Abiola, a millionaire from the west, was declared winner. Jubilation erupted in the streets across the west. Power was finally changing hands. The north had been at the helm of affairs for too long, much to the chagrin of the other regions of the country. However, this jubilation was cut short when Babangida annulled the elections on account of alleged electoral irregularities. The sounds of victory and celebration on the streets were quickly replaced by violent protests. Empty canisters of tear gas littered the streets, and fumes formed black whirlwinds as angry protesters scampered from the police. Citizens called for Babangida to hand over power to the president-elect. Tension grew by the day, and rumors of war began to echo. The Igbos, all too familiar with unrest and massacres, began to agitate as the situation escalated. They knew the pain of war and its devastating aftermath like no other. They had lived through the Biafran war. Igbos in Lagos be-gan their migration southeast. This mass exodus by the Igbos called "Oso Abiola" (Abiola's race), spread like wildfire, and soon many Igbos from all regions of Nigeria began to move home.

In the faraway United States of America, another president,

Bill Clinton, made the news. His boyish looks and daredevil smile filtered through the crystal screen of the CNN news channel. He had defeated the one-term incumbent President, George H.W. Bush, and was sworn in as the 42nd president. Watching a repeat broadcast of his inauguration speech triggered a feeling of utter dejection. I longed for the stable political climate that was America's. Babangida finally caved to the call for his resignation and handed over power to an interim government. Afterwards, the ASUU strike was suspended. It was one of the longest university strikes in history. I lost a whole school year, my graduation date sneaking past unnoticed in the heat of the strike and the looming possibility of a Second Civil War. I had looked forward to graduating and joining the Lagos workforce. I imagined myself in fancy grey tailored suits with perfect creases, walking down the long halls of a corporate office on Lagos Island. I couldn't wait to join the lucrative banking industry.

Students across the country returned to the university campuses. The strike had stolen time from me, something I would never get back. I threw myself into my school work, determined to finish strong. The usual bubbly atmosphere in Naraguta hostel slowly returned, bringing with it an air of steely resolve, and a renewed sense of purpose. As I sat in the rickety taxi that ferried me to class, staring at the faces of my fellow riders, I knew the strike had changed our lives forever.

I thought about the many ways I had metamorphosed, the once insecure child who based her hopes of a better life on finding her father. I thought about that painful weekend when I visited my newly found father in Makurdi after my grandfather's burial. He lived in a nice bungalow surrounded by beautiful flowers. I had looked forward to a time of bonding with him, but that wasn't to be as his girlfriend, a tall, slender nurse, showed up the day after my arrival. This wouldn't have mattered if they didn't stay holed up in the bedroom fighting all day.

The morning I left for Jos, my father handed me an enlarged portrait of himself and money that barely covered my transport fare back to school. I never saw him again after that. In retrospect, that seemed to have been his final farewell and the portrait, a compensation for his absence from my life. I wish I could say it provided me the love I so desperately yearned for, that it filled the vacuum that had gaped open for so long.

Finding my father was my source of self-identity, and that was as good as it would get. Sometimes, in the still of the night when the lights were out and loneliness drowned my soul, I wondered if he shared any bond with his other children. He showed me a picture of his two little girls while I visited with him. I would never know if he was also aloof with them like he was with me.

I had lost a father and found a father. But finding my father had left me with more questions than answers.

With no Cinderella end in sight, I sought to find the will to live and thrive.

Chapter 6

GRADUATION AND RETURN TO LAGOS

THE YEARS FLEW PAST. I WAS IN THE FINAL YEAR OF MY UNIversity studies, preoccupied with graduating with honors and finding a good job. While students from rich and influential homes could depend on their parents' connections for jobs, my fate was a constant reminder that I qualified for no such luxury. The final year long essay was an important aspect of achieving my desired GPA as it was a 6-unit course. A poor outcome could rob me of the opportunity of finishing strong.

Graduation was months away, and students paced their department hallways waiting to have one final word with their respective project supervisors. Dr. Akerele, the macro-economics professor who oversaw my project, was a mild-mannered man in his early sixties.

"The Structural Adjustment Program is a broad topic," he chided gently, his crooked wire-thin glasses perched on his small nose. "Use the resources in the library extensively."

I shuffled to the information center, clutching a folder filled with several sheets of scruffy notes. I slumped into a wooden chair in the library, shutting my eyes for a brief minute, and desperately wishing my problems would all magically disappear. The last few months before my graduation were some of the most challenging times of my life. I didn't know how I would make it to the end or if I could make it to the end. My money was completely depleted, and I had no idea how I would pay for my project. I rubbed my stomach gently, wincing at the sharp pain the gesture elicited. It got worse with each passing day, excruciating pain that started from my upper abdomen and spread like wildfire to my back. Food deprivation in connivance with stress had brought on stomach ulcers. But I didn't worry too much about food, what I obsessed about was money to print my project. I stared at the file before me, retrieving the draft papers from its pockets.

I had meticulously chosen a topic from the list presented to us by the faculty. There was no better time than that moment to write about the effects of the Structural Adjustment Program (SAP) on the Nigerian economy. SAP was a package of loans and measures offered by the World Bank and International Monetary Fund to help boost Third World economies. With Nigeria caving under the heavy burden of corruption, SAP was that Grim Reaper that buried the carcass of the failed economy. Its stringent demand that the country devalues its currency became the final nail to the coffin.

"Why do we need loans from the World Bank and these other organizations?" I asked my supervisor. Surely we didn't need them, especially as they were never used for the cause for which they were procured. If we eliminated corruption and put our revenues from oil to good use, maybe we wouldn't be at the mercy of the IMF and the Paris Clubs. I was determined to present a superior argument that would earn me an A from my fastidious supervisor. As I struggled to set the right tone for my final project, the universe organized my collision with a certain gentleman, a happenstance that carved the path to my graduation.

I met Dapo in Naraguta hostel on one of his many trips to visit his girlfriend who lived a few rooms away from mine. He would smile at me each time he walked past the narrow hallway. He was a man of affluence, often exhibiting his wealth in the brocade material that hugged his torso like a second skin, and the shiny reflection that bounced off his Rolex watch. Many nights, after he was long gone, the smell of his Polo perfume lingered in the hallways. One evening, en route to his favorite destination, he shoved a small white card in my hand.

"Come to my office," he whispered in a deep hoarse voice.

He was gone before I had the chance to look down at the card that had his full name and address. I could tell that he was attracted to me, but I didn't want any problems with his fierce-looking girl-friend who always wore a scowl every time we met in the hallway.

As I neared the completion of my project, anxiety gnawed at my insides. The only thing that stood between me and my graduation was money to complete my project. Stress and anxiety had reached an all-time high, and the ulcer pain had become an ever-present companion.

I was doubled over in agony in front of my room one evening as Dapo strolled past.

"Is everything ok?" he asked.

"No," I replied tersely, wiping the tears that stung my eyes.

"I'm going through so much stress. I don't know what to do."

I was uncomfortable about baring my problems to a stranger, but I had reached the end of my rope at this point.

"Come to my office tomorrow morning." Compassion flickered in his eyes and he was gone. I'm not sure why I made that trip, perhaps the kindness I saw in his eyes emboldened me. The next morning after class, I was seated in his opulent office, bashfully narrating my woes to him.

"How much is your project?" He asked pensively. I mumbled an answer, afraid to demand such an amount from a stranger who owed me nothing. He reached for the grey metal safe beside his chair and pulled out a bundle of naira notes. I walked out of his office that day with more than I needed. The universe heard my cry and handed me respite in a manner I least expected.

Graduation was a quiet affair, much like my graduation from Queens. I slipped into the last row of chairs in my cap and gown, looking on as the provost delivered his final speech to the graduates. The hall was packed with parents, their faces beaming with pride as they watched their young adults shuffle around in their long wrinkled convocation gowns. I was content to be the spectator who sat back and watched the event of the day unfold. I had so much to be proud of. That I was able to graduate, despite the odds against me, was a miracle. A slender man seated in the aisle across muttered inaudibly, his crisp white _babariga_ sweeping the dusty floor as he leaned over to hug his son for the third time. It was a painful reminder that I was all alone on one of the most important days of my life. Swallowing the lump in my throat, I shifted my focus back to the ceremony. Graduates and their families soon began to trickle out of the hall as the event came to a close. It was a clear sunny day. The legendary cool weather was kept at bay by the warmth of the occasion. I posed for pictures with my classmates, every loud click of the small black Kodak camera telling a unique story of determination and resilience in the face of adversity. This phase of my life was finally over, and it was time to look ahead. I hoped life would be kinder. I hoped to find a good job, meet the man of my dreams, and live happily ever after. I dreamed of a house full of children, my framed pictures hanging on every wall in the house. My picture had never made it to the walls or mantlepiece of any home. That was going to change when I had my own home and my family.

Saying goodbye to Jos, my home of four years, came with mixed feelings. While I was happy to have jumped every hurdle set before me and my university education, the void created by the absence of a loving home still gaped wide open. I wondered where to go and what to do with my life while I waited for the National Youth Service Corps (NYSC) to commence. NYSC was a mandatory one-year program for all Nigerians graduating from higher institutions.

I had an epiphany on one of my last nights in Jos. "Why don't you visit Susan in Kaduna, while you wait for NYSC?" a voice in my head suggested. Kaduna was only a few hours from Jos. Susan was my friend from secondary school. She lived in a sprawling house with her husband and two incredibly cute boys. My time in her home was one of the better times of my life. I left Kaduna with a renewed desire to settle down and forge a happy home of my own. NYSC kicked off with a two-week boot camp. This camp was situated on the outskirts of Abuja, the Nigerian capital. I might have enjoyed it if the conditions were not so unsanitary. We spent the day marching in the scorching Abuja sun, and at night I watched the cult boys from the narrow windows of my stuffy dormitory.

Two weeks later, I was on a night bus to Lagos, my primary state of deployment. Not sure how Aunty Irene would react when

I showed up at her doorstep unannounced, I decided to take the chance anyway. I had nowhere else to go. Moving back in with my aunt came with the condition that she could only offer me a place to lay my head and one meal per day. This was an offer I was only too glad to accept. Not much had changed with her, except that my ten-year-old cousin, Ada, now lived with her. She was a pretty girl with sad eyes who reminded me of the little girl I once was. I vowed to love and protect her for as long as I lived with them.

Finding a job was easy, and within a month of deployment, I got a position at Afribank, one of the top banks in Lagos. I walked down the air-conditioned halls of my new office on my first day, clutching my purse nervously. My new manager showed me around the department, as the staff members eyed my baggy pants and platform shoes suspiciously. That first day, I watched as my preceptor pounded at checks with a wooden stamp, the monotony of the sound almost putting me to sleep. It wasn't long before I had a feel of the stamp, its blue ink running amok on my nicely painted nails. I was placed in the clearing department where every check that came in from other banking institutions was processed. It was a physically and mentally demanding task that left me exhausted at the end of each workday. I counted down to payday to receive my first check, dreaming of the many things I would do with it. Coincidentally in the week my money finally came, I received news that my mother had undergone major surgery. As I clutched the fresh mint notes that were the first fruit of my labor, I thought of a million reasons why my mother did not deserve any of it. Against my better judgment, I sent some of it to her. Maybe this one gesture would buy her love, make me the daughter I so desperately wanted to be to her. My job experience at Afribank was replete with frustration. I couldn't go home each evening until I balanced my books.

"I've looked for this two kobo for nearly two hours! Can I just put in my own money?" I cried out to my manager, one evening.

"That's not how it's done," he chided firmly. "Your books have to balance."

Refusing to buckle under the stress and rigor of my bank job, I had fun every evening after work with my new friend, Pauline, who lived a few houses down the street. I met Pauline on my first sojourn to Lagos. Her mother and my aunt were co-workers, and sometimes she came to the house with her mother. Both shy teenagers, we hardly said a word to each other. I bumped into Pauline one evening after my return to Lagos and could hardly recognize the once chubby awkward teenager. The puppy fat was gone, replaced by endlessly long slim legs and a great sense of fashion. We hit it off. It was strange that a few years earlier, we hardly muttered a word to each other, and now we spent our evenings chatting non-stop. Pauline graduated from law school and was working in a reputable oil company on Victoria Island.

While I vented about my job one evening, she said, "Why don't you apply to my office? They might hire you."

I had never considered a career in the oil industry, but Pauline filled my head with this ambition I thought was nearly unattainable.

As I counted down to my last weeks at Afribank, I began to job hunt aggressively. I dropped off my resume at nearly every bank on Lagos Island, and it was on the day of my first trip to Pauline's office to drop off my job application that I met Jide. I stood in the reception area of the glass building that was the reputable oil company, engaged in small talk with Pauline when he walked past.

"That's the chairman's nephew," she murmured.

"He just got back from Yankee and now works with us."

I turned to look as he made his way up the stairs. He was tall, dark, and a sight for sore eyes.

"Oh my goodness, he's cute," I whispered, as he disappeared up the stairs.

Minutes later, he came down, and as he walked past, our eyes locked. Breaking the gaze, I looked down at my feet in a feeble attempt to hide the heat that flooded my face.

I was back at Pauline's office the next week, desperately trying to convince myself that I returned to check on my application status. I left the oil company on the evening of that second visit, disappointed that I didn't get a view of the handsome Jide. I stood on the white pavement of Ajose Adeogun Street waiting to hail a taxi home when Jide pulled up in a white Hyundai.

"Would you like a ride?" he asked.

"No, thank you," I declined at first. But against my better judgment, I got in the car.

Our first date was at a pizza joint off Awolowo road, Lagos Island. I bit into the thin crust of gooey cheese and vegetables with caution. It was my first attempt at pizza and one that I didn't enjoy at all. He watched me closely, sensing my hesitation.

"You can order something else if you don't like this."

"It's okay," I said, chuckling nervously. "I'm just trying to understand the taste."

"I didn't like it at first too. I had to acquire the taste for it."

We both laughed, easing off the initial tension that hovered like an unwelcome guest. We talked about everything and nothing in particular. He was twenty-six, graduated from university, and went to work at his uncle's oil company.

Jide was kind and thoughtful, and in no time, I was sucked into a whirlwind romance with him. But I guarded my heart. I knew our affair would lead nowhere. He was the son of a Lagos socialite, and I was a small-town girl.

On the eve of a trip to America, Jide threw a large grey T-shirt at me as I made my way to the bathroom.

"Can you sleep in this tonight?

My face set in a frown, confused by the request.

"I will be gone for a while. It will smell of you, so I will wear it when I start to miss you."

I slept in the fuzzy grey shirt. The next morning, I took it off, folded it, and placed it in his suitcase.

It was the middle of September, and I hadn't made much progress with finding a job. I had attended a few interviews, all of which amounted to nothing. Jide had been gone for a month, and Aunty Irene was also visiting her children who lived in the U.K. One early morning, I was jolted out of sleep by excruciating pain in my stomach. I gulped down two tablets of paracetamol and tried to go back to sleep, but the pain worsened. Something was terribly wrong; I could tell from the way my intestines twisted in a million knots. I crawled out of bed, barely able to walk. Ada, roused from sleep by my grunts of pain, stood beside me. Her large eyes filled with worry as she watched me writhe in pain.

"I have to get to a hospital. Go and get ready for school," I muttered, waving her off.

"If you come home from school and I'm not here, go to Pauline's house." I got dressed and staggered to the street to hail a taxi.

"Take me to a hospital," I whispered hoarsely as a rickety yellow taxi screeched to a halt.

"Which hospital, Sisi?" the taxi driver asked.

"Any hospital, just take me to any hospital," I mumbled.

My heart raced in sync with the car wheels as the taxi driver weaved in and out of the rush hour traffic. He was a middle-aged man with tribal marks etched on both sides of his dark oily face. I caught his concerned glances through the rear-view mirror as I raised a trembling hand to wipe my sweat-drenched forehead. He drove maniacally until he got to a shabby building in Obalende, a neighborhood in Lagos Island.

Pointing to the entrance of the building he said, "This one na hospital, Sisi."

Thanking him profusely, I paid him, and stumbled through the door of the rundown building, clutching my midsection.

"Acute appendicitis," the bespectacled doctor announced, palpating my lower right abdomen.

He asked for a relative to sign off on my surgery and a deposit of ten thousand naira, both of which I couldn't provide.

"I don't have your deposit, and my Aunt whom I live with is out of the country," I cried. "Please help me. I will find your money."

Thirty minutes later, I was wheeled into the operating room.

It was early evening when I came to. I opened my eyes to the blurry vision of a narrow room on the second floor of the hospital. It was sparsely furnished. A brown chipped cupboard stood on one side of my bed, and on the other side, a rusty intravenous pole loomed over my right arm. A nurse stood by the foot of the bed, her deep blue uniform shimmering in the soft light. Loud noises of bus conductors loading commercial vehicles in the nearby Obalende bus station filtered in through the rusty window. I closed my eyes, hoping to blot out the grating sounds. The horrible pain in my stomach was gone, replaced by a mild throbbing one.

"Please call this number," I said to the nurse, reeling off Pauline's house telephone number.

"Let her know I'm not coming home tonight." I was worried about my little cousin.

I drifted in and out of sleep, the nurses making intermittent visits with vials of different medications. I was out of the woods following the successful surgery, but I was left with an enormous bill that I had no means of paying. I was frustrated by the timing of the appendicitis. Afribank would have paid for the surgery if I was still a staff member. But my one-year youth corps service was over and the bank's insurance no longer covered me. I tossed and turned all night, sick to my stomach with worry. I missed my grandfather, and longed for the times I took healthcare for granted. Here I was, lying helpless in a dingy Lagos hospital, at the mercy of a doctor who would demand payment for services rendered. I didn't know what to do.

My incision was healing well, and there were no signs of infection. The doctor was scheduled to discharge me the following morning. I still had not come up with any plans to pay my mounting hospital bill. I cried most days and at night, the loud chants of bus conductors were my lullaby - "Iyana Ipaja! Iyana Ipaja! Costain! Costain!" I had grown accustomed to the relentless cacophony. They would have driven me crazy, were I not already out of my mind from worrying about my fate.

The morning I was to be discharged, a fair-skinned nurse walked into my room, holding a transparent vial in her hand.

"This is your appendix. Do you want it?" she asked, attempting to hand it to me.

"No," I replied, turning away.

Looking at my eyes, puffy from crying, she chided, "I've told you to stop crying. Your incision won't heal well if you keep sobbing. Those jerking movements tug at the wound."

Checking my vitals, she added, "You will be discharged this morning."

At about noon, there was a light tap on my door. A nurse stuck her head in the room and said, "There's a man here to see you."

Raising an eyebrow in surprise, I wondered who this man might be. No one knew I was there except for Ada and Pauline. Color drained from my face as Jide walked into the room. He wasn't due back for many months.

"I sat on the long flight home and all I thought about was you," he said. "I sensed you needed me."

Tears rolled down my pale cheeks as he spoke. The nurse had left us alone.

"When will you be discharged?"

"I've been discharged."

"Have you paid?'

"No," I whispered hoarsely, my listless demeanor a clear indication that I didn't have the money.

"I'll be back," he muttered.

Ninety minutes later, he returned with the doctor's money. Jide left again ten days later. I like to believe that it was my cry of anguish that lured him home. I never got to find out what the bill amounted to, and I shudder when I think about what might have happened had he not shown up at the door of that hospital room. He was my guardian angel, the one mother nature assigned with the task of shielding me from some of life's vicious trials. He moved to Port Harcourt the following year, and our relationship died a natural death.

As my relationship with Jide ended, the friendship that I had cultivated in my early teenage years reignited. Andrea had graduated from Obafemi Awolowo University and moved back to Lagos for law school. I was excited to see her after many years. She hadn't changed much, she was still the same girl with a great sense of humor. One day, she invited me to a church on Lagos Island.

"It's a funky church. The choir members perform in night-clubs on Saturday nights and head straight to church on Sunday mornings."

"You've come again with your wild stories," I said, raising my brows in mock shock. I had missed her incredulous tales. The next Sunday, I decided to attend this church service with her just to have a peek at these music artists who led double lives. I liked juicy stories, but I liked living them even better.

"You said it's a fancy church. I don't have anything that fancy to wear."

"Don't worry about what to wear," she assured me. "I will find you a nice dress."

I got to her house that Sunday morning, and she handed me a pretty mustard yellow dress.

"This belongs to Yvonne. If she catches you wearing her dress, I didn't give it to you. You took it from the wardrobe."

I chuckled excitedly. Yvonne was her older sister whom she lived with and who was out of town for the weekend.

We made our way to Muson Center, an edifice situated in the Lagos Island area. The church rented one of the halls in the building. I inhaled deeply, cool air blasting from the air conditioning units filling my lungs as we were ushered into the opulent hall. We were early, so we got seats in the front. As the musicians took the stage, Andrea leaned towards me and whispered, "See them, they haven't slept a wink since last night. Straight from the nightclub." I giggled a little too loudly. But if the perfect blend of acoustic guitar and keyboards was anything to go by, it promised to be a lovely morning. It got even better when the lead singer took to the microphone, her long thin braids cascading down her back like a waterfall. She belted out pitch-perfect notes, her voice reverberating through the high quality loudspeakers in an effect only made for heaven. I shivered slightly as I sat on the plush red cushioned chair, not sure if it was from the effect of the music or the freezing hall. Then the pastor, a bald skinny man, approached the podium. Reflections from the translucent platform illuminated the contours of his dark oversized suit. As he began to preach, I shifted uncomfortably in my seat, convinced that someone had told him my life story.

"You don't have to be lonely another day! You don't have to feel rejected another minute!" he screamed, bouncing around the hall, sweat gliding down his bald head.

"You are accepted in the beloveth. God loves you more than you'll ever know."

Does God really love me? If he does, why am I so alone? Why has he plagued me with two parents who do not care about me? Why have I struggled through life? I was conflicted. The pastor's relentless animation and soul-rending sermon slowly chipped away at my defenses until I was submerged in a whirlpool of emotions. I tried to hide my wet face from Andrea. I wasn't supposed to fall for the pastor's sermon, we came strictly to be entertained by a group of mercenary musicians. But I had fallen hard for this church and the heart-soothing words of the skinny pastor.

"He is not the main pastor. Wait till you hear the senior pastor preach," Andrea said, as we sauntered down the stairs after the service. Lost in thought, I could barely wait to get home to reflect on the extraordinary experience that left me feeling vulnerable, albeit in a good way.

I was back at the church the following Sunday and the Sunday after that. I yearned to hear more about this love the pastor so freely preached about, and each service was better than the last. I began to attend the midweek services, and soon I was also attending the daily prayer meetings. I had found a job in Societe Generale Bank and was deployed to the Ikeja branch, a suburb on Lagos mainland. It was ironic that I was saddled with the same task as the one from Afribank, balancing clearing checks. I hated it, and more so, as I now had a strong reason to be out of the bank before sunset.

"Please I beg you, sir, transfer me to another department - teller, customer service, anything," I pleaded with my supervisor.

"You are an important part of the clearing team, and you have a natural knack for balancing checks," he replied.

"Me, natural knack?" I scoffed. I could not balance books to save my life. Nearly every evening, I was the last to exit the premises, looking for missing kobos lost in the twirled receipts of bank checks.

Despite the rigors of my job, I looked forward to my evening church activities. I slipped into the daily prayer meeting one evening, hoping to blend in unnoticed. I was late for the third time that week, after another frustrating ineffectual day at the bank. A new face was leading the meeting. I didn't recall ever seeing him before. His large saucer-like eyes casually perused me before they went back to the leather-encased bible he had before him. I was impressed by his eloquence. He meticulously explained each relevant chapter of scripture, building cohesive arguments before announcing the next prayer point.

He walked up to me as soon as the meeting was over and introduced himself. "Hi, I'm Emeka."

"Joy," I responded.

"Are you new to church?" He asked, extending his hand.

"I should be asking you that," I replied, shaking his hand. "I've never seen you in any of the meetings."

"I'm one of the prayer leaders but I took a few weeks off."

Emeka began to lead the prayer meetings regularly from then

on. His intelligence and deep knowledge of the Bible blew me away. We started to spend time together after the meetings. He spent hours teaching me scriptures, presenting each verse in ways I never heard before.

One evening, after the usual meeting he asked, "Can you make egusi soup and pounded yam?"

"Of course," I replied cheekily. "What Igbo girl doesn't know how to make egusi?"

"It's my favorite soup, that's why I'm asking."

If that was the screening exercise that led him to believe I was to be his wife, I will never know, but a few weeks later, we were formally in courtship.

He was first my pastor and now my fiance. I felt I could trust him with my story. Besides, I had to get it out fast so that if he felt he wouldn't want to deal with a girl with such dysfunctional family dynamics, he could be on his way. I always dreaded telling my story; the shame and awkwardness I felt having to tell it, often left me in despair. But I had to tell this one person, it was imperative.

"Your earthly heritage means nothing," Emeka said as he sat listening to me relive painful memories. "You are accepted in the beloveth. Think about it, what heritage did Jesus have?"

I was beyond relieved that he wasn't put off. As cold as it may seem, I was also relieved that he didn't have parents, and I wasn't going to be scrutinized by adults who would have probably thought I wasn't good enough for their son.

"Promise me something," I said to him.

"What?"

"Promise me you will never call me "bastard". Every time I was called that ugly word, something in me died a little."

"I give you my word that I won't."

Emeka was the oldest of seven children. They were a close knit family. Losing their parents early seemed to have handed them a special bond. They lived in a decent three-bedroom bungalow on Lagos mainland. I was apprehensive about meeting his siblings, but my anxiety was assuaged when I discovered that they were mostly within my age range. His four sisters were beautiful. I hoped that one day when I had daughters, they would inherit their aunts' hourglass figures and thick black eyebrows.

My first Christmas with them was beautiful. It was a sneak peek at the familial love I longed for all my life. An array of dishes was laid out on the old chipped mahogany dining table.. The girls had been up all night cooking, a tradition I suspect was passed on by their late mother. I watched in fascination as they bantered amongst themselves, reminiscing about their late father. I was green with envy. One day, I thought to myself, I will have a house full of children, and we will gather around the table and tell jokes and laugh just like this. I couldn't wait to start a family.

I began to feel anxious when we fixed our wedding date. We had courted for eighteen months. My anxiety heightened as our wedding day approached. Was I making the right choice? How would my family dynamics present at the wedding? I was estranged from everyone in my mother's family, except for Aunty Irene who had categorically told me that my wedding date coincided with her date out of the country to visit her children. I wasn't sure if my mother's brother would walk me down the aisle. I hadn't seen or spoken to him since my grandfather's funeral when he offered me that measley one thousand naira. My father had completely fallen off the radar. I had not heard from him in years. Emeka and I contemplated going in search of him. But I didn't want to. I didn't think I mattered to him. If I did, he would have made an effort to be in my life.

"You can write to him and introduce yourself," I said to Emeka. "It hurts to beg for love, especially from the people whose duty it is to give it to you."

My mother's family was the one I knew. I was going to trust them to at least put in the minimum and show up for my wedding. But first, we had to get the traditional wedding out of the way.

Traveling to Obosi for the traditional wedding brought up many conflicting memories. In the absence of my grandmother, my oldest uncle's wife, Mummy Ibe, took over the role of matriarch. She worked tirelessly, ensuring that the traditional rites were observed. We had a quiet ceremony on a Saturday morning. Toothless old men, most of whom I had never seen in my life, showed up to partake of the bride price. My mother came from Onitsha on the morning of the ceremony and played a fringe role, declining to show up when the visitors asked for the mother of the bride. She was meeting my husband-to-be for the first time, and she was indifferent to him. I was relieved when the ceremony was over. We headed back to Lagos to begin plans for the next phase of our life.

Chapter 7

MARRIAGE
New family; New Drama

MY WEDDING DAY FINALLY ARRIVED, THAT PERFECT ENDING to the Cinderella story I had dreamed of for so long. Fate handed me a fresh canvas, and I was going to paint glossy pictures of a beautiful life on it. As I waited to be joined in holy matrimony, I began to second-guess myself. This was only made worse by Emeka running late for the wedding. I sat at the back of the silver-colored Mercedes waiting for my groom, my stomach twisting in tiny knots with every passing minute. He finally arrived forty-five minutes later, apologizing profusely for underestimating the Saturday morning Lagos traffic.

Shrugging the gnawing emotions away, I focused on the wedding and the hundreds of people who had gathered to make our day special.

My mother, her husband, and her children arrived the night before the wedding, and so did my uncle who walked me down the aisle. I looked beautiful in my cream Victorian-style wedding gown. My hair was pulled back in a tight knot, and fresh beige and orange roses formed tendrils around my temple. Emeka looked handsome in his dark grey suit.

"Do you take Joy Nnenne Iweka as your lawful wife, to have and to hold, from this day forward, for better or for worse, for richer or poorer, in sickness and in health, to love and to cherish until death do you part?"

"I do," Emeka responded, almost too quickly.

My voice quivered as I repeated my vows.

After the wedding, I moved into the family house Emeka shared with his siblings. It was meant to be a temporary arrangement until we found our place, but weeks turned to months and there was no sign that we were moving anytime soon. I wasn't getting along with one of his sisters. Even though we didn't share bathrooms, we shared other common areas like the living room and the kitchen. My relationship with his sister continued to deteriorate and one day, it ended in a shouting match.

"You came here to break up our family," she hurled at me.

"No," I yelled back. "Your brother has a wife now and you need to respect that."

That was it. I had had enough, and so, I began to put pressure on him.

"We need to move," I would say amid tears. "I need my own space."

My pleas fell on deaf ears at first, but as I continued, he became defensive. We began to argue regularly, and one day in the middle of a vicious exchange, he blurted it out.

"Have you ever lived in a house this nice? Bastard!"

Doubling over like I had been dealt a blow to my stomach,

my lips quivered with emotion. I looked him in the eye and asked, "What did you just call me?"

He looked away, knowing he had just broken a promise, the first promise he made to me. I suppressed the persistent voice that told me I had made a terrible mistake, that I had married my detractor.

I found out I was with child one month into our first anniversary. I sat across from the doctor in his small office, mixed emotions flooding my mind. On one hand, I was ecstatic, but on the other, I had no desire to bring a baby into a house I shared with Emeka's siblings. My relationship with his sisters was in tatters. When I was home, I was confined to our bedroom, living like an unwelcome guest.

"I'm not having a baby in this house," I told him many times. To prove I was serious, I launched an aggressive house hunt. I hoped to find a place on Lagos Island.

It was my first trimester of pregnancy and I couldn't keep anything down – not even water. We had just bought our first car, a battered brown Peugeot 505 that had over two hundred thousand miles on it, and had no air conditioning. I was grateful for this car as it ferried me across the heavily congested Third Mainland Bridge to Lagos Island for work every day. I had changed jobs and now worked on Lagos Island again. Opening the heavily corroded passenger door each evening after work was a constant reminder of the unbearably long commute home. I would sit in the stuffy car, drenched in sweat, watching hawkers weave through the stand-still traffic. "Gala! Gala! Gala!" they would chant as they approached my window, waving a couple of dry pastries at me. Gala was the cheap version of the elite sausage roll and the comfort food for Lagos traffic, but not the best choice for a nauseous woman pregnant with her first child. Traffic could span anything from two to three hours. Having lived and worked on Lagos Island for the majority of my time in Lagos, this was a new experience for me and one that I did not enjoy.

A few weeks before Christmas, I bumped into an old friend from the University of Jos. Nneka had graduated from the Theater Arts department, was married, and worked in one of the big banks. As we engaged in small talk, she mentioned in passing, that her family was moving from their three-bedroom apartment on Lagos Island.

"We've outgrown that place," she said. "This is going to be our last Christmas there."

"Wait! What will you do with this old apartment?" I enquired.

"We rented from my sister-in-law. I'm sure she might want to rent it out."

I begged her to put in a good word for us with her sister-in-law as we were hunting for an apartment on the Island.

Fortune was on my side, as one week later Nneka called me with the only news I was dying to hear.

"I spoke to my sister-in-law. You can have the apartment."

I was beside myself with joy. I couldn't wait to share this news with my husband.

"Well, I can't afford the rent right now," Emeka said over dinner that evening. My heart sank. He ran an automobile repair business on the Island and often complained that business was slow.

"We have to find a way," I pleaded. "The offer is too good to pass up. We might not find this kind of deal again."

"If you can make it happen, go ahead. I don't have the money."

The firm tone of his voice told me all I needed to know. That night I tossed and turned, barely getting any sleep. As day broke, it was clear what I was going to do. I walked up to my boss and asked for a loan. We signed a two-year lease later in the week and our new landlady handed us the keys. My job, Emeka's job, and our new apartment were all within a three-mile radius. I couldn't believe my luck. Sitting in excruciating traffic was going to be a thing of the past. I started to feel alive again.

I looked forward to the weekends when we spent time doing up the apartment. We ripped off the plastic tiles on the floor and replaced them with emerald green marble. The nursery was my favorite room to furnish. A perfect blend of blue wallpaper complimented the Winnie the Pooh stickers. We were expecting a boy much to Emeka's great delight. As my due date drew close, I made frequent trips to the market.

Balogun Market sprawled across several blocks on Lagos Island. Having more sellers than buyers, it had a congested feel to it. I weaved in and out of stores, searching for good bargains on baby clothes, bile rising up my throat as I navigated the narrow gutters filled with smelly stagnant water. It never ceased to amaze me how vendors sat by those gutters, oblivious to the stench.

"Aunty, *come buy market*," they would croon, tugging at my hand as I walked past.

While I battled with a third-trimester diagnosis of hypertension, Emeka brandished a "picture" of his unborn son. We had some guests over for a housewarming party one evening, and he passed around the black and white copy of the scan from the doctor's office.

"You should stop showing people that scan and calling it a picture," I told him. "You can't make out anything from it."

"That's my son," he replied, waving me off.

Pastor John chuckled. He was one of our friends from church. I felt a little uncomfortable with Emeka's display as Pastor John had been married for a while and didn't have any children. His dark, slender wife sat beside him, quietly taking it all in.

As the countdown to my due date continued, I paid frequent visits to the doctor. He needed to keep a close eye on my blood pressure. On one of those visits, I saw Rita, a good friend of my cousin's. "I'm having a boy," she announced proudly, running her hand protectively across her rotund bump. I was very happy for her. Having had three girls, she was under immense family pressure to birth an heir. It was a high-risk pregnancy, more so, as she was advanced in age. But the demand by her husband's family to hand them a male child or risk losing her marriage if she did not, was well worth the risk to her. Even though I wanted a girl, I was glad I was having a boy. I could only imagine the pressure Rita endured. I wished her well as she sauntered to her black air-conditioned Mercedes. I believed I would see her again, our due dates were a week apart.

I felt increasingly unwell as my blood pressure skyrocketed. Dr. Dele decided it was best to induce me two weeks before my due date. Gathering my toiletries in the small bathroom of our apartment, I stole a quick glance at the mirror, gasping at how puffy my face had become. I barely recognized myself. An eerie feeling washed over me as I prepared to make that last trip to bring forth my child.

"Please God, let this delivery go smoothly," I muttered, trudging up the stairs of the hospital. It was a Monday evening. The hospital reception was empty except for the nurse who huddled over the polished brown desk shuffling through paperwork. She looked up as I approached her desk, her face dark with emotion, uneasy silence and gloom enveloping the room.

"Is everything okay?" I asked, setting down my stuffed duffel bag on the floor.

"We lost a patient this evening; the woman I saw you speaking to the other night."

I stood rooted to the spot, my head spinning as I tried to make sense of the news. Rita was gone? My mind refused to process the information.

"You must be mixing her up with some other woman," I said to the nurse, my voice trembling with emotion. It had to be a cruel joke, one that had me covered in goosebumps as I dragged my numb legs up the stairs to my assigned room. A tall handsome nurse walked into my room for the fourth time in an hour, "Madam are you feeling any contractions?"

"No," I muttered. She unhooked the empty bag of oxytocin solution, replacing it with another full bag. I lay in bed that night, sleep eluding me as I thought about Rita and the events that led to her death. She had sacrificed her life to birth an heir; paid a costly price to appease the demands of society. Death had snatched her from her three beautiful daughters and the helpless infant son whose gut-wrenching cries across the hall reminded me that he would never be held by his mother. I wiped the tears that escaped my eyelids. Life was transient, fickle like the flame of a candle. You are here today and gone tomorrow. I stared at the IV bag as the solution dripped into the chamber, slowly making its way through the tubing into my bruised right cubital vein. As my body flouted the command of the labor-inducing drug, my mind slowly accepted the news of Rita's death.

Twelve hours later and pumped full of oxytocin, my body continued to flirt with the notorious medication, refusing to budge in the slightest bit. Dr. Dele began to explore other options of labor induction. A nurse came into my room with a doppler which she placed on my stomach. Noticing the frantic motion with which she moved it across my bump, I asked, "Is everything okay?"

"I'll be back," she retorted, a frown furrowing her bushy brows. She returned a few minutes later with Dr. Dele and a sophisticated-looking device which she strapped to my stomach. They huddled over the machine, whispering. I watched them intently, the rapid rise and fall of my chest visible through the blue hospital gown.

It seemed like a lifetime before Dr. Dele turned to me and said, "We have to take you in for an emergency C-Section. The baby is distressed, and we can hardly hear the heartbeat."

I was emotionally spent. The past twenty-four hours were some of the most tumultuous of my pregnancy. I held tightly to the hand of the midwife as I was wheeled to the operating room. Emeka had arrived and stood beside me. He was not one to show emotion. Forty-five minutes later, much to the shock of my husband and my doctor, my baby, a light-skinned girl with a full head of hair came into the world.

I was hazy from the anesthesia when they placed her in my arms. Ketandu was the most beautiful thing I ever saw. The nurse took her away as quickly as she brought her, but not before I noticed that her gums, tongue, and skin were all yellow.

"Why is her tongue yellow... and her gums?" I asked the nurse.

"She has jaundice," the nurse replied, scurrying for the door with my baby held tightly in her arms. I suppressed the eerie feeling that something was terribly wrong with my newborn. I drifted into a drug-induced sleep and woke up the next morning to the news that I feared most. Ketandu was gravely ill. The jaundice had worsened through the night and was not responding to phototherapy. She was born with the hemolytic disease of the newborn, a condition caused by rhesus incompatibility between my rhesus factor and hers. I was blood type O negative and she was B positive. Her blood had crossed the placenta into my body during the pregnancy. My body recognized her blood as a foreign body and mounted antibodies to attack it. These antibodies crossed the placenta into her body and were breaking down her red blood cells leading to severe jaundice. Guilt overwhelmed me. How does my body mount an attack against my child, the one thing I wanted most in this world? Someone must be playing a cruel joke on me. I glanced up at my doctor who stood by my bedside trying to help me make sense of the nightmare.

"The problem is that we can't find the blood type for the transfusion. O negative is a rare blood type," Dr. Dele explained.

"So what is going to happen?" I asked. "And why are you transfusing her with my blood type and not her blood type?"

"We need to transfuse her with your blood type because the antibodies already in her body from your blood will continue to break down her red blood cells if we use her blood type. The antibodies will not break down O negative blood cells because they recognize it."

The explanation flew over my head. I didn't care for the medical jargon. I just wanted them to cure my child. She didn't deserve the pain and suffering that I caused her. I glanced down at my body in disgust, the anatomy that decided it was a good idea to fight her own child. The frantic search for the blood began. Dr. Dele's team scoured Lagos blood banks with no success. They extended the search to the neighboring cities and yet this rare blood type could not be found. In desperation, I reached out to my mother and her family, hoping they might match this blood group, but unfortunately, I didn't share this rare blood type with any of them.

The search continued into the third day. If she wasn't transfused within the next twenty-four hours, she would have a heart attack and die, and if she survived, she might end up with permanent brain damage. As the second hand of the clock above my bed ticked, I knew we were working against time. Every minute that passed spelled doom. I couldn't sleep, not while my baby lay in the ICU fighting for her life. Gathering the catheter and the pole that held my IV, I limped down the hall to the ICU. Barricaded by thick glass, I watched the rapid rise and fall of her chest as she fought to hold on to life. Sadness overwhelmed me. I brought this suffering on her and I would do anything to see it end. A section of her dark rich hair had been shaved off to make way for the transparent catheter that ran through a vein on her head. It was a painful sight to behold. But I could see she was a fighter. I sensed she wanted to live.

"I'm sorry my body betrayed you," I muttered.

"I will make it up to you. I promise. You are all I have in this world. Stay with me." As I watched her, a fleeting smile flashed across her pale face, a sign that she had heard me.

Down the hall on the opposite end, Rita's son cried, his piercing sound of anguish shredding my hearts to bits. I hobbled to the nursery, hoping the nurse would let me hold him. It was barely a month since Rita and I had stood chatting in the hospital lounge, eyes sparkling with love for our unborn children. Fear suddenly enveloped me, terror so strong that all I wanted to do was grab both babies and run; just run and never stop.

The next morning I sat up in bed, nervously kicking the metal frame of my bed as I awaited the latest news on the blood hunt. A nurse walked in beaming. They found the blood at long last. I would never know the full details. A woman walked into the hospital, was a match, and she donated. She was our guardian angel, one that was sent to save my daughter's life. I hoped to find her and thank her, but the hospital was reluctant about giving me her details. I sent her a silent prayer of immense gratitude.

We were discharged seven days later. I was happy to take my child home, away from the depressing hospital environment. My mother refused to come for "omugwo", the traditional postnatal support visit that Igbo mothers made when their daughters gave birth. It did not come as a surprise that she did not wish to meet her first grandchild. She did, however, send a nanny, an older woman who was emaciated to the point that she looked gaunt. She also sent a note along with the nanny. It was a curt letter that read, "Please take Cordelia for a TB test. I noticed she has a dry hollow cough." Cordelia tested positive for the tuberculosis test. Deeply afraid that I exposed my newborn to a debilitating airborne disease, I sent Cordelia back to my mother in the southeast, early the following morning.

Motherhood took its toll on me. Exhausted and sleep-deprived, I began to slip into depression. Ketandu slept all day and was awake through the night. Feeling isolated, I cried every day. My child was healthy, and we were lucky to escape a disease that nearly took her life, but try as I might, I could not shake off the blues that threatened to drown my soul.

I was grateful for the guests who came during the day, guests from church, but I also wished they wouldn't come just so I would sleep when Ketandu slept. I was grateful for my two older cousins, Chiadi and Nwamaka who lived within a ten-mile radius. Their grandparents were my late grandfather's older siblings. They were the closest I had to sisters and also the reason I didn't disintegrate into utter hopelessness whenever Emeka hurled my family circumstances in my face. Our fights were becoming frequent again, mostly triggered by money problems. Both my cousins were happily married. I longed for what they both had – husbands that loved them and financial security. I also recognized that marriage required work. I was willing to put in the work to have what they had.

One evening, Nwamaka pulled into our driveway with her trunk bursting at the seams. I watched in tears as her driver walked up my steps with several boxes of assorted foods. The foods, including dry items, were enough to last several months. Aware that Nwamaka brought food, Emeka didn't think he needed to provide money for food anymore even though we still needed fresh food items. That evening when he returned from work, I asked him for money.

"I don't have any money," he snapped.

"Well, I need money to buy meat," I insisted.

"Didn't your cousin give you money?"

"Am I married to my cousin? You insult me about not having a family, but now you want the same family that I do not have, to feed us."

"How dare you insult me," he roared. "Every item your cousin brought into this house is getting tossed out." He stormed into the kitchen and flinging open the cabinets, began to hurl out the items.

"What are you doing?" I screamed, extending my hand in a futile attempt to stop him. Shoving me aside, he tossed the roll of St. Louis sugar over the banister of the back staircase, to the compound below. Mortified, I ran to the cabinet desperately trying to shut it. He pushed me aggressively, and I staggered, falling on my back. He dragged me by my hair to the hallway as I screamed and kicked. Afraid my Cesarean scar had ruptured, I lay still. The sound of my daughter's faint cry in the nursery reminded me that I needed to stay alive for her. I got up very slowly and walked to the nursery. Picking up my now wailing daughter from her crib, I made for the front door. The crashing sound of the giant tin of Peak powdered milk as it hit the ground, was the last sound I heard as I shut the front door. It was almost midnight and I didn't know where to go. My daughter was barely one month old. I looked down at her cheeks which were flushed from crying. I left the house without a shawl to wrap her in.

Hailing a taxi, I headed to Pastor John's house. He was the only one I could think of. I didn't want to go to my cousins; I didn't want them to know that my husband was physically abusive. Pastor John was shocked to see me at such an ungodly hour. He took my infant from my arms as he held the black gate open for me.

"What happened, Joy girl?" he asked. I didn't know where to begin my story. I was embarrassed at first, but as I began to speak, I let it all out. I told him about the verbal abuse and how it had turned physical, and how he threw the food out of the house.

"Does he know you came here?"

"No," I whispered between sobs. "He doesn't even know I left."

"You will stay here with the baby. Let's see what he does. He had no right to rough handle a woman that just had his baby. No right at all."

"He treats me as he pleases because he knows I have no one to protect me."

"Well... he has me to answer to from now on."

Pastor John went out the next morning and bought us a few necessities. Being under Pastor John's wings offered me protection in ways I always yearned for; he soon became that father figure that I desperately needed. His wife was the perfect hostess, her gentle words helping me navigate my day. At night, when they were asleep in their room, Ketandu would gaze intently at my sad face as I stayed up feeding her, warm tears cascading down my face and soaking her pink jumpsuit. I had never had anyone look at me with so much love. I could almost hear her say, "It's okay, Mommy. You have me now. It's you and me against the world." I vowed to protect this little being I loved so much and who loved me back with equal measure. I decided that I would fight for my marriage, and give my child the stable home I never had. We didn't go back home until one month later. I'm not sure Emeka looked for us until Pastor John admitted that we had been in his house. The first night he came to get us, Pastor John sent him back, saying he didn't think - my husband was remorseful. It took a third visit for Pastor John to let us go home with him. This was after he made him promise that he would not lay his hand on me.

I struggled to find normalcy in my marriage. It was a rude awakening, but my home was going to be no paradise on earth. If there was one thing that brought me joy, it was my daughter. I spent hours sitting by her crib watching her sleep. I didn't think it was possible to love anyone or anything so much. It was during that time, I truly began to resent my mother. Why couldn't she feel this deep inexplicable love that I felt for my daughter? I also concluded that Emeka's shabby treatment was a direct result of my mother's lack of involvement in my life. This was confirmed by one of our many arguments when he said, "No one loves you, not even your mother. If I kill you and bury you, no one will notice." That hurt deeply, more than when he called me "Bastard." It hurt because he was right, deep down I knew that no one really cared if I lived or died. My heart grew cold with each cruel word he hurled at me. Worse still, was that I couldn't confide in anyone. I was trapped and desperately unhappy. I took personal responsibility for every fight, convincing myself that I wasn't good enough; wasn't submissive enough. I tried to be a better wife, the type he espoused through scripture every day at our daily morning devotion. The more I tried, the more I failed at it until the last shreds of self-esteem I mustered to hang on to through the years were left in tatters. I was left to wonder why I was so unlovable, why I could not forge any meaningful relationship. It had to be that I was cursed.

As Ketandu approached the three-month mark, I flipped through pages of baby books in frantic search for social and emotional milestones appropriate for her age. The ordeal at her birth still haunted me, along with the possibility that she might have suffered brain damage. She appeared to meet and exceed most of the standards.

It was our first rainy season in our apartment and the streets flooded every time it rained. This was a recurring problem. Our car was submerged in the flood and for days we were stranded indoors, opting to be ferried out with makeshift canoes if there was an urgent need. The neighborhood youth charged us for this service. The constant floods destroyed electrical transformers and many times we were without electricity, relying heavily on generators for alternate power supply.

I started to feel queasy towards Christmas, the feeling getting worse in the evenings. I had begun to shed my post-pregnancy weight, happy that my equilibrium was gradually getting back on track. Ketandu was eight months old, had mastered her pincer grasp, and was threatening to take her first steps. One day, I was doubled over the toilet bowl regurgitating my stomach contents when Emeka walked in and said, "This reminds me of when you were pregnant." I lifted my head from the toilet bowl between retches to roll my eyes at him. Two nights later, we were both seated in the scruffy office of a doctor we found two blocks from our apartment building.

"This doctor had better not be a quack," I muttered as I opened the unpainted door leading to the bathroom. He had handed me a transparent cup for a urine sample. I was sure I was only plagued by my longtime companion, stomach ulcers, which I was there to get medication for. I reluctantly handed him the urine sample, taking my seat next to Emeka who was holding Ketandu.

A few minutes later, the doctor looked up and said, "Congratulations Madam. You're very pregnant."

"What?" I said, bursting into tears.

"I can't be pregnant. I'm still breastfeeding my daughter. How can I be pregnant?" I asked, trying to bargain my way out of the news.

"You are not breastfeeding exclusively. And even if you are, you can still get pregnant."

I was not ready for another baby. My marriage didn't deserve another baby.

"Madam, if you are not ready for this pregnancy, I can schedule you for an abortion."

"No," Emeka and I spoke in unison. That was one of the few times we ever agreed on anything.

My second pregnancy was tougher than the first. Knowing I wouldn't be granted maternity leave for two consecutive years, I sent in my resignation from my job. Emeka had just landed a big contract, so we were going to be okay financially. This contract came at the time we needed it most. If Emeka managed it well, we would never have to suffer financial hardship another day. I begged him to make me a director of his company. In spite of himself, he acknowledged that I was blessed with the unique gift of financial management. I wasn't sure if my uncanny skill was as a result of the dire financial struggles from my past or if it was a natural flair. It was certainly a gift I was willing to put to good use in our marriage, if my husband would let me. To my pleasant surprise, he made me the financial director of the project. I put together the proposal of how much we would make from the project, what we could potentially invest in, and how much that would change our lives. But it didn't take long for the plan to crumble. Emeka woke up one morning and unceremoniously fired me. "Did I do something wrong?" I pleaded with him to at least give me an explanation as to why I was no longer a part of the project. He offered none. I watched with bated breath as the finances were mismanaged. The project eventually collapsed. The only good thing that came out of it was that we replaced our battered 505 with a decent Peugeot 305 and the novelty of the project helped us secure visas to the U.K.

With the news of my second pregnancy, I began the search for a blood donor. If the new baby needed a transfusion, I wanted to be ready. As good as Dr. Dele was, his prices were not affordable and the last childbirth left us nearly bankrupt and the bulk of that bill was paid by my cousin, Chiadi. Healthcare was generally cheaper on Lagos Mainland, so we decided to look for a new doctor there. We found Dr. Tayo in Surulere. His hospital was located at the end of a quiet residential street. White daisies adorned the entrance of the one-story building, giving it a cozy vibe. He was a soft-spoken man in his late forties and had practiced in the U.K. for several years before returning to Nigeria. We sat across from him on the first visit as he meticulously examined me, taking down all the minute details we provided him. Two weeks later, we were back to discuss my blood work. He confirmed that I was rhesus negative. Out of the abundance of caution, he placed me on a monthly rhogam injection recommending that I didn't carry the pregnancy full term.

I sat back, enjoying the busy scenery of Apongbon Market as our Peugeot jostled in rhythm to the clanks of the old Eko Bridge. Emeka drove me to the next doctor's appointment that day as he wanted to know the gender of the baby. He started to talk about a son as soon as we found out I was pregnant.

"I don't reveal the sex of babies," Dr. Tayo explained to him. "You have a healthy baby on the way and that is what really counts."

I was relieved. Dr. Dele got the gender wrong the last time, so I didn't want to dwell on it a second time. But I hoped for Emeka's sake that it would be a boy. We decided on the last Friday in September for the elective cesarean section. I had found O negative blood in the event that we needed it, feeling more prepared than the last time.

Ketandu was fifteen months old, with a curious mind and a photographic memory. I was relieved that the horrors at her birth were truly behind us. My mother still hadn't met her, and from the look of things, she didn't seem to be interested in meeting her first granddaughter. She did not know that a second grandchild was on the way. One day, Emeka decided to drive to Onitsha to plead with her to come and meet her grandchild. She miraculously agreed to drive back to Lagos with my husband. I had not seen her or spoken to her since the day of my wedding almost three years prior. She was her usual self; detached, listless, and lack-luster. We didn't have much to say to each other. The period when we could have bonded was long gone. I had questions for her but was afraid to open that can of worms. She didn't strike me as wanting to engage in meaningful conversation. She left a few days later and said she would be back when the new baby arrived.

I waddled through the door of Dr. Tayo's hospital on the day of my scheduled elective Cesarean birth, Emeka following behind with my suitcase. My heart lurched at the memory of my first experience. I prayed for a smooth delivery this time. We had done everything we could to forestall any unpleasant incident. My blood donor was on standby in case we needed him. We had crossed all our T's and dotted our I's, yet I couldn't shake off the uneasiness that plagued me.

As soon as we checked in, Emeka turned to the nurse and asked for the consent form.

"Why are you asking for the form so soon?" I asked.

"I have to sign it now before I leave."

"What do you mean, leave?"

"I'm leaving. I have things to do," Emeka replied. He reached into the top pocket of his shirt, pulled out a pen, signed my consent form, and stormed out of the building. I watched his back until he disappeared. I had no idea what just happened. I couldn't fathom why he chose not to witness the birth of his second child. Had he found out that it was another girl? What could be more important than what was just about to happen? We had known about this date for many months. He had ample time to shift his appointments. I wasn't sure I was going to forgive him for this brash behavior. I had forgiven physical, emotional, verbal, and financial abuse but this was a new low, one that I didn't know how to navigate. I sat at the reception area weeping, and a young nurse with kind grey eyes walked up to me and tried to comfort me.

"Madam, please don't cry. Try and focus on the miracle that is about to happen. You need your strength for the next hour."

She was right. I needed my strength for my new baby. I wiped the tears from my puffy eyes and followed her to the room that was prepared for me.

At 7 O'clock that Friday night in September 2002, I welcomed my second daughter, Amara into the world. She was a beautiful girl with a perfect round head and silky black hair. When I laid my eyes on her, I forgot that I ever wished for a boy. I gushed with overwhelming love just like I did for her sister. She weighed a little less than Ketandu since she was four weeks early. A pediatrician was on standby to evaluate her. Her blood was drawn immediately to check for the presence of bilirubin which could be an indication of jaundice. Her results came back clear. Dr. Tayo and I were in a jubilatory mood. It seemed we had beat the condition that afflicted her sister. Her eyes and skin were clear, and her gums were a perfect pink. Emeka came in about three hours after her birth. He wore a deep scowl. I didn't ask why he scowled. I suspected it had to do with the gender of the baby. I didn't ask because I didn't want to know. He hung around for a few minutes and left. That night, Nwamaka and Chiadi came. Their presence gave me the comfort that I needed.

As daybreak approached, Amara began to exhibit signs of jaundice. Her clear white eyes and her skin turned a dark tinge of yellow. The pediatrician was contacted, and after a series of blood tests, she decided that Amara needed a blood transfusion. My heart sank. I thought we had escaped it this time. I thought we had beat the monster. I reminded myself that we were more prepared this time and as such the process wouldn't be as traumatic. As Dr. Tayo and his team took her away, I clenched my fist in apprehension, praying for an uneventful procedure. I paced the long cold corridors, willing them to hurry up with the process. It had been forty-five minutes and Amara's loud shrieks pierced my heart. Fifteen minutes later, the pediatrician emerged holding her in the crook of her arm. It had previously amused me how this doctor held babies like they were some personal trophy. Today, I was anything but amused. As she handed me my baby, I could see the immediate transformation in her color. Her skin was back to its natural glow and her eyes had turned pristine white. Having cried for a solid hour, her voice was hoarse. I ran my fingers through her silky hair as she nursed, relief washing over me. I was also glad that they didn't have to shave her head as they did with her sister. That image of Ketandu lying helpless in the ICU still haunted me occasionally.

We were discharged four days later after we were given a clean bill of health. As the pretty young nurse on duty swaddled her in a pink fuzzy blanket, she asked, "Is her father Indian?"

"No," I replied. "Her father is not Indian." Her very silky black hair gave her an Asian look.

Back at home, Ketandu's eyes glowed with curiosity as she peered down at her sister. I was worried that she might not accept her. "Baby," she said, touching her gingerly at first and then kissing her. Ketandu was very protective of her baby sister from the onset. I had to keep a close eye on them as she always tried to climb into the crib to pick her up.

My mother visited again after I returned home with Amara. Emeka and I had another one of our arguments one evening. We were in the nursery and my mother was holding Amara. This argument wasn't over anything in particular, but it escalated very quickly.

"Bastard!" he yelled.

I instinctively turned to look at my mother, and I could see her recoil. Early the following morning, she left and that was the last time she ever visited.

"What have you done? She wants nothing to do with me, and now you've made it worse! What did you hope to achieve with that? What did she do to you?" I hurled a barrage of questions at Emeka, none of which he bothered to answer. The verbal abuse sadly, had become part and parcel of my life. It hurt less as my marriage grew older. I no longer cried about it. My heart had calloused over the years, and I had learned to give as much as I received. But he knew I longed to salvage my relationship with my mother, and calling me that name, in front of her, was him setting us back.

When Ketandu turned two, we decided to enroll her in a playgroup. We diligently hunted for a school until we found a small one. It was a new school located in Lekki, an upscale neighborhood in the heart of Lagos Island. I knew we were overly ambitious when on the first day of school, I pulled up beside luxury cars belonging to fellow parents. I alighted from our modest blue Peugeot, clutching Ketandu with one hand and her lunch box with the other. I wished I had paid more attention to my appearance as I breezed past a couple of mothers adorned in Gucci shoes and Louis Vuitton purses. A sense of inferiority enveloped me as I inhaled a whiff of designer fragrance. I quickly tossed aside the feeling, focusing instead on what led me to the school, which was to give my child the best possible start in life. Traffic was torturous, and making the commute each day was a nightmare. We needed to beat the early morning traffic if we were to get Ketandu to school by eight. We would leave home at the crack of dawn most mornings, navigating the street sellers who hawked anything from live puppies to bootleg movies in the standstill traffic jam on Falomo Bridge. Ketandu cried every time I dropped her off.

"Don't worry," her class teacher, Mrs. Johnson, assured me. "She will settle in soon." She finally stopped crying after nearly a month, during which I wondered if we enrolled her in school too early. She would come home every day regurgitating everything her teacher said in class. All the anxieties I entertained about what had happened at her birth, and how that might have compromised her mental status dissipated, given what a bright mind she had. She sang nursery rhymes to her little sister who was now three months old and in awe of her. Both girls were growing and bonding, and everything seemed to be going well, except for my marriage which was now in shambles. The fights were not abating. We disagreed about everything under the sun. These arguments sometimes ended in physical fights, but the wounds I nursed the most were the emotional wounds, those cold callous words he threw at me in the heat of the argument.

"You're nothing but a prostitute." "You're ugly on the inside and out." Those wounds gaped open long after the physical scars disappeared. I was certain I had made the wrong choice after all. I had convinced myself that marrying a godly man would shield me, and perhaps even help me heal from the traumas of my childhood, but I wasn't sure anymore. As the altercations became a frequent part of our lives, I decided I was going to leave him.

Amara approached nine months, bright like her sister and obsessed with books. She would spend hours carefully flipping the pages of brightly colored children's books. A few days after she turned nine months, she uttered her first words; "up, down." At first, we were not sure what she was saying, but it became clear as she continued to speak. Her keen interest in books led me to try to teach her to read when she turned two. With the help of her sister's phonetic books and the good old Queen Primer, a tried and tested phonetic book used by nearly every Nigerian parent, I embarked on what I thought was going to be an uphill task. What two-year-old child learns to read? To my surprise, Amara was catching on. She learned the three-letter words very quickly, and soon she was also recognizing the sight words. We did not enroll her in school as we did her sister partly because of the financial constraints, and also because we had learned from her sister that it wasn't exactly beneficial to start school so early. By the time Amara was three and enrolled in the same school as her sister, she was reading fluently.

One day, Amara's teacher told the headmaster about this three-year-old in her class who could read. The headmaster invited her to the school's morning assembly to read *Goldilocks and the Three Bears*. I got to their school early that morning. I wouldn't miss this occasion for the world. At exactly 8:20 a.m., she was ushered to the stage by her class teacher who was ever so proud to unveil her bright student. Amara stood on this wide stage in her light blue shirt and navy blue pinafore, her curly hair swept away from her small face in a loose heap on her head. Holding the hardcover book with both hands with her teacher holding up the microphone to her mouth, Amara loudly read the first page of the book. The whole assembly went agog with cheers and claps. I stood behind two moms and could overhear them arguing.

"No way is that child reading that book," one said.

"I think she's reading it. Her eyes are moving," the other responded in total awe.

They went on to argue about how their children in second grade could not read as fluently. My eyes lazily glanced at their Prada shoes and gold bracelets. They were women of affluence.

"If my son doesn't read this well in two months, I will sack his lesson teacher," the one with the Prada shoes threatened, waving her well-manicured hands.

After school about six weeks later, I picked up Amara and was making for the door when her class teacher chased after me, waving a blue piece of paper at me.

"Look Mrs. Chiedu, Amara wrote this poem in class today, and I wanted to show you."

"She wrote this?' I asked, staring at words that clearly belonged on the sheet of a much older child.

"She did," she replied. "I gave them papers to color and she wrote a poem instead."

At the end of that school year, Ketandu won an award as the best student in her class. It was clear to me that I had two gifted children in my hands, and I wondered about their future. Paying their school fees was now a struggle. I lived in constant dread about the day they might no longer be able to attend such an elite school.

With both girls now in school all day, I began to search for a job. Unemployment was at a record high, and after several unsuccessful attempts at returning to gainful employment, I began to examine other options. During one of my many episodes of self-reflection, a light bulb turned on. Benjamin Franklin might have felt this way when he discovered electricity. The banking industry, unlike the rest of the economy, seemed to thrive amidst the nation's financial debilitation. Banks recruited young attractive graduates as marketers and that meant a big demand for corporate suits. I could make a career out of selling suits to these bankers. I knew someone who sold clothes on a large scale and she was making good money. This vision kept me awake most nights. Emeka did not share the enthusiasm for my business idea, but I was also glad he did not try to dampen it. Two weeks later, I was sitting in front of Nneka (my old friend from University) in her office, negotiating a loan to commence my suit business. It didn't come as a surprise that her bank turned me down. They required collateral which I couldn't provide. Nneka knew someone who could extend me a personal loan. My hands trembled as I read the contract. It was my first big loan, and I was terrified at the exorbitant interest rate. What if I couldn't pay it back? What if nobody bought my suits? Several questions flashed through my mind as I picked up the blue pen that lay on the glass table, nervously scribbling my signature along the dotted lines.

Three weeks later, I stood in the long line at Murtala Muhammed International Airport, Lagos, my green passport and Virgin Atlantic ticket tucked securely in the breast pocket of my snug brown jacket. It was a busy night, large crowds huddled in front of the counters of various airlines. I could almost smell the desperation in the air, and the sense of urgency that filled the eyes of the travelers as they weighed their luggage and bargained prices at the travel desks. My eyes roamed the hall with boredom. It was a shabby building with walls that begged to be repainted. Overflowing garbage cans littered the hall. Two little boys ran past, almost knocking me down, reminding me of my two young daughters whom I was leaving behind to embark on this debut business trip. I worried about leaving them for ten days, but I shrugged off the sad feeling. I left them with an experienced nanny, a widow in her late twenties. They were in good hands, besides, their father was home.

The eight-hour trip to London was mostly uneventful. Apart from being plagued by intermittent turbulence, it was replete with several Nigerian dignitaries who were on the flight to celebrate its debut as Virgin Atlantic - a partnership airline owned by the famous British Billionaire, Richard Branson, and the Nigerian government. Flight attendants dressed in bright red and white uniforms offered complimentary champagne across the aisle. I sat beside a famous Nigerian Nollywood actor, his large frame spilling into my tight economy class seat. I started to strike up a conversation with him but changed my mind. I thought it was best to pretend I didn't know him. He had a look of self-aggrandizement that I didn't care for. No sooner had he gulped a few glasses of the free-flowing champagne, he fell into a deep sleep; the sound of his loud obnoxious snoring filling the entire cabin.

The aircraft landed at Heathrow International Airport in the early hours of the next morning. Grabbing my luggage, I wandered out the main doors in search of the Piccadilly line of the underground station. It was a cold October morning, frost covered the windows of the ancient buildings, giving them a forlorn look. I secured my grey woolen scarf around my freezing neck as I navigated the steps leading to the tube station. Forty-five minutes later, I alighted from Victoria Station to the streets. Red double-decker buses dominated the narrow roads and the smell of freshly baked muffins from nearby cafes teased my nostrils. London was beautiful.

I had a little difficulty finding a place to stay while I was in

London. I spoke to a few cousins who were not interested in housing me for the short duration. Andrea introduced me to her cousin, Larry who took me to stay with his girlfriend, Cissy, a Ugandan beauty and a registered nurse. Cissy and I hit it off from the start. The first night, we hardly got any sleep chatting late into the night. I was up early the next morning, scouting store outlets across the countryside in search of good bargains. Inside a NEXT outlet store in Wembley, I ran my fingers along the lapel of a stunning coffee brown skirt suit. I pictured it caressing the soft curves of a beautiful young banker. Stores overflowed with gorgeous clothes and matching accessories, and my heart leaped excitedly with every bargain I found. I permitted my heart to feel hope that perhaps I could make a success of this business; that I would pay back the huge interest and capital, and make enough money to leave my husband. I thought about all the possible ways my life would take on more meaning if I left him. It was six years and the marriage was as good as dead. I no longer dreamed of that happy home filled with children. I scoffed cynically when I remembered that once upon a time, it was all I ever wanted. Sex was perfunctory, an act that left me gritting my teeth, praying for it to be over. On good days, it felt like I was married to a stranger, and on bad days, it felt like I lived with a monster. I was dead to his vitriol, but I wondered if I would live long with the physical assaults. The month before my U.K. trip, we had just returned from the funeral of his uncle in Ogwuashi Uku, his father's village. We got into an argument over who had the house keys. My two little girls stood beside me as I rummaged through my purse in search of them. He was the last to leave the house, so I was sure he had those keys. I dug into my purse, pretending to look for the keys.

"You have the keys for Christ's sake," I cried in frustration.

"No, I do not," he yelled back.

"This is so dumb…"

No sooner had those words left my lips, than I felt violent punches to my stomach. Once he started, he didn't stop; couldn't stop. I doubled over in pain, using my green purse as a shield. Amara buried her face in my thigh, screaming at him to stop. Ketandu stood rooted to the spot, taking in the chaos that unfolded. He marched downstairs to the car and came up a few minutes later with the keys in his hand. He had suddenly remembered he had the keys.

That night as I tucked the girls in bed, Ketandu slipped her small fingers into my hands and said, "Mommy, I will look for a strong man that will punch daddy in his stomach."

I vowed that this would be the last time my daughters would witness violence. They had seen it one time too many. I had become weary of fleeing the house after each episode. My cousin, Chiadi, was my refuge. I could only hide it from her and Nwamaka for so long. I sat in her bedroom after each episode sobbing my eyes out and wondering why my life was so different, so difficult. These violent episodes were seldom about one isolated incident. It was always a culmination of events that bubbled until they boiled over. So, it was not about the house keys; we had argued on our way to his uncle's funeral. When we got there, in front of his entire family, he called me "a witch," smugly announcing that he was going to "send me out of his house." That we were so different was one of the many causes of our rift. I was the planner, and he was the one who loved to live on the edge. He called it "faith," and I called it "irresponsibility." The morning before we left for his uncle's funeral, he went to fix the car. I didn't bother to ask why he chose to fix the car on the morning we were embarking on a six-hour trip. I already knew why – he was a last-minute person. The roads were bad and unsafe. I was worried that if we left Lagos too late, we might not arrive at Ogwuashi Uku before sunset. I didn't want to embark on a dangerous road trip with two young children.

"If the 305 is bad, why don't we drive the bus?" I suggested. The bus was his work vehicle, but it was apparently in better shape than the car he was going to fix.

"We are going with the 305," he insisted. Minutes turned to hours as we waited for him to return.

He finally made it back at nearly 2 p.m.

"There's no way I'm getting in that car with my children," I said to him. "It's suicide to embark on this trip at such a late hour."

Grabbing some of the packed bags, he made for the door. I followed closely behind, desperate to talk him out of making this dangerous trip.

"We can leave first thing tomorrow morning. We will still be on time for the funeral. The roads are not safe with all the armed robbers at Ore road," I pleaded. My words fell on deaf ears as he continued to hurl the bags into the trunk of the car. Making one last desperate attempt, I said, "What if the car breaks down and we are stranded?"

"You don't have to come, but the children are coming with me."

He knew that I would die first before I let the girls go on that trip without me.

It was past 4 p.m. when we navigated traffic and got onto the ramp leading to the Lagos-Ibadan expressway. My heart palpitated and beads of perspiration gathered around my temple. I turned to look at the faces of the girls sleeping peacefully in the backseat. I owed them better, I thought. They didn't deserve for their lives to be at such risk. Shifting my gaze to the road, the deathly silence in the car fueling my anxiety, I prayed for a safe trip. As we approached Sagamu road, the car began to jerk.

"What's happening?" I asked, glancing at Emeka nervously.

"Nothing," he muttered back.

The car jerked for a few more miles and then the engine shut down. Sighing audibly, he rolled the car off the road. He threw the hood open, staring at the engine with arms akimbo. I sat still in the front seat looking at the road nervously. He fiddled with wires for a few minutes, got in the car, revved the engine and it started. I heaved a sigh of relief as we got back on the road. Fifteen minutes later, the car jerked to a stop again. It was pitch dark at this time, and we were alone in the middle of nowhere. My heart began to race again. I had heard so many stories about armed robbery attacks on this road. I clutched my purse tightly, whispering a silent prayer. The girls were now wide awake; scared and confused, whimpering softly in the back seat. Suddenly, a black car veered off the road and pulled up beside us. My heart stopped beating for a second. I was relieved to see that they were policemen. They peered into the car, shining their flashlights in our faces.

"Wetin you dey do for road this night with your family?" one of the officers asked Emeka whose head was bent over the hood of the car in a futile attempt to hide his embarrassment.

Grinning sheepishly, he said, *"The car get small problem. I go soon repair am."* The policemen berated him one last time and drove off into the dark night. It was eerily quiet except for the sounds of chirping crickets in the nearby bushes. I locked us in the car and prayed fervently that the engine would respond to his desperate effort.

Ninety minutes later, we pulled into a shabby motel, tired and relieved to be safe from the perilous road. That night in the cheap run-down motel, we argued. I accused him of putting our lives at risk. Not being one to back down from any argument he charged back at me. We barely said another word to each other for the rest of the trip except for when he gloated to his kinsmen in Ogwuashi Uku that he was going to "put the witch away."

And I replied, "The witch will leave before you put her away."

So, it wasn't about the house keys. It was about the events leading to the trip. He hated to be wrong. He disliked the fact that I was right about not embarking on that trip so late in the day with a faulty car.

I inhaled the cool London air, grateful that I was given to introspection. I was not sure where I wanted to go when I left Emeka. I liked the U.K., but I liked America better. With the girls so smart, I wanted an opportunity for a sound education for them.

Ten days later, I stood in line at Heathrow Airport with five overstuffed suitcases. The past few days had gone by quickly. Waiting for my flight to be announced, I strolled past duty-free shops, stopping briefly as my eyes caught a book titled: "How to kill your husband." I chuckled loudly, wondering why anyone would kill their husband. "Just leave him like I plan to leave mine," I blurted out to no one.

Nine hours later, the plane touched down at Murtala Muhammed International airport. Hot humid air laced with exhaust fumes assaulted my nostrils as I exited the swivel doors. It was an all too familiar odor; one that I associated with congestion, something I had grown to dislike. For a minute, I longed to be back in London inhaling the morning aroma of freshly baked muffins. I pushed the thought away. I was happy to be home to my girls.

I started to comb several banks in diligent pursuit of customers as soon as I returned home. Two weeks later, I got my break. The suits were an instant favorite with the young bankers. We huddled in the bathrooms during their lunch break as they tried on the different styles, digging into the pile of clothes like excited children in a candy store. "Can I get this in size ten long?" Anita asked, pointing to a coffee brown pantsuit. She was a slender, ebony beauty with endlessly long legs.

The suits were gone in two weeks. I sat in my living room the following weekend nervously reconciling my books, hoping that I at least broke even. After paying back the loan and interest, I had made enough to make the trip worthwhile. And so continued my suit business in earnest. Aware that I had competition, I made my prices lower than the market rate. That way, I was selling off fast and making more frequent trips albeit at lower profit margins.

Another year rolled by, and our house rent was due. It was common practice for Emeka to shirk financial obligations every time he thought I was buoyant. I was bearing huge financial burdens around the house, more responsibility than my young business could handle. I was mindful that Nneka had put her integrity on the line when she asked her sister-in-law to rent us the apartment. So, when she called early one morning casually asking when we would pay the rent, I panicked.

"When can you come up with the rent?" I asked Emeka. I was certain I could not add the rent to my growing list of responsibilities.

"I don't know," he answered nonchalantly. I rented this place, and it was my reputation that was on the line. I also did not want to do anything that would jeopardize my friendship with Nneka. In addition to the apartment, I also secured my business loan through her. There was too much at stake. I had recently returned from a trip and gathered my capital. I had a whole month before the next interest was due, so I offered to pay the rent with the capital.

"You have to give me back the money within a month, so I don't get charged interest," I said to Emeka.

"Don't worry," he said. "I have some money in a fixed deposit. It will mature in a few weeks, and I will give you back the money."

A few weeks passed and he made no mention of the money. The due date for the interest was approaching, and I was growing apprehensive. It was a lot of money in interest, besides my next trip was imminent which meant I also needed the money.

The morning the interest was due, I got up at the usual time to get the girls ready for school. Our green concrete walls vibrated gently as the Muslim cleric chanted the words of the early morning call to prayers. That loud sound from the shabby speakers at the nearby mosque served as my second alarm. Emeka was awake but still lying in bed as the girls and I scurried around the apartment. I approached him just as I was about to leave with the children, reminding him that the interest was due. He leaped off the bed, and pointing to the door, he told me to get out of the room.

"What is the matter?" I queried.

"Do not ask me for that money so early, just get out of here!"

"The last time I checked, I also live in this room. So, ordering me out is hardly the way to talk about money that you owe…."

The blows caught me off guard, crashing down on my face like deep turbulent waves. Ripple after ripple cascading down my head as I cowered, shielding my eyes with the door frame. I didn't dare scream as the girls were in the living room. I had vowed that they would never again witness another violent episode. I stopped feeling pain after a few punches, convinced I had died. I soon realized that I was only numb. I staggered to the living room and grabbed my purse from the couch. Careful not to let my daughters see my face, I opened the door and walked out. If they were curious about why I left the house without them I would never know, but I couldn't bear to have them see my battered face. My head throbbed. Liquid leaked from my right eye. I was afraid to touch it, not sure if they were tears or moisture from a damaged cornea. I couldn't tell the difference and I didn't care. I just walked.

The day had broken, the sun slowly peeking through thick white clouds, giving off the illusion of a good day. But nothing was good about my day. Car horns blared in the distance as I made my way to the mini taxi rank, half a block from the apartment. It was unusually full for that time of day. Okadas, the commercially operated motorcycles, lined a section of the park. Rickety yellow taxis stood on the opposite end, waiting to pick up their share of morning commuters. I approached the first taxi in the line, shielding my battered face with my arm.

"Lekki Phase One," I muttered at the elderly taxi driver.

"Pay four hundred."

"Two hundred."

As we haggled back and forth, a blue Peugeot pulled up. My blood turned cold as I recognized our car. Emeka was behind the wheel, and the girls sat in the back seat. It happened quickly, much too fast. Emeka wound down the window, poked his head out of the car, and screamed, "Ashawo!" "Prostitute!" Satisfied that he held the attention of the entire taxi rank, he drove off. The dust from his screeching tires formed a misty cloud around my face, but no mist was enough to conceal the humiliation I felt when all eyes turned to me. I got into the taxi without another word, and the driver drove in silence. Once inside the taxi, I let the tears flow. I wondered what kind of man would humiliate the mother of his children in front of such a large crowd. The domestic verbal and physical abuse no longer sufficing, we had hit yet a new low.

The taxi pulled up in front of Chiadi's house, thirty minutes later. I handed the taxi driver his four hundred naira. He extracted two hundred and returned the rest, a gesture that signaled he was sorry about what just happened to me. I thanked him profusely and walked through the black metal gate.

My actions in the following months were crucial to my survival. My plot to walk away from my marriage consumed my every waking moment. First, I knew I had to leave the country if I was going to have a shot at survival. There was no place for divorced women in Nigeria. They were the scorn of society. I couldn't live in ridicule anymore. I had lived in derision as a bastard child from the Biafran war. I had allowed life to treat me as it pleased. I no longer wished to sit back and take whatever it threw at me. I deserved better. My girls and I deserved better.

While I grappled with plans to exit my comatose marriage, I struggled with a myriad of health problems. My body seemed to be gradually shutting down. My hypertension, no longer pregnancy-induced, was back in full force. I suffered frequent bouts of hemorrhoids, gastritis, and bronchitis. My shoe size went up two sizes and strangely, my tongue and jaw also grew in size. It had been several months since the humiliating incident at the taxi rank. I cowered in shame every time I walked past that area, wondering what they thought of my husband calling me a prostitute. I was sure that the news had spread through the neighborhood. Perhaps, they thought he caught me cheating and beat me to a pulp, hence my battered face. I wondered if I could ever repair my reputation; if I should go from door to door explaining that the cause of the fracas had nothing to do with infidelity, but everything to do with the money that he borrowed and refused to pay. I shifted my focus from the events of that dreadful morning. I was going to rise from those ashes of shame, I owed that to myself.

One fine Friday, I received an August visitor, my Aunt Stella from Makurdi. She was in Lagos to attend the wedding of a friend's daughter. I knew it was not the right time to host anyone. My husband and I had not spoken in months following the incident. The tension in my home was palpable. Aunty Stella was not aware of the travails of my marriage. I didn't think she would care, so I spent the next few days desperately trying to pretend that everything was normal. One evening when I got home, she called me into the room and asked me to shut the door.

"Your husband and I talked, and I know that all is not well with your marriage."

"Okay, Aunty," I sighed, exhausted even before the conversation began.

"Talk to me. What is wrong?"

Now that she knew, there was no point in hiding anything. I talked nonstop for two hours, not holding back a single detail. When I was spent, Aunty Stella looked at me with tears in her eyes and said, "You are going to kneel and beg your husband."

Staggering back like a slap had been dealt to my face, I retorted, "What! Aunty! Did you hear a single thing I told you?"

"I heard everything you said. The bible says we must submit to our husbands."

It had been months since I last attended church. It no longer held any appeal for me. Each time I sat beside Emeka in church or I heard him speak "bible language" to a church member, my stomach churned and bile rose in my mouth. I couldn't bear the hypocrisy and the two-facedness so I stopped attending altogether.

"How can I kneel and beg this man who did all of these terrible things to me, Aunty? " I sobbed.

"Obey God and watch him honor you. Also, remember that it is the responsibility of a wife to build her home. You cannot let the devil destroy your marriage."

A few minutes later, Emeka walked into the room, smugly taking a seat beside the bed. Aunty Stella looked at me and gestured with a nod of her head. I got down on my knees and begged my husband to forgive me.

In all my years on earth, that was arguably the most difficult thing I ever had to do. That night, I cried myself to sleep, thinking about the many ways in which my family had failed me.

Aunty Stella left a few days later and we continued from where we left off. One morning, two months later, he called me to our bedroom and told me he was leaving for the U.S. in a week. He had gotten an inheritance from his late father, and he was going to use it to study abroad.

"What provision do you have for the children?" I asked.

"I will manage and pay their school fees, and the rest is up to you," he said.

Seven days later, he was gone. Nothing shocked me anymore. I had seen it all. Life had thrown it all at me. I only had to step back and restrategize. He paid the school fees like he said he would but that was all he did. I was left with enormous responsibilities that threatened to drown my resolve. But I wasn't going to give up. My girls deserved better and so did I. Come hell or high water, I was going to give them a life that would be better than the one I led. My determination was the compass that charted the course as I rode out this latest storm.

Chapter 8

AMERICA
BECKONS

Like a jaguar in the Amazon rainforest, I clung to the sliver of survival. My routine comprised attending to daily needs as they arose and sighing in relief at the brief respite from financial worries. I was grateful to get past each day but fazed by the reality that living from hand to mouth could be a lifelong experience. This was something that I certainly didn't want to bequeath to my children. My eyes were set on one prize – leaving Nigeria and breaking the jinx of stagnancy. Every fiber of my being was devoted to making this dream a reality.

The first item on my checklist was securing U.S. visas for my daughters. For that to be possible, they had to have a travel history. From my frequent trips to the U.K. for my suit business, I had a two-year U.K. visa and both girls had their U.K. visas issued in my passport. While Ketandu had used hers, Amara's had expired unused. I needed to get them off my passport, and then renew their visas. No sooner had I gotten their international passports, than I applied for their U.K. visas. Confident that they would be granted, I was shocked and disappointed when they were both denied. That night, after I put them to sleep, I lay in bed tossing and turning, the cacophony of my neighbor's laughter and the noise of his "Tiger" generator gnawing at my frayed nerves. I thought of all the ways in which my plans could go wrong. It frightened me that I might never get the break I so desperately needed. Just as I was drifting off to sleep, I decided that I was going to appeal the decision of the U.K. consulate.

Over the next week, I compiled the appeal, drafting a strong missive to the consulate and stating reasons why I thought they had made a mistake in denying my daughters entry into the U.K. The weeks that followed were filled with anxiety and trepidation. I spent my days worrying and my nights engrossed in fervent prayers. After what seemed like an eternity,, I heard back from the consulate. The judge in charge of the appeal reversed the decision: "Please grant this family their visas to enable them enjoy their vacation in the U.K." I was beside myself with joy.

One month later, I boarded a flight to London with the girls. Emeka's friend, Ade, picked us up from Heathrow. He was a comely man with a pleasant disposition.

"I have done my good deed for the day," he said as he dropped us off at Cricklewood. Emeka had good friends. For a fleeting second my mind wandered back to the previous year when Yomi, another good friend of his, visited us. I had just finished mopping the living room floor when I heard the doorbell. As I ushered Yomi into the living room, he halted suddenly, grimacing at the dirt marks his shoes left on my squeaky clean floor.

"I'm so sorry," he said, tugging sheepishly at the lace of his black Adidas.

"It's okay," I said. "You don't have to take off your shoes."

But I was pleased that he was mindful of my floor which was more than I could say for my husband who on many occasions would come home and smear my polished floors with muddy footprints. He knew I was house proud, and that an orderly house was the gateway to my sanity, but he refused to let me score even that one victory.

So, when Yomi apologized for staining my floors, I started to cry. In retrospect, the tears were not about the floor, they were about everything that was wrong with my marriage.

We returned to Nigeria ten days later, just as the school year was coming to a close. I was relieved that school runs were going to be one less thing to worry about. With the car constantly breaking down and the electricity supply getting worse by the day, I had a growing list of problems. There were also my health concerns which every time they popped up, I tucked away for a later time.

Two weeks after we returned from the U.K., I applied for U.S. visas for my daughters. I was moderately optimistic. But as their interview date approached I began to despair. What if they denied them? What would be my alternative? Anxiety gnawed at my insides and fear crippled me. I had not been religious in recent times, but I began to pray again, beseeching God daily for a miracle. The day before the interview I decided to fast for twelve hours.

"I will fast with you, mommy," six-year-old Ketandu said.

"No, you are too young to fast."

She refused to eat, so I finally succumbed and let her fast with me. Later that evening, she told me she wanted to do something nice for the beggars that lived under the bridge. We cooked some noodles and packed them in plastic containers. She went to her wardrobe and brought out some of her best dresses and said, "Mommy I will give these to the little girls that have no clothes."

Two hours later, she was seated in the backseat of the car, clutching the bag of food and clothes as we drove to Obalende in search of the homeless beggars that lived under the bridge. I wound down the window as skinny children with dirt-stained faces approached the car. Ketandu handed them the food and clothes and we drove home.

Later that night, I reflected on the significance of the day and wondered what would inspire a six-year-old to suggest such a kind gesture. I was glad that she did. It felt right to have done it.

We were up and out of the house at the crack of dawn the next morning. Holding both girls on each hand, I made my way to the taxi park, maneuvering the flooded streets that were typical of the rainy season. The American Embassy occupied a corner piece at Eleke Crescent Victoria Island. It was an intimidating building overlooking the Eko River. Small crowds had begun to gather in batches by the narrow street that wound around the building. I paid the taxi driver and we made our way across the street to the entrance. I had come prepared to spend a chunk of the day.

We walked into the air-conditioned hall and settled into the plush seats. I strained my ears to hear what a security officer was saying to another visa applicant. It was no doubt a nerve-racking interview. I fiddled nervously with the big brown envelope I brought with us, my hands trembling gently as I went through the checklist for the umpteenth time. It wasn't long before the first applicant was called up to the kiosk. The American embassy was a tough place to navigate. They were notorious for denying more visas than they granted. As I sat waiting our turn to walk up to the kiosk, it dawned on me that our fate was swinging on a precarious pendulum, one that could easily sway against us. The voice of one of the interviewing officers grew louder as the day progressed. He sounded angry, and I prayed feverishly that we wouldn't be sent to his kiosk.

The first applicant was denied the visa. He stormed out of the building, his face dark with rage. I began to pray fervently, "God, if we are denied these visas, what will I say to the six-year-old who fasted with me?" I glanced at my daughters as I tried to suppress the sinking feeling in the pit of my stomach. I was almost jealous of the calmness with which they carried on, oblivious to my inner turmoil. We were finally asked to approach the kiosk. Sure enough, we were sent to the angry officer. My knees threatened to buckle as I walked towards what would be the greatest verdict of my life. He smiled at us as we approached and that was my cue that perhaps it was going to go well.

"Where is their father?"

"He is currently in school in the U.S."

"Where in the U.S.?"

"Arizona."

I started to push the documents through the window. He pushed them back at me.

"I don't need them."

Too scared to breathe, I clutched tightly to Amara's hand as I watched him scribble furiously on a pile of papers. Were we going to be denied? I was not sure. His demeanor seemed to have lightened up when we approached him, but that did not mean much. He was probably tired of barking at people, or maybe he didn't want to scare my girls. It was the longest three minutes of my life.

Finally, he looked up and said, "Come back on Monday at 10 a.m. to pick up the visas."

I suppressed the urge to burst into tears as emotions overwhelmed me. Thanking him profusely, I marched out of the building, grinning widely as we walked past security. Time had suddenly paused. Everything seemed to happen in slow motion. Could this be a dream? Was I going to wake up? It was past noon and dark clouds had given way to rain. I ran into the streets, and throwing my hands to the heavens, I began to laugh and cry. The future, once bleak, suddenly looked bright. I could dream big for myself and my daughters. Rain cascaded down my face, sweeping my tears as I chanted over and over. "We are moving to America. We're moving to America."

Getting the visas was only one hurdle to surmount. There was still the obstacle of where to go and who would house a woman and two children. I called Emeka to inform him about the visas. Many times in the past when I told him I was leaving him, his response was, "You can leave whenever you want, but you can't go with my children." He knew that there was no way I would leave without the girls. I would die first before that happened. I needed to figure out a way to leave with the girls without incurring his wrath. I also recognized that he had a say in the fate of his children. He loved them. It was me that he didn't love. Finding a way to solve this dilemma was a tall order. I turned to God. He had heard me in the past when I cried out to Him. I was confident He would hear me again. When I spoke to Emeka again after a series of midnight prayers and fasting, I was not surprised when he said, "You can take the children." I believed in the efficacy of prayers and I also reasoned that he was enjoying his stay in the U.S. too much to care about life beyond the moment. Whatever his mindset might have been at the time, that was my window of opportunity to leave with my children, and I was going to seize it.

Even though I had an uncaring family, I knew I had been immensely blessed with good friends. As I journeyed through life, I discovered that making good friends and sustaining healthy friend-ships seemed like second nature to me. I liked to think of it as com-pensation. I went to pick up the girls from school one afternoon and that was the day that I met Freda. As we both stood by the door of the classroom waiting for the dismissal bell, a mother sashayed past us, covered in a plethora of designer brands. Almost instinctively, we looked at each other and smiled knowingly. I felt an instant connec-tion with her. I could tell that she was amused by the garishly dressed mothers who made up the majority of parents in the school. Amara rushed to my side just as the bell rang, and Freda said,

"I always wondered who the mother of this little girl was. She looks just like my daughter."

I looked at her daughter who had also left the class and was holding on to her mother's hand shyly.

"It's true. They actually do look a lot alike," I replied, chuckling.

We hit it off almost instantly. She had an older daughter who was also in Ketandu's class, so each girl had a playmate. It wasn't long before we began to spend time together. We took the girls out to the movies and restaurants on the weekends, and many afternoons after school, we spent time in each other's houses. At the end of the following school year, Freda and her girls moved to the U.S.

As the reality of our journey loomed ahead, I called Freda to see if she would house us. She was the only one I knew who would be willing to open her doors to us.

"Oh my God. Do you need to ask?" her voice reverberated at the other end of the call. I was confident that she would take us in, I only wanted to be doubly sure. The last hurdle standing between me and my dream was money for our flight tickets. Fortunately, many of my bank customers bought the last batch of clothing I had for sale and gave generously towards the trip. In a bid to raise extra money, I had a yard sale, disposing of most of my personal belongings. I was ready to start afresh in a new country and there was no looking back.

The night before our departure, I took the girls to say their final goodbye to my cousin, Nwamaka. As we made our way to the living room, the sound of Beethoven's *Fur Elise* echoed through the walls. Her oldest daughter, Somkene, was a fine pianist. Ketandu and Amara scurried towards the finely polished Yamaha piano and watched in fascination as her delicate fingers stroked the keys flawlessly. I stood by the door watching my daughters as they huddled over their cousin in rapt attention. One day in America, I thought to myself, my girls will play like that. I believed it with all my heart. After all, America was a country where you could achieve anything you wanted if you really wanted it. My girls were going to be great. I could feel it already. Chiadi stopped by to say goodbye as we piled the rest of our belongings into the taxi en route to the airport the following evening. I was grateful for both cousins and for the roles they played in my life.

We landed at O'Hare International Airport on a late summer evening in September of 2007. Clearing customs and immigration with unexpected ease, we picked up our luggage and stepped out of the Terminal Five exit where Freda and her daughters waited in a green truck. It was a beautiful day. The sun cast shadows on the white pavement as we walked towards Freda's truck with our oversized suitcases. I had heard horror stories about people refusing to open their doors to family members abroad. But here was this woman, who did not know me from Adam, letting me in with two children. It was one of the kindest things anyone had done for me. I was eternally indebted to her. She got out from the truck as she sighted us and enveloped the girls in a bear hug. It was a long trip. We had a layover in Amsterdam for several hours. I couldn't wait to take a long cool shower once we got to Freda's house. We were out of the airport and onto the I-94 East in no time. The roads were wider than any roads I had ever seen and the motorists drove at an alarming speed.

"Wow! You guys drive really fast," I said to Freda, holding firmly to the roof handle for extra support.

"We do," she chuckled as she weaved in and out of lanes. "You will get used to it."

I wondered if I would ever get used to the pace on this highway or any other road in this city for that matter.

Freda's apartment was on the fourth floor of an old building in Rogers Park, Chicago's northside. It was a well-kept apartment with a grey wall-to-wall carpet and a matching grey sofa set. The bedroom contained a bunk bed and one queen-size bed. Freda's girls slept on the lower bunk while Ketandu and Amara shared the upper bunk. The four girls all got along much to my relief. We settled into our life with remarkable ease.

Freda enrolled Ketandu and Amara in the school her daughters attended. It was a neighborhood public elementary school right across from our apartment building. I marveled at the convenience of getting the girls to school. It was more than I could ever wish for. I shuddered as I remembered the gruesome Lagos traffic and the many hours it took to get the girls to school and back.

I woke up early on their first day of school and ironed their uniforms, creasing the navy blue khakis pants with straight parallel lines. Ten minutes to resumption time, I walked all four girls across the street, holding the two younger ones with either hand. I dropped them off at the playground and watched with pride as they joined their respective groups.

Six hours later, I was back at the school to pick them up. Excited to hear all about how her first day went, I barged into Amara's class-room with a wide grin. She was sitting alone in a corner, looking indignant. It was a neat classroom. Brightly colored pictures adorned the walls, and sets of building blocks sat on the round red tables. Her teacher, Ms. Baker, approached me wearing a stern look.

"She wet my carpet."

Alarmed, I replied, "That is unusual. She is almost five and past potty training."

Amara got up from where she sat and walked towards me. "Nne'm, did you pee on yourself?" I asked. Very slowly, she nodded her head in affirmation.

I started to apologize to her teacher. "I'm so sorry. It must be because she's in a new environment."

Turning to Amara I said, "Tell your teacher whenever you need to go. Don't be shy."

It seemed that we were off to a rough start with her new class teacher. I had to come up with a clever way to forge a relationship with this teacher. Ketandu, on the other hand, had an uneventful first day. The next day, I walked into Amara's classroom and was greeted with a smile. I was relieved that the second day had gone well. At the end of the first week, Ms. Baker pulled me aside and said, "Amara's reading is above the kindergarten level. Starting next week, I will start to send her up to second grade for reading."

We were in a new country and a new school system. I didn't want to be that obnoxious mom who bragged that her children were smart, so I kept my fingers crossed, hoping that their talent would be noticed.

Six weeks later, we moved to our own place. It was a one-bedroom apartment, three blocks east of the children's school. It had a spacious wooden porch and lots of storage. I had enough money to pay for it, but I had to get a job if I was going to sustain the monthly rent.

Long summer days made way for fall, as dry amber leaves dangled loosely on trees, yielding to the blast of Chicago's fiery wind. I found a job in a group home working with individuals with mental disabilities. There were about eight residents in total, some of whom were nonverbal. It was different from anything I had ever done. I worked the second shift and that meant I needed someone to mind the girls while I worked. My pay was low and adding the cost of babysitting was not sustainable. Freda watched them after school until I found an affordable babysitter who charged a dollar per hour per child. She was a petite silver-haired Indian lady who lived across the street from the girls' school. So, I picked them up from school at 2:15 p.m., dropped them off across the street with the babysitter, and hopped on the bus to my shift which started at 3:00 p.m. We quickly settled into our new routine, one that I was not too pleased with. Helping them into their coats at 11:15 p.m. each night and dragging their tired feet into the cold Chicago night consumed me with guilt. Their teeth chattered as we made the three-block walk home. I needed a car and a better shift. As I tucked them into bed every night, I prayed for a miracle. I knew it wouldn't be long before we all caved in to the pressure. It made me sad that I couldn't do homework with them every evening as we did back home in Lagos. This came with the territory of a new country and a new routine. I was hopeful that we would find our equilibrium soon.

One evening in November, Emeka called to say that he had completed his studies in Arizona and was coming to Chicago to see the girls. My heart sank at the news. My marriage was dead and I had picked up the pieces of my life and moved on. Letting him back in was not a good idea, but it was one that I was willing to consider.

He could watch the girls while I worked my shift, at least until I found a better job. The memories of the last violent episode still haunted me. I wanted nothing to do with that life.

He arrived a few days before Thanksgiving. That evening, I left him with the girls and went to work, relieved that the girls would be in bed at 8 p.m. Having them in the warmth and comfort of their home was worth the sacrifice of enduring a dead marriage. It snowed the weekend after Thanksgiving. We peered through the windows in awe as light flakes cascaded in quick succession, enveloping the trees and streets in a blanket of immaculate beauty. It was the first time we had seen snow and we were all excited.

"Mommy, can we go outside and touch it?" Ketandu asked.

Helping them into their newly purchased Walmart winter boots, I ushered them outdoors. While Ketandu and Amara rolled in the snow, making snowballs and throwing them at each other like they saw on television, I marveled at the beauty of this ice and how much our lives had transformed in the span of two months. It was barely twelve weeks and the girls' accents were beginning to change, sounding less Nigerian and more American. I always worried when they came home and told me that a classmate had called them, "African booty scratcher." They were singled out and bullied because of their foreign accent. But their intonation was fast-changing and soon they would blend with the American children.

We soon realized that snow was only beautiful when it had just fallen. Its nuisance value rivaled its beauty once it melted and turned to dirty brown slush. After we slid and fell in slush and ice a few times, we decided it was time to buy a car. Emeka found a ten-year-old Nissan Quest on Craig's list. It was heavy on mileage, but the price was right. The Chinese couple who owned it wanted two thousand dollars. We settled for twelve hundred. As Chicago's brutal winter unleashed subzero temperatures often accompanied by frequent snow and black ice, I was happy that my girls were co-cooned in the warmth of the old truck. I also felt more at ease that they were in their own house and not with a babysitter.

Early in December, I was scheduled to attend a workshop for my job. I walked into the third floor of the corporate building feeling nervous. Signing in at the reception area, I strolled into the hall where the training was to take place. It was a large hall and a huge monitor was suspended from the wall. A box of freshly brewed Dunkin Donuts' coffee stood on a table at the corner of the hall. American coffee was much too strong for me. One cup would keep me awake for days. I made a mental note to avoid it. The training commenced with the instructor, a Caucasian registered nurse, split-ting us up into small groups and asking us to practice taking blood pressures on one another. My partner, a young African American girl wrapped the cuff of the blood pressure machine around my right arm and inflated the pump. A few seconds passed and looking at the dial she gasped. "Oh my God! Your blood pressure is very high," she blurted out. She checked it again, and after recording a second high number, she called for the nurse.

The nurse took my blood pressure again and said, "You have to go to the emergency room immediately." I was asymptomatic, but be-cause I had a history of hypertension, I knew I had to take it seriously.

Grabbing my backpack, I jumped on the southbound Red Line train to John Stroger Hospital. I had never been south since we ar-rived in Chicago. I stared at the colorful graffiti that graced the walls of each station as the train made its scheduled stops. My mood was pensive as the train raced towards downtown Chicago. I wondered what had caused my blood pressure to rise so sharply and concluded that it was the coffee I drank a few days prior.

Jackson Train Station bustled with crowds. The saxophone tunes of street performers reverberated through the walls as I alighted the train and walked briskly towards the approaching Blue Line train headed towards the Illinois Medical District.

The emergency room was busy. People of all age groups sat patiently waiting for their names to be called. There was a look of despondency on many faces. I took my seat beside the exit door waiting for my turn. Six hours passed and my name hadn't been called. I suppressed a yawn, wishing I brought something to read. It was close to midnight when I finally heard my name. I leaped off the chair and followed a nurse to a small room behind the waiting area.

"What is your name and date of birth?" the nurse inquired as she hooked the blood pressure machine to my left arm. The reading was still elevated. Disconnecting the machine, she left the room for a brief second and returned with a young, skinny resident doctor.

"What brings you to the emergency room today?" the doctor asked.

"I have a headache and my blood pressure is high," I responded.

"We will give you medication to bring the blood pressure down, and we will also do a CT scan of your head."

Forty-five minutes later, I was wheeled into a cold room. A donut-shaped contraption was stationed in the center of the room. The muscles around my temple tightened as my body slid through the tunnel of the machine.

"It's only taking pictures of your brain," the technician assured me, sensing my frayed nerves. It was not long before the doctor returned with the result of the scan.

"We found a tumor in your brain."

"Tumor in my brain," I said, staring wide-eyed at the doctor. I blanked out for a few seconds, not sure what to do with the news.

"Am I going to die?"

"We have to run further tests and an MRI to see what kind of tumor it is."

My head began to pound aggressively. My mind went to my children. What would happen to them if I died? I wished I never came to the hospital. I came for an elevated blood pressure and by some twist of ugly serendipity, a brain tumor was discovered. How long had I lived with this tumor? How did I get it? A million and one questions flooded my head as I tried to hold back the tears.

"From its position, it looks like a pituitary tumor which is benign a lot of times," the young doctor explained, offering me the ray of hope that he sensed I desperately needed.

I began to sob. The doctor's words did nothing to comfort me. I had made it to America against the many odds that life threw my way, and now I was going to die from a strange brain tumor. It was the scariest night of my life. I called Emeka and the girls to let them know I was not coming home just yet.

I was discharged the next morning with a long list of appointments scheduled for the following month. Week after week, I got calls from the hospital for visits with endocrinologists, cardiologists, ophthalmologists, primary physicians, and brain surgeons. I thought about my latest diagnosis and how it could potentially change our lives forever. I wondered how I would keep my job with the barrage of unending hospital appointments.

As I grappled with the uncertainty of my health prognosis, I was also left to contend with the skyrocketing heating bill. The frigid winter raged. As Christmas approached, I began to solicit for extra hours at work. I was slowly beginning to unravel under the massive weight and Emeka seemed oblivious to my plight. One day, when I could no longer bear it, I asked him to find a job to assist with the bills.

"I can't work menial jobs," he retorted. "They are beneath me."

"I don't like them either, but there are bills to pay," I explained.

He seemed content to be home with the children while I worked. I would not have minded so much if he "picked up some shifts" around the house. But every night I got home I was met with a pile of dirty dishes in the sink, dinner to be cooked, and children to bathe, none of which he was remotely interested in assisting with.

"You can at least shower the children," I pleaded. This also fell on deaf ears.

As the bills mounted, so did my resentment for Emeka. One evening at work, I reached out to my supervisor about working extra hours.

"I can send you to Greenhouse on the weekends. I don't know if you will like it," he said. "It's a tough place to work."

"I will go," I said to him. "I need the money."

Greenhouse was situated in Evanston, a close Chicago suburb. There were four individuals in total, who were all wheelchair-bound and totally dependent on staff for all activities of daily living. I could tell it was going to be a challenging job.

"Be careful with Steve," the first shift staff whispered, pointing to a resident with dark unruly hair. "He will get you fired in a second."

Shrugging off the advice, I got to work. I came to earn extra money. I was going to try my hardest not to get fired.

It was a long, grueling shift. I was in and out of their rooms, getting them out of bed onto the toilet, fixing dinners, feeding them, assisting with phone calls, opening mail, giving showers, and cleaning rooms. Two of the residents were non-verbal, making it even more challenging to identify their needs. I went home that night emotionally and physically spent, my back hurting from lifting so much dead weight. I went back the following weekend. There were shifts waiting to be picked up.

Greenhouse soon became a regular feature. As time went on, nonverbal communication with the clients got easier. I relied on their eye movements to guide me as to what they wanted. Sometimes, I got it right by sheer intuition. But as I fine-tuned my communication skills, the physical aspect of my job got harder. Lifting them from their beds and onto the wheelchairs soon took its toll on my back. But I loved my job. I loved working with these very special people. I admired their strength. Fate had dealt them a hard blow, but they found the courage to keep living. I could tell they liked me too. Their eyes lit up every time I arrived for my shift. Rachel was my favorite. She was a buxom African American lady with an equally large personality. Her loud voice, often booming with laughter, welcomed me at the start of every shift. She was born with cerebral palsy and had spent all her life confined to a wheelchair, but it didn't deter her from enjoying life and appreciating the simple things that came with it. She could talk, but with great difficulty, and the more time I spent with her, the easier it became to understand her. One day, I got to work and she said to me, "Joy, I had a dream last night that I could walk."

I searched her face for traces of sadness, but there were none. She was simply telling me about a dream she had.

"So where did you go, when you found yourself walking?" I asked.

"I didn't go nowhere. I got up and danced." Rachel loved music. She was a great fan of Jackson 5.

That day, after I completed my tasks I said to her, "You may not be able to get up and dance, but you know what you can do? You can dance right here in this chair."

She shrieked with laughter, raising both legs off the pedals of her wheelchair like she always did every time she was excited. Her laughter was contagious. Turning on Jackson 5's, *I want you back*, I walked to the center of the room.

"Come on, let's dance girl."

Rachel spun her wheelchair and followed me. Together we danced to the music. She glided her wheelchair back and forth to the rhythm, her body rocking in time to the beat. I held onto the back of the wheelchair, cheering and swaying with her.

"Yeah…go girl…yeah, go…go…"

As I lowered her to bed that night with the grey Hoyer lift, she looked me in the eyes and smiled. I knew exactly what that smile was saying to me. It was worth more than the extra money I came to Greenhouse to earn. I was finally sent to Greenhouse to work on a permanent basis.

January was arguably the coldest month of the season. Fierce winds raged, worsening the bitterly cold morning as I took the girls to school. Digging my frostbitten fingers into the pocket of my black woolen jacket, I ushered the girls to their classrooms, envious of how they seemed oblivious to the biting cold. They loved their lives in the new country. They had lost their Nigerian accents and were fast adapting to their new environment. I dropped Amara off and as I turned to leave, Ms. Baker gestured that I wait.

"I've been meaning to speak with you." Moving close, she whispered, "You have to get Amara out of this school. She's way ahead of the curriculum."

Shoving a white piece of paper in my hand, she continued, "This is the information on how to apply to the magnet elementary schools. Don't let anyone know I gave you this. The principal won't be happy with me if she finds out. She would hate to lose a good student."

Clutching the paper tightly, I thanked her and left. I had noticed that the curriculum was a watered-down version of what they were used to in Nigeria. I often worried that they were not being stimulated enough. I was relieved that Ms. Baker validated my concern. I immediately went to work, applying to three of the top magnet schools in the city. The girls' education was a top priority. It was one of the major reasons for our relocation.

I worked the third shift and most weekend shifts at Greenhouse. I was making the extra money I needed to cover the basic bills. Emeka had bought his plane ticket back to Nigeria and this meant that I was faced with babysitter issues again.

As Emeka's departure loomed, so did my despair about what to do with the girls when they got out of school in the afternoons. Our relationship had degenerated over the last month. We could barely stand each other. During one of our many arguments, he shoved me, and I fell back against the wall, flashes of our life in Nigeria flooding my mind.

"You can't hit me here," I said. "This is not Nigeria where I had no one to defend me. I will call the police."

"I dare you to call the police. You do not have papers. You will be deported," he mocked.

I picked up the phone and dialed 911. Two officers showed up at the door in ten minutes.

"If you hit her in Nigeria, you can't do that here," they said to him.

They left him with a warning and that sufficed for me. I felt safe knowing that he understood that it was no longer business as usual.

It was ten days to Emeka's departure. I was up most nights tossing and turning, praying for a miracle. I did not want to send the girls back to a babysitter and disrupt their equilibrium. I was desperate for answers. That week, my miracle appeared in the guise of Jane. She was a first shift staff at Greenhouse. Jane had worked the shift for seven years and enjoyed it by her own account. Out of nowhere, she put in her resignation.

"I'm tired of this job. I'm leaving," she said to me as she clocked out at 3 p.m. that afternoon. I called the office and asked for the shift. It was approved immediately. It was a full-time position with full benefits including paid vacations and sick days off. It was a morning shift, just what I needed. I could leave with the girls in the morning and we would go home together in the afternoon. I was dumbfounded at the timing of this job opportunity. There was no better time to believe in miracles. That night, I got home and hugged my daughters a little tighter, knowing that an awkward shift would soon be a thing of the past. Two months after Jane quit the morning shift, she came back asking to be reinstated to her position. The company said the shift was no longer available. She claimed she didn't know why she had the sudden urge to give up the shift. I like to think of it as an act of kindness by the universe towards me and my daughters. Jane settled for the second shift position after it was clear that she was not getting the first shift back.

The morning Emeka left, the girls and I stood by the door and watched as he dragged his suitcases down the stairs to the waiting yellow taxi. Amara clutched my leg, sobbing quietly into my faded jeans. Of the two, she was the daddy's girl. Ketandu seemed indifferent. As I shut the door that last time, I knew I was shutting the door on my marriage for good.

Our lives took on a whole new meaning once I started my new shift. We left the house together each weekday morning and were back home at 3:30 p.m. Homework was usually done in thirty minutes and we had the rest of the evening to read and prepare dinner. The girls were in bed by 8:00 p.m. I gave up the weekend shift altogether. I loved my new life and the stability it afforded me. Routine was my comfort zone and the unknown, my greatest fear. There was still a lot unknown to me about my diagnosed brain tumor. I had an upcoming appointment with my endocrinologist and fear gripped my heart every time I thought about it.

On the morning of my appointment, I dropped off the girls at school and headed south on Lakeshore Drive. Crystal white sheets of ice covered the surface of the sun-starved Lake Michigan, giving it a forlorn look. The lake seemed in dire need of spring. An hour later, I was seated before my doctor, nervously waiting for the verdict on my tumor.

"Your blood tests came back and your growth hormone level is very high. This is consistent with what we thought the tumor might be," the doctor said. She was a middle-aged woman with auburn hair and kind, grey eyes.

"Does that mean I'm going to live?' I asked, a ray of hope suddenly appearing from nowhere.

"The tumor is not malignant, but if it's left untreated, it can cause your vital organs to swell and eventually shut down."

"What are my treatment options?"

"The first line of treatment for a tumor of this nature is surgery."

The beacon of hope disintegrated at the mention of surgery. My body began to tremble and tears welled up in my eyes.

"I can't have brain surgery, doctor. I'm new in this country. My children are both under eight years old, and I have no family or social network."

"We will start you on monthly injections to see if we can lower your growth hormone levels and we will take it from there."

I nodded in agreement as she further explained my diagnosis.

"What happens with an elevated growth hormone is that it makes things in your body grow, including your heart, kidneys, hands, feet, nose, and tongue. If it's not treated, you will wind up with an enlarged heart and kidney failure."

This solved the mystery of why my shoe size went up two sizes and my jaw and tongue were growing. I had lived with this condition all these years and didn't realize I was sick. I was suddenly overwhelmed with gratitude that I found myself in an environment where my disease was diagnosed and treatment was a possibility. I vowed to overcome my fear and worry and replace them with gratitude.

Two weeks later, I was back in the clinic for my first dose of Sandostatin. I winced as the stern-faced Filipino nurse jabbed my rear end with the thick syringe, sending waves of pain down my left limb. I stood paralyzed for a few seconds as the thick medication traveled down my leg, the excruciating pain I felt in the moment causing me to reexamine my decision to opt-out of surgery. I was going to ride it out, I said to myself. The pain was transient, but a brain surgery was permanent and involved too much risk. This was the beginning of several trips to the endocrinology clinic. I was back there every twenty-eight days for my injections. And in between, I had to see the cardiologist to assess if the disease had done any damage to my heart. I also had to take tests for my kidneys, undergo MRIs to see if the tumor was getting bigger, and see an eye specialist to confirm that the tumor was not encroaching on my optic nerves. I felt like a guinea pig, an experiment of some sort, but I was grateful to be alive and to be in one of the greatest countries in the world. I was thankful for a new lease on life. Had I not made the bold move to leave Nigeria, I shudder to think of what might have become of me.

I had come face to face with a new hurdle, but there was light at the end of the tunnel. Fate had sanctioned the pilgrimage to my new country, and there was no looking back. The die was cast.

Chapter 9

FLIGHT
OR FIGHT

RESILIENCE IS A SKILL THAT YOU HONE AS YOU NAVIGATE VARious bends in the journey of life. I was an old student of bounce-backs, and coming to America presented me with the opportunity to exhibit my hard-won grit. Greenhouse was a good place to work because it tested my resolve.

On days when I woke up consumed with self-pity, I would look into the four pairs of helpless eyes that depended on me for virtually everything, and that sadness would disappear. Steve was one of the individuals I cared for. He was a forty-year-old Jewish man and a first-generation American. His grandparents and their three-year-old son arrived on the shores of America in the 1930s. Sharing stories about his family's immigration experience was one of Steve's favorite things to do. We bonded over those stories.

"My grandparents are not originally from Russia. They are from Slovakia, but the quota for Slovakia was full, so they had to fake that they were Russians to be admitted into the United States."

"They could do that?" I asked, perplexed by the information.

"Apparently, they could. I'm here," he chuckled.

Steve had a great sense of humor and joked about nearly everything. But he also had a dark side. This grim side made him unpopular amongst the staff. Seeing how disliked he was, set me on a mission to befriend him, an act I didn't realize was noticed until I was nominated for the employee of the year award.

One afternoon just as I was rounding off my shift with Steve, there was a slight tap on his door. A slender middle-aged woman walked in.

"Hello. I'm Irene," she said, extending her hand. She was employed to drive Steve to the store on a biweekly basis, and this was her first day. We engaged in small talk as I got Steve ready for his outing. She was originally from Russia and taught piano at her local Young Men's Christian Association (YMCA).

"I've always wanted my daughters to learn to play the piano," I said.

"How old are they?" Irene asked.

"They are seven and five." Chuckling sheepishly, I added, "I can't even afford the lessons."

Handing me a piece of paper with her phone number, she said, "Call me, let's talk."

My conversation with Irene reignited a desire, one that I had placed on the back burner in the wake of my economic and health battles. I shoved the paper in the pocket of my blue scrubs, trying not to think about the financial implications. But it was okay to dream big. We were in the land where big dreams came true. It was time to work towards those dreams; that American dream that says you can be anything you want if you work hard for it. Meeting Irene was not a coincidence. It was a collision with destiny. It was a vital aspect of our American Dream. I was going to call her.

As our lives slowly transitioned, so did the season. Birds chirped in nearby trees as day broke, and daffodils sprouted out of the once barren, snow-covered ground. The long-drawn winter was behind us, and I was glad to shed my heavy coat for a lighter spring jacket. Our first Easter break was uneventful. We took long walks on the lakefront, enjoying the sunlight that had eluded us in the winter months. Summer break was around the corner and I fretted about what I would do with the girls when I went to work in the morning. I decided to seek Tiana's opinion. She was an African American who was originally from Mississippi. Tiana had worked in Greenhouse for twelve years and knew the neighborhood. She was the first close friend I made at Greenhouse. Tiana had an answer to every question, a trait I was most grateful for. We spent lunch breaks engaged in small talk. One afternoon after lunch, while I stood waiting for her to finish a cigarette, she said:

"My big brother is getting out, and we're having a cookout for him. I would like you to come."

"Wow! Congratulations. What university is he getting out of?" I asked, waving away the smoke she blew in my direction.

"Girl, he's not getting out of no University. He's getting out of jail."

"Jail? You throw parties for people getting out of jail?" I asked, my eyes widening.

"Y'all don't welcome your family when they get out of jail in your country?"

"Of course not! If a family member ever goes to jail and they are released, they sneak home at night when no one is awake."

This was part of the culture shock I experienced in my new country. I did attend Tiana's brother's "get-out" party in their family house on Chicago's south side. Driving through the derelict streets of Englewood, Chicago's most violent neighborhood, I wondered why I accepted the invitation. Perhaps curiosity had gotten the better of me to witness a get-out-of-jail party, or maybe it was an effort to compensate for my rude reaction.

Smoke rose from the black barbecue grill in a corner of the yard and the aroma of grilled chicken and roast corn teased my nostrils as I approached the white picket fence that enclosed the faded brown bungalow. Tiana met me at the door with a huge grin.

"I'm so happy you could make it!"

Grabbing my jacket, she led me to the living room. Large red antique settees dominated the room and portraits of family members lined the pale walls. I sat on an armchair clutching my purse as guests began to trickle in: cousins, aunts, uncles, and neighbors. Soon, the living room buzzed with laughter. I could barely keep up with the names and faces as Tiana introduced me to everyone.

"Meet my co-worker from Africa," she announced proudly.

The celebrant finally made his grand entrance. I watched intently as the guests took turns hugging and kissing him. An older gentleman gave him a friendly slap on the back, reminding everyone of the name he called him when he was a little boy. He was a burly guy in his mid-forties. He had an intimidating aura that was softened by the obvious love he received from his family. He was dressed in a pair of oversized brown khaki shorts and a t-shirt that revealed bulging biceps. A thick gold chain hung on his neck. Solid black tattoos that looked like an abstract combination of dragons and numbers shimmered down both arms. If I ever saw a warm welcome, this was one. Food, drinks and laughter dominated the evening.

As I headed home hours later on the Dan Ryan expressway, I thought about how lovely an evening it had turned out to be. Tiana's family had taught me the many layers of familial love, a lesson I was grateful to learn.

Tiana came through and found me a summer camp for my daughters. It was four blocks from Greenhouse. I could rest easy knowing that the girls were going to have an engaging, fun summer. Chicago's summer days were as hot as its winter nights were cold. Temperatures of 75 degrees Fahrenheit ushered in the sunrise as humid air tickled our faces. The girls and I left the house at 6:30 a.m. each weekday morning. I dropped them at the summer camp on my way to work and picked them up a little after 3 o'clock. I was grateful for the camp. I had applied for a scholarship to assist with the cost, an offer that was available to struggling single mothers.

Being our very first full summer in Chicago, we were determined to make the most of it. We spent evenings at the lakefront enjoying a swim in the lake or just basking in the sunlight. The girls built sandcastles while I lay on the Mickey Mouse beach towel reading a book or watching teenagers play beach volleyball. I liked Chicago and with the arrival of summer, I decided I loved it. Rogers Park, our northside community, was culturally and socioeconomically diverse. It was home to Loyola University, and Northwestern University was only a few miles north. The Red Line train ran west of the lake adding to the contemporary feel of the community. Grocery stores and laundromats were accessible, and small coffee shops were the signature of most corner lots. My favorite African store was three blocks north.

On the third weekend of summer, we hopped on Bus 147 headed downtown. Strolling down Magnificent Mile, we toured the historic Old Water Tower place, one of the few structures that survived the Great Chicago Fire of 1871. We stopped to visit The Bean at Millennium Park as we continued south on Michigan Avenue. The Crown Fountain was an instant hit with the girls. They loved the huge billboards that displayed the images of Hollywood stars, and giggled as water spouted out of Marilyn Monroe's eyes and ears. White chariots plied the immaculate streets and tourists could be seen taking pictures with policemen on horses. We stopped to grab lunch at a nearby Potbelly's and some ice cream cones from McDonald's.

The sun had begun to set when I ushered two very tired girls on to Bus 147 headed north. As I tucked them in bed that night Amara asked, "Can we go again tomorrow Mommy?"

"We will go again soon. We will take your bathing suits so you can splash at the water fountain."

"Yay!" they both chorused. It was an eventful summer, filled with fun days at the lakefront and the beautiful streets of Downtown Chicago.

Summer gradually took a graceful bow as the sun began its cycle of early descent. The temperature dipped at nighttime and loud noises often made by air conditioners began to slowly diminish. My apprehension grew as fall navigated the corner. The heating bill was outrageous, something I couldn't afford for a second winter. I started to hunt for a new apartment. One evening as we drove home, I spotted a "To let" sign on the building next to the girls' school. Bringing the car to an abrupt stop, I jotted down the number of the realtor and called immediately. The owner was a nice Jewish man named Jeff. He had a studio apartment available on the fifth floor. It was an old building with rusty windows and frayed carpets that begged to be replaced. But it was clean and affordable. Heat was included in the rent, and because it was next door to the elementary school I couldn't go wrong with it. I signed the lease three weeks later, and Jeff was kind enough to hand us the keys a week early.

The smell of wet paint welcomed us as we moved in a few non-essentials. The polished wooden floor glittered in contrast to the pale white walls. A paint-coated radiator stood in the far corner of the bedroom/living room, reminding me that I no longer had to worry about heating bills. The tiny kitchen, barely big enough for two, overlooked an alley. A huge dumpster sat directly underneath the window. Loud singing could be heard from the building next door which was home to a Spanish church. Our new home was small, but it was all we needed at the moment. I was going to be saving about $180 every month by downsizing to this smaller place and getting rid of the heating bill. It was money that I planned to spend on piano lessons for my daughters. I never stopped thinking about Irene, the piano teacher. She never came back to Greenhouse. I assumed she didn't get along with Steve, but I was certain of one thing - that the universe brought her to Greenhouse on that day just so our paths would cross.

Moving house was no easy feat, but we got most of our belongings into the studio apartment by the end of the week. The heavy Queen-size mattress was the last thing we lumbered up the stairs and into the studio apartment. It was a tall order securing it to the roof of the Nissan van. I heaved a sigh of relief as I slumped to the floor beside Ketandu, glad that every last piece of our belongings was finally moved. It had been a long week, and we were all bone tired.

"My body hurts, Mommy," Ketandu cried.

I felt guilty about working her so hard. I often forgot how young she was.

"I'm so sorry," I said, rubbing her back. "I will give you a warm shower. I'm sure you'll feel better."

We slept in the next morning, thankful that it was a Sunday.

With the new apartment offering me the respite that I desperately needed, I was able to focus on the new school year.

Ketandu moved on to second grade and Amara started first grade. I applied to the magnet schools like Ms. Baker, Amara's teacher, had suggested. There were a couple of good ones on the Northside where we lived. I ranked Walt Disney Elementary, first, and Stone Academy, second. Admissions were strictly by lottery, and we were not going to find out if they got accepted until six months from the date of application. Fingers crossed, I prayed for a miracle. The desire for my girls to acquire a world-class education consumed my every waking moment. My ambition crackled like wild flames and was stoked every time I watched a success story on the Oprah Winfrey Show. My girls were going to attend Ivy League schools. I didn't see what could possibly stand in the way of this American dream. I knew that getting accepted into top schools was no walk in the park. Aside from strong academic achievements, an applicant also had to exhibit strong passion in non-academic areas. I began to explore activities that I could enroll the girls in.

The park district offered free swimming lessons, but spaces were limited. The only way I was guaranteed slots for the girls was to stay up until midnight to enroll online. The spaces filled up in five minutes, barely allowing me enough time to enroll both girls. We went to the indoor pool during spring break for the first of many lessons, and I watched with excitement as they splashed in the water, inflatable pink floats attached to their arms. It wasn't long before the floats came off and they were swimming in the deep end under the strict supervision of the coach.

There was no word on the Magnet School application as the school year drew to a close. Ketandu and Amara both surpassed academic expectations, and there was a growing agitation to move them to a better school. I remained hopeful that the girls would still land spots in some of the Magnet Schools. But as they entered the final week of the school year, my faith began to wane.

"I don't think Amara is getting a spot in any of the Magnet Schools," I said to Ms. Kaitleen, her class teacher. "We haven't heard back from Chicago Public Schools."

"If you haven't heard back by now, it means she wasn't selected," Ms. Kaitleen replied. "But it's fine, you can apply again next year."

My heart sank. I did not want them to spend another school year in their current school. I was doing everything in my power to keep them challenged. Their teachers sent home extra worksheets. Both girls were avid readers and spent evenings after homework buried in storybooks. I slowly came to terms with the fact that the girls would spend another year in their current school. I would try again as Ms. Kaitleen suggested. While I was at work the following Monday, my phone rang.

"Can I speak to the parents of Amarachukwu and Ketandu Chiedu?"

"This is she," I said hesitantly.

"I'm calling to let you know that your daughters have been offered spots at Walt Disney Magnet School."

"Both of them?" I asked.

"Yes ma'am, both of them."

It wasn't April Fool's Day, was it? Or was it a prank call? What were the odds that out of thousands of applicants my daughters' names were both drawn in one school year? Could two family members win the lottery in one day? I was beside myself with joy.

The next morning, I drove to Walt Disney Magnet to complete the registration. As I walked into the tall brown building, my gait had a certain bounce to it; the springy steps of a person who had just won the jackpot. I felt very fortunate.

It was a beautiful school in the uptown neighborhood, just west of the lake. The entrance was modest until you got past the swivel doors and into the common area. The atmosphere held a superiority that our neighborhood school lacked.

I rummaged through my bag for the girls' birth certificates as a staff member recounted the steps they had taken to contact us. The offer letters were sent to Freda's old address which happened to be the address we had on file with the school. Freda had moved, and the letters were returned to the office of Chicago Public Schools. I was grateful for the efforts that were made to contact us. Our spaces could have been offered to some other accessible students.

I took a quick tour of the school. They operated a pod system where the homerooms were collectively in an open space and teachers were rotated for core subjects. I was intrigued by this system.

"Aren't the students distracted by this concept?" I asked the staff who showed me around.

"No. Not at all."

I walked out of the building convinced that Walt Disney was the right school for my daughters.

I had to call Ms. Baker, Amara's kindergarten teacher. I owed her a ton of gratitude as she was the one who started me on this quest.

"I'm so happy for Amara and her sister," she said, her excitement traversing the telephone glued to my ear. "It's rare that both girls were accepted at the same time."

"I know. I feel blessed and my lips hurt from smiling."

"I had a student who transferred to Walt Disney the year before Amara joined my class," Ms. Baker continued. "They are Nigerians and I think you will like her mother, Iyabo. Call her. She will help you settle."

She gave me Iyabo's number and we met for the first time the next weekend. It was odd that they lived across the street from us and we never bumped into them. That day, I walked up the narrow wooden staircase that led up to their apartment, clutching both girls in each hand . I was a little nervous, not knowing what to expect. She held the door open as we made our way into the spacious living room, her face lighting up with a warm smile. The girls eyed one another for a few awkward minutes before they decided they would get along.

Iyabo and her daughter, Kanyinsola became an integral part of our life. Iyabo had been a high school teacher in Nigeria and valued education as much as I did. I didn't have to peer too closely to notice that she had similar aspirations for her daughter as I did for my girls, a platform upon which we formed a close bond. We began to spend a lot of time with our new friends. Iyabo and I combed libraries for resources for the girls. Ketandu and Kanyinsola, classmates in their school's gifted program, were often embroiled in healthy competition.

Time flew by. It was our second summer in America and the first in our studio apartment. The apartment whose warmth had cocooned us from the terror of Chicago's cold seemed to unleash hell as we navigated summer. The heat made it impossible to sleep at night. After yet another sleepless night, I went in search of an air conditioner. I found a rusty old one in our local Salvation Army thrift store. Loading it on my cart, I wheeled it to the checkout counter, hoping it would work when I took it home.

That night, the girls and I were excited to mount our newly acquired contraption. As we moved furniture around in readiness to install the air conditioner, something darted across the room and slid underneath the refrigerator. I screamed in terror. "What is it, Mommy?" Amara asked, her eyes bulging with fear.

"I think it's a rat. I just saw a rat," I said, taking giant strides towards the bed.

"Oh, a mouse. Don't be scared, Mommy. It doesn't bite."

"I hate them."

I didn't sleep a wink all night. First, it was the heat and then mice. The next day after work, I bought a mousetrap from the hardware store and installed it behind the refrigerator.

We got home the next evening to the loud and desperate squeak of the mouse. It had been caught in the trap.

"I can't look at it. I just can't," I said to the girls.

"Don't worry mommy," Amara said. "I will throw it out."

I opened the kitchen window that overlooked the alley and told her to throw it in the open dumpster directly beneath the window. I hid in the bathroom, awaiting the completion of the mission.

"Stop wriggling around, okay?" I heard her say to the mouse as she attempted to place it in the plastic bag I had provided her. All of a sudden, she let out a loud shriek and dropping the mouse, she ran towards the bathroom where I was hiding.

"A wasp! Mommy! A wasp!" She was terrified of flying insects, and a wasp had flown in through the open kitchen window. The big, black wasp buzzed loudly as it darted across the room in rapid zigzag motions. Amy was crying hysterically, her face firmly glued to my dark jeans. She didn't want to see the wasp, didn't want to hear it. Her hands were secure around both ears. I could hear the mouse squeaking loudly in the kitchen. My seven year old who was bent on rescuing her mother from the clutches of a mouse suddenly needed rescuing. It was a Catch-22 situation. I was the Mom and I had to put on my big girl pants. I finally left the bathroom and let out the wasp and Amara completed her previously aborted mission. It was a night to forget.

The fear of wasps however, didn't keep Amara indoors. That summer she learned how to ride a bike alongside her sister. Taking turns, I propped each girl up on the brightly colored Huffy bikes I bought on sale at Walmart until they learned to steady themselves, and in no time they were cruising down the streets in drag races. Some evenings, I cut their fun short, so I could go indoors and watch *Everybody Hates Chris* – my favorite TV show.

Teaching the girls to ride a bike was something I wished their father had done. I had to fill that role. I had filled other roles and this was not going to be an exception. I wasn't sure if they missed him. They didn't talk about him except for the times he called. Every time my phone rang and it was him, I gave the phone to the girls. We hadn't had a conversation since he left. We had nothing more to talk about. I was making dinner one evening when he called. Ketandu handed me the phone,

"Daddy wants to speak to you."

He had never attempted to speak to me in the past. I was surprised that he wanted to. Grabbing the phone with my oil-stained fingers I greeted him, "Hello, good evening."

"I want you to come home with the girls."

Taken aback for a second and not sure I heard correctly, I replied, "I don't understand."

"I said you should bring my daughters home to Nigeria."

"You know that is not even possible. They have settled in nicely. And what is bringing this kind of talk?"

"I don't care. I'm giving you one month to come home or I will take action."

"Action such as what?"

"You don't want to know."

He hung up.

That night, I tossed and turned in bed wondering what instigated Emeka's behavior. He gave me his blessing to leave with the girls. He knew I was relocating for good.

That was the beginning of an onslaught of threats that changed my life forever.

The following week, I received a call from Aunty Stella, "Your husband has asked me to tell you to come home."

"Aunty, I am not coming home. This is my new home. My marriage is over, and as soon as we've been separated for two years, I will file for a divorce."

I received a call from a different person each day; old friends in Nigeria, church members, and even from my mother whom I hadn't been in contact with since I left Nigeria.

"Emeka said he will call the immigration to deport you if you don't come home," she warned.

"He can go ahead and do whatever he wants. I am never going home to him."

Returning to a dead marriage filled with physical and emotional abuse was not an option. But after a few weeks, I began to buckle under the pressure from the barrage of calls and threats. When it seemed like my family was not getting to me, Emeka deployed his family.

His aunt called me one evening and said "Emeka has drafted the first letter to immigration. If you don't come home in a week, he will send it."

I knew whom I was married to. I knew the lengths he could go and I also knew he was not one whose bluff I could call. But I didn't know what to do. Fear and worry began to eat away at my insides. I woke up many nights drenched in cold sweat from nightmares where the girls and I were deported. I was constantly looking over my shoulder, afraid I was going to be pulled over and handed to immigration. I slowly unraveled. Driving home from work on many afternoons, I would pull over to ride out a bout of violent panic attacks.

In desperation, I reached out to a Nigerian immigration lawyer who said she could file asylum for the girls and me. But upon hearing that Emeka had potentially written immigration to get me deported, she decided against the asylum application.

I walked around feeling like I was living on borrowed time. Emeka's threats mounted pressure on my already fragile health. If he got his desire and I got deported, my chances of surviving the brain tumor were slim. I still managed the diagnosis with regular visits to specialists. The future suddenly looked very bleak.

While I hovered at the edge of a nervous breakdown, the girls were excited about starting at their new school the following week. We went shopping at Walmart for bookbags, and stopped at Marshall's for a few new clothes. School uniforms were not required in the new school, so we were shedding the blue pinafores for some fancy clothes. That night, the girls displayed the new purchases on the bed, and while Ketandu leaped on the bed in excitement, she fell and twisted her thumb. I applied a cold compress to the swollen thumb and sent her to bed. The next morning, I took another look at the thumb and decided to take her to the emergency room. It was a Sunday morning, so we walked into an almost empty urgent care unit. It wasn't long before she was seen by a doctor who ordered a scan of the thumb. While we waited in a small room, a social worker was sent to interrogate us as to the cause of the injury. Bone-related injuries were often considered a red flag for possible child abuse. The doctor walked in about thirty minutes later with good news.

"The x-ray doesn't show any fracture. But I'm going to put the hand in plaster and send you to a specialist tomorrow."

My heart sank. She was starting her new school the following day and the injury was to her right hand.

"Why does she need to see an orthopedic doctor, if the bone isn't broken?" I asked the young doctor.

"The orthopedic surgeon will take a closer look since it's his specialty."

Thanking the doctor, we left the emergency room with Tylenol and the entire hand wrapped in plaster of paris.

"You have to learn to write with your left hand like me," I teased Ketandu. "At least until you see the new doctor tomorrow."

I drove the girls to their new school the next morning, stopping to take pictures at the school entrance. It was a historic day for my family and not even the huge plaster on Ketandu's hand could dampen the atmosphere. Ketandu walked towards me as I picked her up from school six hours later, brandishing her cast coated in different colors.

"Look, Mommy. My new friends wrote nice things on my cast."

"Nice. Let's hope this doctor decides you don't need it. How did you write in school today?"

"My teacher helped me, and I tried to use my left hand."

Amara giggled. The orthopedic doctor wasted no time in peeling off the plaster of paris. He confirmed that it was a strain and not a fracture. Ketandu was happy to have her hand back.

The new school was everything I wished for and even more. Each morning as I ushered them into the big yellow school bus, I muttered a silent prayer of immense gratitude. We adjusted to our new routine as quickly as we did the old one. I would put them on the school bus at 6:45 a.m. and drive manically to Greenhouse to meet up with my shift which started at 7 a.m. They got off the school bus at 2:45 p.m. and my shift at Greenhouse ended at 3 p.m. I left my job at 3:05 and drove manically to pick them up from the bus stop before someone noticed they were alone and called the authorities. I was late to work on the days the school bus was late, and I was late to pick them up on the days that my co-worker ran late for work. I was constantly on a rollercoaster during the weekdays and couldn't wait to unwind on the weekends. One day, Amara came up with a brilliant plan, "Mommy, we can wait for you at the library when we get off the bus." There was a public library next door to where the school bus dropped them off. A light bulb had suddenly turned on.

"That is so true," Ketandu added. "You don't have to be driving so fast to come get us."

We tested the idea the next day and it worked perfectly. Amara was thoughtful, she came up with brilliant ideas every time we struggled with decisions. Life's burden seemed to ease off with the new arrangement, and the constant threats from their father seemed to have dissipated until one Tuesday evening when I got a phone call that rocked my heart to its core. It was another school night and

Ketandu was sprawled on the floor tackling a math problem while Amara lay cross-legged on the bed flipping the pages of a science fiction book. The loud hiss of the radiator masked the sound of my cell phone as it vibrated on the TV stand. Making a quick dash for the Samsung phone, I flipped it open.

"Hello, is this the parent of Ketandu Chiedu?"

"Yes, this is she."

"This is a call from the Department of Child Protective Services. We are on the way to your apartment. There's a report of child abuse leveled against you."

"Child abuse?" I stuttered, looking at the phone as the voice on the other end tapered off. My hands trembled as I tried to make sense of this strange call. As I set about gathering my thoughts, my phone rang again.

"This is the Chicago police department calling to inform you that we are on the way to investigate a case of abuse."

The night that started off as another regular one was fast becoming a nightmare. I searched my mind for what this could be about but I found no answers. My heart pounded, sweat fast drenching my forehead. I turned to the girls, searching their faces for clues as to what the mayhem could be about.

"Did anything happen in school today?"

They both shook their heads in unison.

"Please girls, tell me the truth," I pleaded. "Somebody has reported mommy to the authorities and I need to know what happened before they get here."

"I don't know, Mommy," Ketandu said. Amara started to cry.

Time was ticking. I paced the floors of the studio apartment, at a loss for words. My worst fear had come upon me. I lived in dread of the Department of Children's Services taking away my children. That was the first thing I was warned about upon my arrival to America.

"They will take your children and place them in foster homes and you won't see them for many years."

If they took my children, was my life even worth living? I began to shake violently. I had to speak to someone before I lost my mind. Hands trembling, I called Freda.

"I don't know what to do. DCFS just called me. They are coming to take the children. I don't know who reported me."

I was now hysterical.

"Jesus! Who did this?" she queried.

"I don't know."

"Did you ask the children?"

"They said they don't know."

"Okay, calm down. Just answer their questions. Remain calm. You hear me?"

The girls and I huddled closely together on the couch as we awaited their arrival. I hoped for the best outcome. I had to plead my case and try to convince them that I was not an abusive mother. But first, I had to know what I was being accused of. There was a soft knock and I opened the door to two police officers and a slender African American lady. She introduced herself as Ann, a staff member of the Department of Children's Services. She led me away to the kitchen. The girls remained in the living room with the police officers.

"The department received a call from a male residing in Nigeria who claimed to be the father of the children. He alleged that you were hitting your daughter and broke her arm in the process."

Heaving a sigh of relief, I muttered, "Oh, that."

"Why do you say that?" the lady questioned.

"He is an estranged husband who only wants to see my downfall," I said.

"Did your daughter have an injury recently?"

"Yes. She sprained her thumb a few weeks ago."

"How did their father know?"

While I was interrogated, it dawned on me that the pictures I sent Emeka of the girls' first day at their new school were the evidence he used against me. I felt like a fool.

Satisfied with my answers, she whisked the girls away to the bathroom for their round of interrogation. While they were in the bathroom, the police officers questioned me.

"Your husband reported that you are living in the United States illegally."

"Yes, Officer."

"Why do you think he made this call?" the older of the two officers asked.

"He wants to destroy me because I refused to go back to him. He was abusive."

He jotted down notes as I spoke. "We will visit the hospital where your daughter was treated and corroborate your report about the injury."

"No problem, Officer. Here's the address of the hospital." I handed him the address and they left.

What was potentially the worst night of my life was coming to an end. The DCFS lady stayed behind and watched some T.V with us. American Idol was on. Simon Cowell's voice filled the room as he harshly critiqued a contestant. For a long time, I couldn't watch the show without thinking about the events of that cold Tuesday night. I was investigated and the case was finally dismissed, but not without Emeka constantly calling DCFS in an attempt to sway the outcome of the case.

I realized that I had shot myself in the foot when I sent him pictures of Ketandu with the bandaged arm. But I sent them in good faith, to keep him abreast of his children's progress which I thought would make him proud. Going forward, I learned to be circumspect. If he was bent on dragging me home by any means possible, I was not going to be caught napping again. We gradually put the horrors of that Tuesday night behind us. I had so much to be thankful for.

The girls thrived in their new school, coming home most days with complex Mandarin homework. On many weekends we were in Iyabo's house till midnight, putting final touches to Ketandu and Kanyinsola's projects. I was not going to be derailed by Emeka's antics. I had a purpose and I was going to achieve it. I also believed in the power of the spoken word. I decided to incorporate daily confessions into our morning routine. Every morning before we left the house we would pray and confess the life I aspired to for the girls:

I'm a child of God
I'm born to win
I'm above only and never beneath
From Walt Disney Magnet School, I'm going on to a gifted High School
From a gifted High School, I'm going on to an Ivy League College
I will meet my husband at the right time
He will love me as Christ loved the church
Divorce will not be an option in my marriage
The peace and love of Christ will reign in my home
I shall not die, but live to declare the works of the Lord
I shall be a voice to the voiceless
I shall fight the cause of the poor
I shall fulfill destiny
I shall leave my mark on the sands of time

The Daily Confession became an integral part of our lives for the next decade. Summer approached as we wrapped up the school year at Disney. We had a few interesting things lined up including starting piano class with Irene. I felt it was time. One fine Friday evening in June, I took the girls to meet Irene. She lived on a quiet street in Winnetka, a northern suburb of Chicago. She led us into a spacious living room with her two white Persian cats following closely behind. A brown, old Steinway piano stood in the middle of the room. Music books were scattered on the floor, adding a casual ambiance to the room's appearance.

"Hello, hello," she said, shaking my daughters' hands, one after the other.

"My name is Irene, and I'm a classical piano teacher."

The girls responded with shy smiles as they reached for Irene's hand. They both sat on the piano stools as Irene took each of their hands and examined their fingers. "Your fingers are stiff," she said to Ketandu as she moved her fingers around testing for dexterity.

"Most good pianists start lessons by age six. You're nine. You have to work hard." Ketandu nodded. Amara, who was only seventeen months younger, was not given a free pass either. Irene asked them to play a few notes on the piano and to clap after her in a particular sequence, this was to check their rhythm. That marked the beginning of piano lessons that spanned nearly a decade, and the beginning of a great mentorship that birthed many important life lessons.

Our first "piano" was a Yamaha keyboard which I purchased for $50 from a resident at Greenhouse. It was in great shape and came with a stand. We mounted it in a corner of the studio apartment. Friday evenings were sacred; it didn't matter what was happening, we made that forty-minute trip to Winnetka. We showed up in snowstorms, in torrential rain, and holidays were no exception. Irene was basically offering us the lessons for next to free. What better way to appreciate her kind gesture than with diligence?

Every evening after homework, I ensured the girls practiced for forty-five minutes. There were no exceptions and no off days. In no time, they were breezing through simple pieces like Chopin's *Prelude in E minor* and *Ode to Joy* by Beethoven. It pleased Irene that they were such dedicated students.

I was glad that Irene did not pamper my girls. She was stern with them and would yell occasionally if they made the same mistakes too many times.

"ALL COWS EAT GRASS!" she yelled at Amara, one evening.

It was an acronym she taught them to help read notes. Amara had hit the wrong key for the fourth time, much to Irene's exasperation. It did not bother me that she yelled at them. It pleased me that she felt comfortable enough to do so with me sitting a few inches away. My daughters had a mixture of fear and adoration for Irene. On our way to their lesson and on rare occasions when they didn't perfect their homework, Ketandu would plead with me to put in a good word for her.

"Mommy, would you please tell Irene that I had a lot of homework from school, so I couldn't learn the last line?"

"I will do no such thing," I would reply.

"She's going to be mad at me," she would say.

"Get your homework completed next time, if you don't want her angry."

Irene was a combination of steel and mush. She would berate them one minute and heap praises on them the next. I trusted her wholeheartedly with my daughters. She was a Russian immigrant who had similar values as I did. Her daughter, a pre-med student at Harvard, was proof.

"I am going to introduce you to another one of my good students. She is Nigerian too," Irene said one night after a grueling lesson.

Irene introduced us to Kay and her daughter, Ngozi. A few weeks into our weekly lessons, we drove up to their home in Glenview to meet them in person. Kay was one of the kindest people I had ever met. Her soft brown eyes lit up every time she smiled which was quite often. I was thrilled to find out she was also Igbo. I didn't know a lot of Igbo people in Chicago and missed being around my tribe. We struck up a friendship. Ngozi was one year older than Ketandu. She was smart and driven, just the right influence I wanted for my girls.

Kay and her daughter became family. We were in her house most weekends. She was a great cook and had a knack for improvisation. She would create a delicious Nigerian dish of *peppersoup* out of nothing. She also had a great love for the outdoors and many weekends she came up with tickets for concerts or passes to Museums downtown. We were reintroduced to Chicago in ways that we hadn't known.

I shoved aside the traumas of our recent past, choosing to dwell on our newly found friendship and the joy that came with it. It had been a while since Emeka's last dastardly act. My stomach lurched every time I thought about him, leaving me to wonder what next he had up his sleeve. I didn't have to wait too long to find out.

One school night, after homework and piano practice were out of the way, the girls lounged in the living room. Ketandu's nose was buried in *Percy Jackson and the Last Olympian*, a book that was the most recent in her obsession with Greek mythology. Amara scribbled the lines of a short story on a pink notepad. I had just put dinner on the stove when my cell phone rang.

"Mommy, here," Ketandu said, walking towards me with the phone.

"Who is it?"

"No name, Mommy."

"Answer it then."

It could be their father. He often called with a hidden caller I.D. Ketandu flipped open the phone and pressed the speakerphone button.

"Hello."

"This is Immigration and Customs Services. Tell your mother we are on our way to pick her up."

The line went dead. Ketandu stared at the phone, color draining from her panic-stricken face. She had heard her father threaten me enough times to understand the implication of the call. Rushing to the shoe rack, she grabbed a pair of shoes and made for the door. Amara followed closely behind.

"Where are you going?" I asked Ketandu, refusing to process what we just heard.

"You heard it, Mommy. They are coming to get you!" She swung open the door leading to the back and leaped down the dark stairs. With barely enough time to grab a pair of shoes, I hurried to catch up with her and Amara. Chicago's freezing air gnawed at our scantily clad bodies as the girls pushed open the back door. Only then did I realize that we hadn't stopped to grab coats. I looked back at the building for a split second, toying with the idea of rushing back to grab our coats. I decided against it. We stood by the big dumpster beneath our kitchen window. I needed a few seconds to clear my thoughts, and make sense of what was happening. Amara had started to shiver violently. She was the one who was most susceptible to the cold. Goosebumps formed underneath her lime sleeveless top. We couldn't be out in the vicious cold for too long. My daughters would freeze to death. I had to come up with a plan. But my mind seemed to have frozen with the weather. As I stood there contemplating what to do, where to go, a police patrol car approached us, its flood lights shining into our faces. Ketandu began to cry hysterically, "Mommy they are here. They have found us."

She hugged me tightly, her teeth chattering to the cold. "It's not immigration," I said, holding her tightly. It's the police and they are just passing."

Pressing their cold faces to my stomach to shield them from the view of the police vehicle, I waited nervously for the police car to drive past. I prayed that the police would not stop to ask why I was outside at that time with two little girls who were inappropriately dressed for the weather. Holding the girls tightly in each hand, I began to walk. I had no idea where I was going. I just walked. My mind had deserted me, but if I couldn't think, I could at least walk. I do not recall how we made it to Iyabo's house, but I remember standing in front of her building with two little girls who were on the verge of a hypothermic crisis. With my frost-bitten fingers, I frantically pressed the buzzer.

"Who is it?" Iyabo's raspy voice echoed through the intercom. "It's me Joy."

Iyabo threw warm blankets around the two shivering girls as she waited to hear my story. She had a calm demeanor and didn't ruffle easily and she was no stranger to the ordeals of my dead marriage.

"That was a fake call," she said, after I narrated my story. "Immigration will not tell you that they are coming to arrest you."

Then, realization suddenly hit me like a cannonball. Why would Immigration call to say they were coming? And why would they tell my daughter?

"Who do you know that might want to play this sort of prank on you?" Iyabo asked.

Staring into each other's eyes, we both knew who it was likely to be. My body suddenly began to shake, bile welling up my throat. I felt sick.

"While we were running along the alley, he called with his number. When Ketandu answered, he asked her where we were."

"Remember, you told me he can feign an American accent," Iyabo said.

"The jerk ass," I muttered, fighting back tears. How could he stoop so low? Making a prank call and putting the health of his daughters at risk.

"These girls could have suffered hypothermia or frostbite," I cried.

"Let's call an immigration lawyer, just to be sure," Iyabo said in a bid to reassure me.

She dialed the number of a lawyer friend, and handing me the phone, she listened as the lawyer assured me that it was a prank call.

"Immigration does not call to give notice. They just show up and whisk people away," the lawyer said. My fears assuaged, I headed back to my apartment with two very tired girls bundled in coats from Kanyinsola's wardrobe.

Thick dark smoke filled the hallway as we approached our apartment. Two of my neighbors stood by their doors looking towards my apartment. I had an eerie feeling that something was terribly wrong. As we got closer, I could see the building janitor by my door, holding a fire extinguisher. Then it hit me – I had forgotten to turn off the stove before we fled the apartment. The food had caught fire, nearly burning down the building. A cocktail of emotions besieged me: shame, guilt, anger, and sadness. Nico, the janitor, had opened all my windows to let out the thick smoke. We waited in the hallway as the smoke receded. Forty-five minutes later, I walked into a kitchen I barely recognized. The pot was charred and dark soot covered the entire kitchen. I shuddered violently as I thought about the danger I had subjected my co-tenants to.

That night, long after the girls had fallen asleep, I lay in bed, inhaling the residual smoke of the fire that nearly destroyed our lives. Suddenly, it all came crashing down like an avalanche; deep violent sobs wracked my body. I was tired of being afraid. I was tired of looking over my shoulder. I was tired of being sick with a brain tumor and not knowing if I would live past the next year. I was tired.

The next morning, I ushered the girls into their school bus, called off work, and went in search of a new apartment and a divorce attorney.

It was time to begin afresh.

Chapter 10

FORGING NEW PATHS

SKIPPING CONTINENTS TO ESCAPE THE WRETCHED CLAWS OF affliction was a good idea. But pain seemed to know my address. It followed me around like a shadow, casting its grim contours along every path that I dared to tread. It seemed like I would never get a break. Every time I tried to put up my feet, adversity came charging in like a bull. Tribulation was my longtime companion, one that I had learned to placate. There was no giving up, and there was no time to wallow in self-pity. The girls' future was at stake and there was too much to fight for.

My landlord, Jeff, offered me a one-bedroom apartment three blocks north of my studio apartment. "I like renting to you foreigners," Jeff often said to me. "You don't give me any trouble and you pay your rent on time."

What Jeff didn't know was that I was running from an estranged husband who had sworn to make my life a living hell. We had not taken any of Emeka's calls since the night of the immigration fiasco. I decided that it was in the best interest of the girls. We never talked about the event of that dreadful night either. I didn't learn just how much of an impact it made on them until I read an essay that Amara wrote about it. It was time to push back. He would no longer control my life like a puppeteer. We moved house and did not leave a forwarding address or telephone number, an action that seemed to fuel his rage. I would only get to hear of his latest antics from a friend whose neighbor was a Nigerian attorney.

"Name your price and help me deport my wife," Emeka would pester the attorney with a barrage of calls. When it was clear that the lawyer would not take his case, he moved on to several other lawyers, all of whom rejected his case. I could heave a sigh of relief once the ugly incident was behind us and we settled into the new apartment, a step up from the studio apartment. It had a large dining room detached from the living room which we converted into a second bedroom. The girls were now playing more advanced pieces than the Yamaha keyboard could accommodate and since we now had a spacious living room, I decided that it was time to trade the Yamaha Keyboard for a proper piano. We found an affordable piano on the southwest side of Chicago. Families donated their old pianos to an organization called Keys for Kids and they sold the pianos to the public for a meager amount. That Saturday morning, we strolled through the aisle of the open store, testing different pianos. Ketandu instinctively walked to a battered, light brown Steinway and Sons. Chipped on all edges and dented in several spots, it looked like it had been around since the 1800s. Perching on the brown stool, she began to stroke the worn black and white keys in a seamless fashion. I watched with pride as she played a near-perfect rendition of Beethoven's *Turkish March*.

"That one," I whispered to the salesman, pointing to Ketandu. "We will go with that one."

"You've made a good choice," the salesman said. "It will sound great when it is tuned."

The following weekend, our piano was delivered. It took all of four men to lug it up the narrow stairwell, their loud grunts and sweat-drenched shirts the indication of the drudgery of the task. One of the men, Joey, stayed behind to mend a pedal that fell off. He became our piano tuner and every six months for many years, he dropped by to tune the piano for a token fee.

"I like this a lot," Ketandu said, as she settled in to play a rendition of *Moonlight Sonata* by Beethoven. Amara edged her off the stool attempting Debussy's *Golliwog's Cake-walk*. As time went on, soft classical music serenaded us in our apartment every evening, cascading through the walls and into the rooms of our delighted neighbors. We became the beloved of the building.

"It's like I'm in a classical music concert every night," one neighbor said as we met in the hallway one morning. The Jamaican lady who lived in the apartment beneath us said she rushed home from work every evening, just so she wouldn't miss Beethoven's *Fur Elise* by 6:05 p.m. It appeared that she had a good knowledge of our routine.

Getting a proper piano proved to be a catalyst. The girls advanced to more difficult pieces in little time, a development that pleased Irene. Amara had just finished *Sonata No. 15* in C by Mozart. Irene's eyes welled up with tears as she polished off the piece with her.

"I have never had a student play this piece as beautifully as you do," she said. "I think you're ready for competitions."

Not confident in her ability, Amara started to decline, but I stepped in and said, "It's okay. She will practice hard and enter the competition."

Illinois Musical Association hosted competitions for piano protégés every year. Talented classical piano students from all over the state converged to exhibit their impeccable talents. The next competition was exactly one year away. Irene and the girls had drawn up a list of pieces that would impress the judges.

"*Prelude* and *Fugue* No. 12 is a good piece," Irene said. "It's a very difficult piece by Bach and not many people can play this piece very well. The judges will like you."

Amara settled for Irene's choice while Ketandu opted for *Wedding Day at Troldhaugen* by Edvard Grieg, a less complicated piece. The next fifty weeks flew by with the girls on a quest to finish their pieces for the upcoming competition. In the weeks leading to the competition, Friday classes were marathons with Irene pushing them to advance to the finish line.

As the girls struggled to impress Irene, I struggled with bills. The house rent had gone up significantly and my income from Greenhouse no longer sustained us. I found myself falling behind, and each month I had to decide as to what item I struck off the list. The list grew longer as my income stretched thinner. One night, after I tucked the girls in bed, I sat in the kitchen drowning in self-pity, and a sudden epiphany came upon me – I could drive a taxi. That would give me a decent income and still afford me time to be home with the girls when they got back from school. I didn't know any women who drove taxis in the city of Chicago, but I knew a male church member who did.

"You want to drive a taxi?" Charles asked, glaring at me like I was an alien. "You can't be serious."

"I'm very serious, Brother Charles. Too serious, in fact!"

Armed with all the information I needed, I went down to Harold Washington City College of Chicago and enrolled for the forthcoming taxi class.

Saying goodbye to my clients at Greenhouse was one of the most difficult things I ever had to do. Rachel, my favorite client, held my hand, tears welling up in her eyes as she begged me not to leave.

"I will come back to visit, I promise," I said, fighting back tears of my own. I had come to love working with these unique people. It had been five incredible years. They had stolen my heart with their infectious laughter and dogged spirits. They had taught me how to ride the rollercoaster of adversity in ways I had never imagined. They had loved me as hard as I loved them, nominating me time and again for the employee of the year award, an award I eventually won. Tears drenched the collar of my light blue scrubs as I walked to my car for the last time. It felt like I was leaving a piece of my heart behind.

I found a part-time job with an agency, caring for Eddie, a hospice patient while I waited to start taxi school. Eddie was an unpleasant man with terminal lung cancer. Each day when I got to work, he would snarl at me and demand that I "get the hell out of his room." The days I wasn't at work, I was told he asked for me incessantly. Eddie passed away on my first day of cab class. I was getting ready to go to work when the agency called me with the news. I said a prayer for Eddie, got on the Red Line to Olive Harvey College to begin the taxi class.

Sixteen pairs of hostile male eyes bore through my soul, threatening to rip it apart as I scurried into the room on that first day of class. The scorn and derision were palpable. The taxi industry consisted predominantly of foreign conservative men. It was uncharted territory, but still, nothing prepared me for that steely reception.

Grumpy men in faded white kaftans and bushy beards looked like they were getting ready to pounce on prey. I didn't scare easily. I glared back at them.

Cab school was more challenging than I anticipated. The curriculum was insanely difficult. We were expected to memorize all the streets downtown, what direction they ran and how far they ran in those directions. We were also supposed to know the addresses of hotels, museums, government buildings, train stations, and hospitals, in three weeks. It was impossible to cram all that detail in such a short time. I was bad with directions, couldn't tell which was east or west to save my life.

As days progressed, I became increasingly overwhelmed. I began to regret my decision to quit my job and enroll in cab school. I made flashcards and went about memorizing the addresses. There were over five hundred flashcards in total. My train rides to school and back were spent huddled over those cards. They consumed my every waking moment. On our way to church on Sunday mornings, the girls would quiz me while I drove.

"Where is Halstead?" Ketandu would ask.

"Eight hundred west."

"Good job mommy! And Madison?"

"Oh, that one is easy," I would brag. "Madison divides the city into north and south, so it's zero north and south."

"Way to go mommy, way to go!" Amara would chant.

On the last day of class and after the final exam I stood in the line waiting patiently for my result. My heart pounded loudly as it approached my turn. What if failed? I would have to repeat the class, a luxury I could not afford. I rubbed my sweaty palms together as the instructor rustled the small pile of papers. I had a D in the mid-session quiz, an indication that I struggled immensely. Finally, he pulled out a piece of paper, scowling at it for a split second, he looked up and said, "Congratulations."

I snatched the paper from him and ran out of the room. "I passed! I passed!" I chanted, waving the thin white paper at my very nervous classmates who were still in a line awaiting their fate.

It had been a grueling three weeks. Only eight people had passed the class out of twenty. I felt lucky to be one of them. But there was one more hurdle I had to scale and that was the state license exam. It was reputed to be a near-impossible exam to pass. If you failed on your third attempt, you had to go back to cab school. I shuddered as I thought about the state license exam. Pushing the thought out of my mind, I focused on the girls' piano competition coming up over the weekend.

It was a late summer evening and the clouds swirled around the sun as it slowly set. The car was uncharacteristically quiet as we drove to the last lesson before the Illinois Musical Competition.

"The important thing is that you enjoy yourself," Irene said to Amy, as she put the finishing touches to her much-rehearsed piece.

"Remember to keep your elbows straight and use your pedals," she reminded Ketandu.

"And don't worry about winning, make sure you have fun. Remember you are my champions." Irene hugged them as they got into the car.

The day before the competition, I asked them not to practice at all. Irene had told us a story of how she forgot her notes at a concert in Russia. She felt she over-practiced the day before. I decided it was wise to give them a break. We spent the day picking out what to wear and watching a movie on Lifetime. Amara settled for a light blue summer dress. Ketandu chose a pink floral one.

We set out early the next day, navigating the interstate 290W on a not-so-busy Sunday morning. Arriving early, we sat in the lobby and waited. The competitors trickled in, stern-faced in their impeccable suits and perfect Cinderella gowns. I glanced at the girls' clothes, wishing for a second that they had worn something fancier.

Amara was up against sixteen competitors. I sat at the back of the room and watched as each competitor went up to the polished grand piano. Amara's fingers were twisted in a tight ball. Each performance was better than the last. My stomach rumbled audibly, and I shuffled my feet to detract from the noise. I had to be calm for my daughters. I had reassured them time and again that we were just going to have fun and have a feel of what the competition was about, but I wondered if I didn't expose them prematurely.

A young Asian boy performed an impeccable Chopin's *Nocturne* in E flat Major, his fingers gliding across the keys in perfect precision. His calm confidence gave off an aura of someone who performed at Carnegie Hall. Next was Amara, she walked gingerly up to the stage, and adjusted the stool, pausing for a few seconds to wipe her damp palms on the skirt of her dress. She started off a little aggressively, her fingers running to and fro over the keys in fast motion. I held my breath, hoping she wouldn't miss a note. My heart somersaulted as I glanced at the judges' stoic faces. It was over as quickly as it started. She walked back to her seat, hanging her head. I knew from her gait that she thought she did poorly. But she was my champion – mine and Irene's. It didn't matter that she felt outplayed by the other children. I was immensely proud of her and I couldn't wait to tell her.

There were two runner-ups and the winner, as with most competitions. The third and second places were announced, and I was a little disappointed not to hear her name. I got up and started to make my way to the front to hug her and tell her how proud she made me and how it didn't matter that she didn't win.

"…First place is Amara Chiedu."

She turned towards me and grinned. Time stood still. I watched with pride as she went up to the judges to grab her trophy. Holding it gingerly and unsure of what to do with it, she ran towards me. I stretched my arms and enveloped her in a bear hug. It was a win for her, but it was also a win for me and Irene. It was a victory for the many Friday evenings, tired from work, I would will myself to take them to their lessons. It was a triumph for Irene's selfless service and trust. It was our American dream that unfolded before our eyes. Ketandu did not win a medal. We knew she might not, as her piece was not complicated enough to "wow" the judges. She was too proud of her little sister to care.

As soon as we stepped out of the building, we called Irene with the news. "That's my girl! That's my girl!" She chanted in her raspy voice.

As I basked in the euphoria of Amy's trophy, I also worried about my mounting bills - a problem that would vanish if I passed the state taxi license examination. The first time I went to write the exam, I carried a ton of confidence. In addition to studying very hard, I relied on the residual knowledge from cab school. The test took place in a small room of a city building on the southwest side. It was a second attempt for many, and the last attempt for some. I rested my head on the square desk, making doodles with my sharpened HB pencil as I waited for the test to begin. The still air in the room reeked of tension. A third failure meant you had to go back to cab school.

The test lasted sixty minutes, and I was confident that I had done well until I heard my name. If you heard your name, it meant that you failed the test. As I took the walk of shame towards the door, I wondered what questions I had flunked. Not accustomed to failure, my ego took the worst hit. How was I going to tell the girls that their mother failed a test? This was the same mother who was so big on school work and good grades.

The second time I attempted the test, I wasn't so confident. I had studied a little harder and learned those routes that I hated. Why would routing a trip from Thompson Center to O'Hare International Airport be so cumbersome? It seemed that whoever wrote those routes did so solely to see cab students fail. I recognized one of the men from the last test as I walked into the testing center. He was huddled over a scruffy piece of paper doing some last-minute revision. It was his final attempt.

I clenched my fists as we awaited our results. I couldn't fail a second time. There was too much at stake. My heart pounded loudly, but as the list of names shrunk, my faith grew. Perhaps, this was my time – second time's charm I suppose.

"Joy Iweka," the instructor bellowed with a voice fit to announce an Oscar winner. But it was no red carpet walk for me, it was another walk of shame. I stumbled out of the room, head bent, and shoulders slouched.

Revving the engine of my car, I headed north on Western Avenue, tears blinding my eyes as I drove. My rent was due in a few days, and my plans were crumbling before my eyes . Maybe, leaving Greenhouse wasn't a good idea after all. I rubbed my temple in an attempt to suppress a wave of anxiety. Screeching to a halt at a traffic light, the car behind pummeled into my trunk, sending shockwaves through my head and down my spine. Shutting my eyes for a split second, I awaited my death.

"Oh my God! I'm so sorry…. Are you okay?" I heard a voice say as I stumbled out of the car. She didn't look a day older than four-teen. Ignoring her inquiry, I inspected my trunk. There wasn't much damage, and my tail lights were intact. I heaved a sigh of relief. I recalled passing her and noticing her head was bent over her phone.

"This is why you shouldn't text and drive, honey," I said.

My day had gone from bad to worse. We pulled over onto the shoulder to commence the usual protocol and as I waited for her to approach me, I heard her speaking with her mother.

"I'm sorry, Mom, I'm so sorry!" she sobbed over the phone. Moments later, she handed me the phone.

"My insurance will call you. Please do not go to the police," her mom pleaded. In retrospect, I realize how naive I was, not to have gotten a police report as they could have denied the accident. But my trust paid off when I got a call from their insurance company two days later. I took in my car for evaluation, and one week later I received a check for the damages. This check covered my rent for the month as well as my utilities. The car repair could wait, the damage wasn't conspicuous. The Man upstairs was looking out for me, meeting my needs in the most unusual ways.

With my rent worries out of the way, I returned to fretting about my third and last attempt at the cab test. As the exam day approached, my apprehension grew in leaps and bounds. I realized it would be foolhardy to do things the same way and expect differ-ent results, so I decided to re-strategize. I met an African American lady who had passed the test on her last attempt. Felicia was the only female taxi driver-prospect that I knew, as such I felt a kindred spirit with her. On the eve of my final test, I drove to her home in a southwest suburb to gather tips on how to pass the much-dreaded test. Her Belize boyfriend, a burly veteran taxi driver, was present to quiz me.

"Where is Intercontinental Hotel?"

"Michigan and Upper Illinois," I answered.

"How about Four Seasons?"

"Michigan and Delaware."

"What is 800 West and 2400 North?"

"Halstead and Fullerton."

"You've answered most of the questions right," Felicia said. "Girl, trust yourself that you will nail it this time."

But I had no trust in myself. Nothing had changed since the last test, if anything, I was now a bundle of raw nerves.

Lightning sketched jagged lines in the dark sky as I headed home on 290 E after a grueling seven hours with Felicia and her boyfriend. It was 2 a.m., and I could barely see one foot ahead as torrential rain pounded my noisy wipers. I was emotionally and physically spent, and I didn't think I had any more to give. I was ready to accept the outcome of the final test. I could crawl back to Greenhouse. They loved me and would take me back. I just had to look for other means of supplementing my income. The girls were rounding off elementary school, and I needed to be present – physically and emotionally for their high school journey.

I was desperate for this taxi license. I hoped that, somehow, I had done enough for the final attempt.

The next morning, I loaded the girls into the car, and as we headed to catch their school bus, Ketandu reminded me that we had to do our daily confession. Sometimes, when we were running late, we would have that part of our prayers in the car.

"Whose turn is it to lead the confession?" I asked.

'Amara," Ketandu said.

"Nne'm ngwa, Nne'm come on, lead us in the confession and declare that mommy will pass her final test," I said to Amara, peering

at her through the rearview mirror. Nne'm was the pet name I called
her when she was in my good books.

I'm a child of God
I'm born to win...
Mommy will pass her cab exam
And she will start driving and making a lot of money....

I dropped them off five minutes later and got on Lakeshore
south to the test venue. The atmosphere was somber as we walked
into the small room for the test. Sixty minutes later, we surrendered
our answer sheets and waited with bated breath as the instructor
went off to get them graded. I sat cross-legged, tapping the wooden
desk lightly. I had no emotions left to feel. I caught a whiff of sweat.
The Middle Eastern man beside me was also on his last attempt. I
started to feel sorry for him but decided to reserve the pity for myself.
I probably needed it more.

The Instructor returned fifteen minutes later with the pile of
answer sheets. I knew the drill. Not wanting to watch the pile of papers shrink and raise my hopes like the last time, I shut my eyes and
placed my head on the desk. The roll call began and people exited
the room as they heard their name. The room suddenly went quiet.
I was still seated. I looked up, and the Middle Eastern man beside
me was still present. There were just a handful of us left in the room.

"Congratulations to you all seated," the instructor announced.

The room went wild with celebration.

I placed my head back on the desk and sobbed.

With my Chicago taxi license under my belt, I could breathe
easy but that was cut short as my health issues took on a new twist.
Dr. K, my resident endocrinologist, opened the door to the waiting
room and Dr. A, the attending endocrinologist followed closely

behind. I had been waiting for nearly thirty minutes. Almost immediately, I knew something was not right. Usually, the resident would see me first, then the attending would come in later.

"How are you, Joy?" Dr. A inquired, a mild frown furrowing her forehead.

"I'm okay..." I replied, staring at her suspiciously.

"I decided to come in and see you with Dr. K. Your IGF-1 levels are still high. Joy, we need to have that tumor removed."

I knew this day would come, but I had hoped against hope that it wouldn't.

"Can't you increase my dose for the injection?" I negotiated, even though I already knew the answer.

"You are on the highest dose of Sandostatin and Cabergoline," Dr. A said. "Usually, surgery is the first line of treatment for Acromegaly like we discussed. We've tried medication for too long. It is not working. I'm sorry Joy."

I began to shiver. I was not ready for surgery. That, in my opinion, was a death sentence.

"I can't have this brain surgery. What will happen to my children if I die? I have no family here to care for them. No, Doctor A. Please find me something else that would work…please," I sobbed uncontrollably.

"I understand your fear but it's not as scary as it sounds," she said. "Dr. D is a fantastic neurosurgeon. You will be in good hands, Joy."

My throat tightened as I gasped for air. A brain surgery would surely be the end of me. What if I survived but ended up a vegetable? My mind traveled to the girls and my hopes for them; the dream of an Ivy League education. Everything dangled on a precarious balance. My heart raced and skipped several beats as I pleaded over and over to be exempt from the life-threatening surgery.

"You are barely forty. If we don't get this tumor removed, it will start to affect your heart and kidneys," Dr. A interjected.

I did not want my heart enlarging or my kidneys failing. Those would kill me too. I was between the devil and the deep blue sea. I might survive the surgery but would I survive a series of organ failures? Mustering every shred of courage I had left, I wiped my tears and said,

"Okay, doctor. I will have the surgery."

Dr. A's face lit up instantly. She seemed to care deeply about her patients.

"We will schedule you for an appointment with Dr. D."

I spent time ruminating on the vicissitudes of life on the days leading up to my appointment with Dr. D. Everything that could go wrong, went amiss in my life. I wondered if I could overcome this current obstacle in my path. I prayed earnestly for my daughters' sake, that I would survive. Like a cow handpicked for slaughter, I waited helplessly for Dr. D's arrival. She was a blonde woman in her mid-fifties. Her kind aqua eyes perused me as she walked into the waiting room. She gazed intently at the computer screen, reviewing my MRI results.

"The tumor is not so big. It's best we have it removed now," she explained. "The bigger it gets, the more complicated the procedure."

I started to panic again, clawing at every reason to dodge this frightening surgery.

"I have no one to care for my girls. I'm a single mom."

"You can bring them to my house. I'll watch them."

I wasn't sure if she meant those words, but hearing them triggered a rollercoaster of emotions. I began to sob.

We agreed to have the surgery the following summer. The girls would be on a long break and I wouldn't have to worry about school and homework. I wasn't sure about the recuperation time, but first I would have had to find who would watch them. Kay offered to have them move in with her. "Of course, I will keep them. Ngozi will be on summer break, so they will all be home together." I felt a heavy burden leave my shoulders. I had no doubt that my daughters would be safe with Kay.

My sense of apprehension grew as the surgery date approached. I woke up many nights drenched in a cold sweat from nightmares in which I was a vegetable and my daughters were pushing me around in a wheelchair. The girls and I moved to Kay's a day before the surgery.

"Please behave yourselves," I chided them. "Don't disgrace me. Thank Aunty Kay after each meal and pick up after yourselves. Don't try that nonsense you do at home!"

It was a tough night. I hugged them a little tighter as they went to bed, wondering if I would be cognitively present the next time I saw them, or if I would even ever see them again. They didn't seem to grasp the gravity of the situation, and if they did, they did a good job of suppressing their feelings.

Kay drove me to the hospital the next morning. I watched as she tossed a thick hardcover book onto the backseat of the car. She was going to stay with me during the surgery, and it was going to be a long day for her. We arrived as dark clouds gave way to light. I was quickly ushered to a private room and given a grey hospital gown. Left with my thoughts, I pondered on the possible outcome of the surgery. I thought about Dennis, a young Kenyan child I sponsored through a charity organization. I had logged into the organization's website one evening while we lived in the studio apartment and his large, sad eyes did a number on me. I knew I had to sponsor him. The girls called him, "Mommy's son."

"Spare my life for Dennis," I negotiated with the Man upstairs. Asking that I be kept alive for my children seemed self-serving, and I had to come up with a better bargaining chip. Dennis was that chip; that anchor. He was the last person I thought about as the medical team wheeled me into the ice-cold operating room. Dr. D held my hand and whispered, "I will take good care of you, I promise." Her kind blue eyes were the last thing I saw, before I surrendered to the cold grip of the anesthesia.

Blurred images danced before me. I blinked in an attempt to clear them.

"She's awake," I heard a voice say.

A nurse rushed to my side. "Ms. Joy, can you hear me?"

I blinked again. I was flat on my back, both nostrils stuffed with thick white wool, making it impossible to breathe through my nose. I gasped for air with my mouth. Kay was sitting by my bedside. She smiled and only then did I realize I was out of surgery alive and not a vegetable. I smiled back.

"The surgery went well. I have to go home to the kids."

I nodded slowly.

I drifted in and out. Lying flat on my back and breathing through my mouth was no easy feat. I shifted uncomfortably, asking for a pillow.

"You have to be on your back until the doctor changes the order," my nurse explained. The surgery was trans-sphenoidal - the tumor was removed through my nose.

Kay came with the girls the next day. Ketandu approached the bed cautiously, not sure what to do with her mother who was tangled up in several wires. Staring at me for a brief second, she reached out and held my hand. Amara was too scared to come close. She stood wide-eyed, taking in the view.

With my nostrils relieved of the densely packed gauze and wool, I slowly began to learn to breathe through my nose again, something I thought left me constantly dehydrated.

"Please, can I have more water?" I asked the Asian nurse. It was the third time I had asked for water in fifteen minutes. I worried that she would grow weary of answering my call light. She returned a minute later with a pitcher of water which I gulped down. My throat felt dry, and the more water I drank, the thirstier I got.

"You've developed Diabetes Insipidus," Dr. D explained, standing over my bed with a hoard of fellows. "Sometimes, in taking out the pituitary tumor, some hormones are deranged in the process. It resolves in some patients. We will wait and see, if it doesn't resolve, we will place you on medication to replace the hormone."

Part of the risks of the surgery was losing some or most of your hormone functions, in which case, you go on hormone replacement. It was part of my pre-surgery education. I was hoping to escape that risk.

My body felt like one huge tunnel as water entered from one end and immediately exited through the other. My mouth constantly felt like I had just run a marathon.

My first MRI post-surgery revealed that most of the tumor was successfully taken out and my IGF-1 levels returned to normal for the first time in many years. I woke up one day and the incessant thirst had disappeared. I didn't need hormone replacement for Diabetes Insipidus or any other condition for that matter.

I closed my eyes to the cool evening breeze that caressed my face as I rode home. Dr. D finally gave me a clean bill of health. I caught a glance of myself in the mirror, gasping as I touched my face. I hadn't seen a mirror in two weeks. Gone were the puffy nose, the swollen tongue and the protruding jaw. Only then did I realize the full impact of this disease that tried to take everything from me. I was grateful for the team of doctors who worked tirelessly to save my life. They had given me a new lease on life. I could dream and hope again.

I was grateful for the United States of America.

I began my new job as a taxi driver in the city of Chicago soon after a not-so-lengthy recuperation from my surgery. Securing a license to drive a taxi in the city of Chicago was one thing and operating an actual taxi was another. I soon discovered that the license was the least of my problems when compared to ferrying impatient, sometimes rude men to their destinations. My very first passenger was a young Caucasian boy. I noticed his tattooed right arm raised above his head as I approached the traffic light. I screeched to a halt, my heart in my mouth.

"Wrigley Field," he said, slamming the door of the taxi.

My mind suddenly went blank. What direction was I facing? The address of Wrigley Field was a question in one of my tests and I answered it correctly, but it eluded me as I stared blankly at my passenger through the rearview mirror. Summoning up courage, I said, "Today is my first day driving a taxi and you are my first passenger. I have no idea how to get to Wrigley Field. Could you direct me?"

"No worries," he said. "Make a left at the next stoplight."

That evening, the Chicago Cubs were playing against their arch-rival, the Cardinals. It was a big game. Large crowds took over the streets, chanting happy songs as they trooped to the stadium, armed with kegs of unopened beer.

"You can pull over right here," he said, as we crawled behind hordes of people dressed in blue and white jerseys. He reached into his wallet and pulled out two twenty-dollar bills.

"Keep the change." His fare was barely eight dollars. "Good luck with the taxi," he said, disappearing into the crowd.

It was a good start, but over the next week, I was met with a torrent of angry passengers.

"Dang it! Maybe you shouldn't be driving if you don't know where the hell you're going," an angry passenger swore. And getting out, he slammed the door so hard it rattled. I made him late for his meeting when I took the wrong turn. This was the third passenger I had made mad that day. I grew weary with each disgruntled customer. I began to think that maybe this taxi thing was not for me.

"Always, tell them you are new," said a Nigerian Yoruba man that I met in the line while I waited to sign my daily taxi lease. That seemed to work, but not in all cases as some of them were too impatient to teach a new driver the routes. They preferred an aggressive driver, who knew where she was going and knew the fastest way to get there. I was none of those things. As days passed, my anxiety worsened. I feared going out in the mornings, and I dreaded being yelled at or belittled. I began to toy with the idea of quitting. I wondered how Felicia would handle disgruntled customers, but I would never know . She never drove after she got her license. She said she was too scared.

My lucrative dream of driving a cab was quickly evolving into a nightmare. I wasn't making money because I drove half of the passengers for free. "When you miss the road, turn off the meter and don't charge them," said another well-meaning Nigerian driver. If I drove them all for free, I was going to be bankrupt.

One morning, as I waited in line at the taxi company to sign my lease, I struck up a conversation with a dark-skinned bespectacled young Nigerian man.

"I'm Francis," he said, stretching out his hand. Francis was a pharmacist in the process of acquiring a Master's in Public Health. He drove on the days he wasn't in school.

"This job is hard," I complained. "I don't know where I'm going most of the time, and when they shout at me, it makes me forget the few routes I know."

"I was that way as a rookie," Francis said, nodding empathetically. He devised a plan, one that helped me conquer my fear and got me making money.

"Be on the phone with me permanently and always have your Bluetooth in your ears," he said. "As soon as you pick up a customer, announce the address loudly and where you are, and I will direct you."

It was the perfect plan. I began to rely heavily on Francis; he taught me all I needed to know about the taxi business. He showed me the routes and the fastest way to get there. He taught me where to find fares. "Be at the train stations in the mornings and at hotels by noon." He taught me how to get customers to tip me generously. "Talk to them, smile. That is how to dig into their pockets," he said.

Many fares tipped me well because of the fact that I was a female driver. There were just a handful of female taxi drivers in the industry. People would get excited every time they opened the taxi and discovered I was a lady.

"Oh, a female taxi driver," they would say, smiling. The novelty of my gender in the industry, combined with "digging into their pockets," got me some really generous tips.

I began to master the routes as weeks turned into months, and I relied on Francis less. But we had formed a close bond, one that transcended surviving the busy streets of Chicago. When he got married and had his first daughter, he named Ketandu her godmother.

A few months into my driving career, my confidence at an

all-time high, I decided to venture to the airport. I heard many stories about airport trips and how your fortune could change from a single trip.

"Ah, Aunty Joy! I been get one trip from O'Hare to Indiana and the fare with tip na two hundred and fifty dollars," Francis boasted, speaking the Nigerian Pidgin English we often used to communicate. He was my cab mentor and every word that proceeded out of his mouth was gold. That morning, I took my cab to the car wash and polished it to a squeaky white. The cleaner your cab, the bigger your tip, Francis' voice echoed in my head. I got on 190W to O'Hare.

Purchasing the airport stamp as Francis had taught me, I proceeded to the staging area where I waited. I pulled into Terminal 3 Arrivals almost ninety minutes later, and two pleasant gay men in matching brown khaki shorts got into my taxi.

"Embassy Suites, Lombard," the taller of the two men said. Armed with a GPS, I pulled out of the airport onto the highway. I struggled to keep pace as cars passed us at terrifying speed. I swerved quickly as a black truck cut in front of me, almost brushing my side mirror. Other road users were not kind to cab drivers. I learned quickly from the numerous fingers and cuss words flung at me, and the close brushes I experienced daily. I felt as if I was handed a death sentence every morning when I got into my taxi.

The GPS suddenly went quiet, I looked down and a blank screen stared back at me. I slapped the screen a few times, desperate to restart it. I started to hyperventilate, scared that I might have missed my exit. I thought about calling Francis, but I had to keep my eyes on the highway and the aggressive motorists who drove like they were on cheap drugs. My mind went blank and the headache I always got whenever I was under pressure, began to creep up. The two men behind chatted away, oblivious to my turmoil. Out of options, I kept going, hitting the GPS and hoping it would turn back on. The men suddenly went quiet and then resumed talking with a whisper.

The taller one said, "Ma'am, we are going to Lombard, Illinois and my map says you've gone forty miles past."

I wished they had yelled at me like the men downtown in fancy suits. Their silence was deafening. I dropped them off two hours later, a fare that should have taken forty-five minutes. I could barely meet their eyes as I lugged their heavy suitcases out of the trunk. I had turned off the meter as the Nigerian cab driver told me to, whenever I made a blunder. Even if I didn't, they didn't seem interested in paying me. "I'm terribly sorry," I mumbled as they walked away, the wheels of their suitcases scraping the white pavement.

I avoided O'Hare International Airport like the bubonic plague for a very long time. But eventually, I overcame my anxiety, returned to the airport, and became a regular. One morning a slim brunette got into my taxi, she had arrived from Boston and had missed her connecting flight to Wisconsin. She asked if I could take her. My legs trembled slightly as I got on the highway to Wisconsin. She was there to attend a short interview and then she would head back to Boston. She asked if I could wait for her and drive her back to Chicago. It made sense to drive her back and make double the money. While I waited for her, I wandered the aisles of the local Walmart, looking for nothing in particular. Forty minutes later, we were on the road back to Chicago. My hands shook almost violently as I handed her back her American Express card. Her total bill was $472.98. I headed home after I dropped her off. I had hit my jackpot for the day, and so I didn't need to put in any more hours. Hope for fares like these were the reason cab drivers made those diligent trips to the airport. But they only came once in a taxi career for some and never for others. I was blessed to be one of the few lucky ones.

My taxi business boomed as both girls thrived in Walt Disney Elementary. It was everything I hoped for in terms of putting more money in my pocket and being home in time to care for the girls. They continued to thrive in their Mandarin classes in school.

"Now that I'm making decent money with the taxi, maybe I should find you a private Mandarin teacher."

"No, Mommy," Ketandu said. "You should be teaching us Igbo instead."

I looked away uncomfortably. She was right - I should start to speak Igbo at home but I had put it off for too long.

"Your dad and I spoke English at home, so it was hard to teach you Igbo. I will start now."

Even though I had failed in teaching them my native language, I tried to hold on to other aspects of our culture. We cooked Jollof rice and Ogbono soup at home, leaving the American foods for when they were at school or out and about. We sang Nigerian songs when we had our daily morning prayers and I still tried to convince them that black cats with piercing eyes were an evil omen. One Friday evening, after piano class, I hauled both girls and two loads of laundry down to the basement. It was close to midnight when we pulled the last batch out of the dryer. As we made our way up the stairs, a pair of translucent eyes stared down at me. I ran back, almost bumping into Amara.

"What's wrong, Mommy?" she asked, peering over my shoulder.

"It's a black cat!"

The cat started to climb down the stairs towards us. I turned and fled back to the laundry room, the girls following closely behind.

"Where did this cat come from?" I asked, not expecting an answer.

"It's likely a neighbor's cat," Amara said.

"Neighbor, from where?" my eyes widened in agitation.

Just then, we heard a hissing sound and scratches at the door. "Oh my God! Is that the cat? What does it want? Blood of Jesus!"

"Calm down mommy, it won't do anything to us."

"It's midnight and a black cat is after me and you say I should calm down. What did I tell you about black cats and midnight?"

The hissing got louder, and when it seemed we would continue to ignore it, the cat began to squeeze itself through the crack underneath the door.

"Wait, oh my God! It's trying to get in here. Oh Jesus! My enemies are after me!"

"Mom, it's scared too," Amara said.

"Scared, how? What kind of logic is that? When things are scared they run away, they don't run towards the thing they're scared of."

"I bind you evil cat. I send you back to the abyss where you came from in the mighty name of Jesus," I prayed, pacing the scruffy concrete floor.

"Mom, stop!" Ketandu yelled.

The hissing cat was steadily gaining entrance. One hairy paw had successfully gotten through the crack and it was waving it frantically as it continued to hiss aggressively, squeezing the rest of its body through the crack. Now delirious with fear, I began to look around for a weapon, anything I could use to defend myself against the deranged animal. A rusted metal old pipe sat in the corner of the room. Grabbing it with both sweaty palms, I made for the door, brandishing it at the cat. "What are you doing Mom?" Amara screamed, snatching the pipe from me.

After several failed attempts to gain entrance into the laundry room, the cat sauntered into the dark of the night, taking its loud hiss with it. We opened the door thirty minutes later, leaping up the flight of stairs in multiple bounds.

It's been several years and Amara still insists the cat was scared and harmless.

"Well...first of all, for a cat that was harmless, it had a lot of aggression," I argued. How do you convince me that something that hisses, or snarls at me does not mean harm?

I knew about aggressive animals. I knew enough to steer clear of them.

I was ten-years-old when I encountered Lassie, my neighbor's German shepherd. It was a rainy evening, and Aunty Stella sent me to return the tray with which our neighbor had sent her home-baked pastries. I walked through the neighbors' black metal gate, oblivious to the danger that lurked ahead. I had gone halfway to the front door when I heard a deep snarl. I looked in the direction of the sound and the huge dog stared at me like a lion would a puppy. My heart froze. I was looking death in the face. I looked towards the door, hoping someone would come to my rescue. The canine snarled again, approaching me slowly. My blood curdled and I could barely utter a sound. I did what a frightened ten-year-old would do. I turned towards the gate and fled. It galloped after me and as it leapt on top of me, I let out a shrill cry. I landed on my butt, and the pastry tray flew out of my hand.

"Lassie come here!" a voice said behind me. It was our neighbor's young son. The crazy dog waddled back to its owner, leaving me to pick up the fragments of my pride amidst my mud soiled dress. I thought animals were erratic. I tried my best to avoid them.

One of the perks that driving a taxi afforded me was time to micromanage the girls' school work. I had just gotten home from work and stared at their quarterly report card. "*Bia*, come, you know better than to bring home a B to this house," I said to Amara, waving the white paper at her.

"Don't worry about it mom, it will be an A by the end of the term."

We were in a race for the top high schools in the city. Walter Payton College Prep, Northside Prep, and Whitney Young High School were the top three. Landing a spot in one of these schools was akin to landing a spot in an Ivy League, it required perfect test scores and perfect grades. Ketandu was slowly approaching seventh grade. I looked back, wondering where all the years had gone.

"Ketandu is brilliant and will get into any high school of her choice," Mr. Rhinehart, her 6th grade teacher said to me. He was her favorite teacher of all time, and she rewarded his impeccable teaching skills with perfect grades. Her deep love for math was reflective in the manner in which she breezed through complex algebra problems. Mr. Rhinehart thought Walter Payton College Prep would be a good fit for Ketandu as it was known for its excellent math program. We narrowed down our top two choices to Payton and Northside Prep.

Seventh grade was a rollercoaster of events, the year we had to work the hardest before high school. There were also the Disney Track team events which led us to waking up early Saturday mornings for practice and competitions. Both girls ran track.

I was grateful for the quality of education the girls received at Walt Disney Magnet. Both girls being in the gifted program meant exposure to accelerated course materials. Sometimes, they were accelerated by two grades. The children in the gifted program were treated like sacred cows, they were the kids with the high Measures of Academic Progress (MAP) scores.

Each year, the kids in the gifted program held shows, and dignitaries like the city's Mayor and Diane Disney, daughter of Walt

Disney, were in attendance. Ms. Disney was a huge supporter of the school. She was a big contributor to the state-of-the-art computer lab, an addition that boosted the quality of the school. Every time I walked through the doors of this very special school, I was reminded of how blessed I was to have both girls there. And each year, when I got to meet the class teacher for the first time, I was blown away. It seemed the teachers were cherry-picked for the gifted classes.

Ketandu's seventh grade class was in full swing, and so was our quest to land a spot in the prestigious Walter Payton College Prep. That year, it was voted the number one public high school in the country. Rumors were already flying around about how difficult it was to land a spot in this high school.

"Did you read the article about selective high schools?" Agatha asked. She was Abby's mum, a good friend of Ketandu's who also ran track. We caught up on high school news every Saturday when we met for track.

"No," I responded.

"Payton admitted 5% of its total applicants. That's crazy. A recent survey says it's easier to get into Harvard than to get into Payton."

My heart lurched at the news. My Ketandu was getting into that school. I didn't care how tough it was.

"Abby is going to try for Lane Tech. That's where her dad went. I don't think it's fair to put these young kids through so much stress."

"True," I mumbled distantly. She could settle for a less competitive school, but as for my girls, they were going to get the best.

I made decent money with the cab business, so I was going to enroll Ketandu in a class to prepare her for the entrance exam, but first, we had to focus on ensuring she maintained her straight A's and MAP scores. Seventh-grade MAP scores and grades were used to determine selective high school placement. The MAP test was a computerized adaptive test. Walter Payton required a ninety-nine percentile to guarantee a spot. Ketandu couldn't afford to slip in that either.

On the eve of her MAP test, I tucked her in bed early. "You know how important this test is Ki," I said. "It has to be a ninety-nine percentile, if we want Payton to look at us." She nodded, as she yawned.

The MAP test result arrived in a brown sealed envelope. Ketandu brought it home one Friday afternoon. I had grown weary of waiting for it. My hands shook slightly as I ripped open the envelope.

"Yes! Thank you, Jesus," I screamed, staring at the perfect ninety-nine in black print. The school year ended and Ketandu maintained straight A's. The last hurdle between us and our dream school was the entrance exam. It would take place towards the first quarter of eighth grade. First, we must bask in the victory that came with seventh grade.

Saint Patrick's Day in the city was a special event for taxi drivers. They looked forward to this day as much as they did New Year's Eve.

"Ah, Aunty Joy," Francis bragged. "You will drive with your meter on, non-stop. In eight hours you will go home with eight hundred dollars."

I looked forward to Saint Patrick's Day all year. But as the day approached, I realized it clashed with the girls' Mandarin Speech contest. They were now almost fluent in Mandarin, so we decided to enroll them in the competition. They had both worked hard for the competition, practicing their speeches every evening after school. I listened attentively as they recited them in the shower, the complex language rolling off their tongues with seamless effort. I knew I couldn't miss the competition for the world. I devised a plan: I would drive for a few hours and then rush back and drive them to the competition.

Lake Shore Drive was bereft of its usual morning traffic as I traveled south in search of my first St. Patrick's Day's customer. The Chicago River glistened in the early sunlight, a mixture of forest and jade green. It had been dyed the day before in keeping with the St. Patrick's Day celebration. Crowds had begun to slowly gather at the bridge; men and women dressed in green attire, their faces also covered in shades of green. The Saint Patrick's Day parade took place on Michigan Avenue, along the stretch of the magnificent mile. Young men wore their green caps backward, clutching kegs of beer. Francis said it was a day they drank themselves to a stupor.

"By eleven in the morning, they are already drunk," he warned.

I was nervous about having a drunk person in the taxi. What if he refused to pay the fare or to get out of the taxi?

"Call the police," Francis said. "They will get your money for you."

The day got off to a slow start but as it began to pick up, I had to leave for the Chinese Mandarin competition. Rushing north, I picked up the girls and headed for Northside College Prep, the venue of the competition. The participants were split into small groups and each group made their way upstairs to the room where the judges waited. The girls' Chinese teachers were both in attendance, patting them on the back and encouraging them in Mandarin. I walked into the auditorium, not sure of how long the contest would run. I sat beside a slender Caucasian woman who looked up from a book on her thigh and smiled at me.

"Is this your first time?" she asked.

"Yes," I said, chuckling awkwardly. She made small talk for a few minutes and then went back to her book, leaving me to my thoughts.

Forty-five minutes later, the girls emerged, each dangling a gold medal on their neck. They had both won the gold medal for their groups.

"Good job," I said, stretching my hand for high fives.

That spelled the beginning of many Mandarin competitions. The girls participated every year, growing their repertoire of gold medals.

I took them home and made my way downtown, determined to make the most of this famous St Patrick's Day. Downtown Chicago bustled with large crowds as I approached. The parade was over and it was alcohol time. A young girl staggered into the street. I swerved sharply, avoiding her. It got very busy from then on. There weren't enough taxis in the city to feed the demand. I would drop off and pick up from the same spot. Young boys and their drunk girlfriends fought for taxis. They were mostly happy drunks who tipped heavily. Francis had said they tipped stupendously when they were drunk - it was true. But they did other stupid things like the drunk man I took home. I arrived at the address he gave me and looked in the back seat to find him fast asleep. I honked aggressively, the noise jolting him from his drunken stupor.

"Sir, we've arrived at your destination," I said, turning off the meter. Swiping his credit card on the machine in front of him, he opened the door as if to climb out but changed his mind.

"This isn't my house," he slurred.

"Yes, it is. This is the address you gave me, sir."

"No, it's not," he said.

"So, what is the correct address?"

Mumbling a few incoherent words, he went back to sleep. I had to be back on the streets, it was a busy evening and I was not about to waste it on one drunk. There were more fares waiting to be picked up. I woke him up again and said, "We are approaching your house." I drove round the block and came back to the same spot.

"You're home."

He looked out the window as if he saw something new.

"Hic...Yeah...yeah hic... This is my shit." He staggered out of the cab, smiling sheepishly.

Four hours later, I decided I had had enough of crying drunks, shirtless drunks, vomiting drunks, happy drunks, and clueless drunks who didn't know where they lived. They had come in all shapes, sizes, and hiccups. I headed home with bundles of dollar bills. I was too busy to stop and count, but I knew I had a successful St. Patrick's Day debut.

As the transition to high school loomed closer for Ketandu, I set my plans in motion by enrolling her in a prep class for the high school entrance exam. It was a small class run by a middle-aged couple who boasted of several years of unparalleled success with entrance exams. I walked into the orientation session to a room full of stern-faced Caucasians. My eyes traveled casually to the ginger-haired man seated beside me, his beer belly stretching his Cubs T-shirt. We were in a race against each other. It was going to be survival of the fittest as our children competed for the limited spaces in some of the best high schools in the city. I braced myself for what was ahead, relishing the silent spat and the adrenaline surge in my veins.

"Your students will get a diagnostic test the first week...." My mind wandered as the instructor gave the welcome speech and guidelines to the class. The journey was no easy one. The grades, MAP scores, and entrance exam were only a part of the determining factors; there was also the socio-economic aspect. The city was divided into four tiers for this high school selection process, with tier one being the poorest neighborhood and tier four being the richest. The children from the rich neighborhoods were expected to score higher than the kids from the poorer geographical regions. This was done to foster diversity in these selective high schools. This meant that a tier-one student could gain entrance with an 860 score ahead of their tier 4 contender with an 880 score. This allowed the minority students to be represented in these elite high schools. The process was divided into three parts that totaled 900 points. Straight A's in seventh grade earned you 300 points. 99 percentile in MAP earned you another 300 points and a perfect score in the entrance exam earned you the last 300 points. Ketandu had 600 points in her bag. She just needed a perfect score in the entrance exam to land the final 300 points which would guarantee her a spot in Walter Payton or any other selective school for that matter. We resided in tier 3 and had to work almost as hard as tier-4 students. But none of that would matter if she got a perfect 900. She would be considered "rank." Rank were students whose outstanding performance automatically placed them in schools of their choice. I hoped she would bag these last 300 points.

I'm a child of God
I was born to win
I'm above and never beneath
From Walt Disney Magnet Elementary
I'm going on to Walter Payton College Prep
From Walter Payton College Prep
I'm going on to an Ivy League College….

Our daily confessions took on a new meaning as the entrance exam approached. At the same time, Amara was in her 7th grade - the year she had to work the hardest, if she were to stand a chance at getting into a selective high school.

"There will be no B this school year, Nne'm," I warned Amara. A Single B meant 25 points off the 300 and that would make it impossible to get into a top selective high school. I was extremely nervous for Amara. She had a penchant for bringing home one B every school year.

My anxiety heightened as the date for Ketandu's entrance exam drew close. Rumors trickled in that the rich parents from tier 4 were renting houses in tiers 1 and 2 neighborhoods to improve their children's chances.

On the day of Ketandu's entrance exam, we drove to Whitney Young High School, the venue of the test. It was a cold November morning. I made sure she got nine hours of sleep and a good breakfast of oats and blueberries. I heard berries were good for brain stimulation. Ketandu buried her head in the hood of her black jacket as we drove down the quiet street of Ashland Avenue. "Are you okay, Ki?" I asked for the umpteenth time.

"I'm finc mom."

"Your HB pencils are sharp enough right?" I asked. She nodded.

There was a long line outside the grey school building. Hundreds of students from across the city had gathered for the test.

"They should make more of these elite schools," I thought out aloud. "Too many children vying for too few spots."

Ketandu kissed my cheeks as she exited the car. I pulled over and watched until she disappeared into the building. I started the car and headed north, praying silently for her as I drove past Washington Boulevard.

"Mom, the test was easy," Ketandu said, as she hopped in the car five hours later.

"Thank God. So, it's a perfect score then?"

"I hope so, mom."

"That HB pencil you used, throw it in here," I said, opening the glove compartment.

"Your sister will use it next year for good luck." I believed in charms like that.

We waited four months for the results of the exam. It was the longest four months of my life.

As if the nervousness of awaiting the verdict of Ketandu's entrance exam was not enough, Amara decided to add to my apprehension.

"What is this Nne'm?" I asked Amara, my gaze shifting intermittently from the paper in my hand to her face. She came home with a B in science, causing me a near heart attack.

"Are you mad?" I asked. "And I don't mean American mad, I mean crazy."

"No," she answered, shaking her head indignantly.

I told them time and again that it was a question that didn't need to be answered; a rhetorical question borrowed from my Nigerian upbringing and imposed upon my now very American children.

"This is 25 points off your grade points. If you think you will go to these useless neighborhood high schools where they smoke wee-wee and beat their teachers, then think again. I will send you home to Nigeria and your eyes will clear."

"What is wee-wee, mommy?" Ketandu asked.

"Drugs," I said, still glaring at the report card.

"If you don't convert this to an A by next quarter, I swear to God, I will go and drop you at the fire station! Let them find you a foster home."

"It will be an A, Mom. I promise."

Amara was a child that liked to live on the edge. She loved to toy with near misses even when she played. I had to do everything in my power to make sure the science grade didn't remain a B.

"Did you meet anybody interesting in the cab today, mom?" Ketandu asked, diverting the conversation to ease the tension.

"Not today," I replied. They looked forward to the stories I told them about the characters I met in the course of my job. Sometimes, they were sad stories. Like the beautiful doctor I picked up from Northwestern hospital who was dying of leukemia. I loved meeting people. Chicagoans are mostly good people and as soon as they got over the shock of "Oh Wow! Lady cab driver," we had really good conversations. I soon discovered that not only was I their cab driver who ferried them to doctors' appointments and board meetings, I was also their shrink as with the case of the woman who told me she was so angry at her husband, she wanted to have an affair with a George Clooney lookalike.

"A customer offered me drugs today, can you imagine?' I said to my wide-eyed daughters one evening.

"He pulled this vial out of his pocket and said, try this...this shit is good."

"What did you say to him," Amara asked.

"Well... I said no, thank you. I don't smoke and drive." They both giggled.

My cab stories never ceased to fascinate them. A gay couple was making out in the back seat late one evening.

"I think they were high, so I sped up and dropped them off."

"Why didn't you tell them to stop?"

"I don't know. I didn't want them to think I was gayphobic."

"Homophobic, mom," Ketandu corrected.

I got home one evening after work and opened the rusty grey mailbox. Ketandu's entrance result was lying in the pile of envelopes.

I gasped loudly holding up the white envelope with the Chicago Public School's blue emblem. My heart raced as I made my way upstairs to our apartment. I turned the key in the lock and Ketandu ran to the door.

"Mommy, the results are out. Stacy and Gabby got theirs already."

"I have yours," I said, waving the thin envelope at her.

She snatched it from me, ripping the edge of the envelope. I stared at her face as she read the result loudly.

"It's a perfect score, Mommy, I have a perfect three hundred!"

"Oh, my God!" I screamed, sweeping her into my arms. "We are going to Payton, we are going to Payton. The best school in the country," I repeated over and over, dancing and singing. Amara rushed into the room, joining in the celebration.

Now that Ketandu had secured a spot in the elite school, my full attention shifted to Amara. She was on track with her grades except for science which still remained a B. She was in the 97 percentile for MAP score, two points short of 99. It would suffice because it translated to a 297 which would land her a spot in an elite school if she maintained perfect 300s in both her grades and entrance scores. We had until the end of the year to worry about the entrance exams. First, we had to do something about that science grade. A B-grade in science left you with a 275 out of 300.

"There is no way you would get into Payton or Whitney Young or Jones," I said to Amara.

We spent many evenings at the kitchen table obsessing over her science homework and projects. Everything else meant little. I reviewed every minute detail of her work as we prepared vigorously for her final science test. By the end of the school year, the science grade became an A much to my relief. All we needed was a perfect 300 in the entrance exam to secure a spot in Payton like her sister.

Ketandu's high school journey began in early fall. The changes that came with this journey filled me with apprehension. The girls were going to be in different schools for the first time in history and I dreaded every minute of it. Amara had to walk three blocks south to get on her school bus. Chicago Public Schools did not provide bus services to their high school students, so Ketandu had to get on the Red Line to go to school. The closest Red Line station was half a block from our house. I suppressed the gnawing fear about Ketandu riding the train alone, reminding myself that I had raised smart independent girls who could hold their own in the world.

"I don't want to go to Payton," Amara confessed, one day. "I prefer Whitney Young."

This didn't come as a surprise. Whitney was better suited to her because it was more "artsy." It was an excellent school, made even more popular in recent times because former first lady, Michelle Obama, was an alumna. I wanted Amara to join her sister in Payton for selfish reasons. I wanted to keep them together for logistics. I didn't want to run back and forth to different schools for report card pick-ups and conferences, so I convinced her to rank Payton as her number one choice and Whitney Young as the second.

My heart burst with pride as I led Ketandu down the polished floors of Walter Payton College Prep, still reeling with euphoria. It was a small school that housed the children of many dignitaries. The daughter of the state governor had graduated from Payton. Children of politicians, surgeons, and finance gurus attended this very prestigious school. A wave of inferiority swept over me for a moment as I perused the shiny plaques on the walls that read "Number one high school in America 2015." I shrugged the feeling away, reminding myself that Ketandu had earned her spot. She soon blended into the academically rigorous environment, taking all the Advanced Placement classes that were offered to freshmen. It was a predominantly white school with only 7% black students, a trend she was used to, coming from the gifted class in Walt Disney Elementary. She had no trouble integrating socially. She joined the Math team as well as the Science Olympiad team and thrived in her AP calculus and AP Human Geography classes.

As Amara's entrance exam approached, I enrolled her in the prep class that her sister had attended. Since I had gone down that lane the previous year, I knew just what to do. "You will finish every single test in this book," I said, pointing to the fat textbook the instructor had sent home with her. Amara was good at reading and spelling. She was a spelling bee champion. We only had to polish other aspects of the test that consisted of graphs and their interpretations.

I dropped her off at the test venue on another cold November morning. It had snowed the night before and the crystal white flakes were beginning to turn into dirty brown slush as snow trucks spread salt across the streets. Opening the glove compartment, I handed her the HB pencil from the previous year.

"Here, use this one. Kiki used it last time, and she got a perfect three hundred."

She grabbed the pencil from me and jumped out of the car.

Amara was not forthcoming with her exam experience when I picked her up four hours later.

"How was it?"

"I don't know, mom."

"Jesus! What do you mean you don't know? Are you not the one that wrote the exam?

"I don't know if I will have a perfect three hundred, Mom."

My heart sank, and I felt a hollow pain in the pit of my stomach.

"I don't want to hear this sort of thing. Not right now."

"Okay, can we just stop Mom? I don't want to talk about it."

We drove the rest of the way in silence. I had done everything humanly possible. It was now down to this final test and we had a few months to find out.

"Please, put my good luck pencil back in the compartment," I said to her.

Apart from the agonizing wait for Amara's test result, I had my health results to contend with. My most recent MRI results showed that the brain tumor had not grown back. It was great news, but my IGF-1 levels were slowly creeping up again. Dr. A said it was a result of the residual tumor. I had to resume the monthly injections to curb the spike. I was saddened by the news.

"At least, the tumor hasn't grown back," Ketandu said, offering comfort as she knew how.

"I guess… But those injections are very painful. The syringe is as big as my pinky finger."

"I'm sorry, mom."

I didn't have the luxury of wallowing in self-pity. I had a lot on my plate with Amara's pending high school admissions. Soon, we would find out how she fared with the exam - the last link to her high school entrance. I was counting down to the day already.

"Your result will be out tomorrow, Nne'm," I said to Amara, searching her face for a clue as to how she performed.

The next day, I could barely focus at work. I could feel the blood rush to my head every time I pictured the white envelope lying in the mailbox. I finally caved in to my obsession with the result and left work early. I spotted the USPS mail truck at the end of my block, an indication that the letter must be in the box. I walked briskly to the lobby and opened the box. With the letter firmly in my hand, I marched upstairs to the girls.

"The moment of truth," I said, handing the letter to Amara.

Her hand trembled, and passing the letter to her sister she said, "I can't. Do this for me."

Ketandu grabbed the letter and without hesitation, ripped it open. Glancing at the contents she said, "You did it, Amy! You have a perfect three hundred."

Amara burst into tears and I burst into a song of jubilation.

"My baby is going to the top. She is joining her sister at Payton. Glory be to God." Tears streamed down my face. For so long, I wasn't sure how it would end, but now I knew.

"You did it, Amy! You did it," Ketandu chanted, hugging her sister.

That night, I slept soundly for the first time in many months. Knowing that both my girls were in the top high school in the country filled me with a sense of joy and pride. They were made for greatness. I could feel it now more strongly than ever before.

The next Monday, it was Amara's turn to lead us in our daily confession after our morning prayer and she started:

I'm a child of God
I'm born to win
The devil is under my feet
From Walt Disney Magnet
I'm going to Walter Payton College Prep…

"But guess what?" I said, interrupting her mid-way. "You are now officially in Walter Payton, so you can cross that confession off the list."

She continued, "…From Walter Payton College Prep, I'm going on to an Ivy League College…"

Ketandu was a sophomore and continued to take as many AP

classes as were available. While she thrived with advanced classes, Amara trailed socially. She struggled to make friends in the predominantly white school. I began to regret not letting her attend Whitney Young. Young was more diverse and might have been a better fit for her. But I wanted to keep them in the same school for my own selfish reasons. She dreaded lunch periods because there was always the issue of what group she would sit with.

"I hate it here mom, I really do," she cried, one day after school.

That night, I had come home with problems of my own. A young girl got into my taxi and upon getting to her destination refused to pay her fare.

"You drove in the wrong lane. I will not pay you," she said.

"You're kidding right?" I asked. It turned out she was not. She opened the door and started to walk away and when I tried to stop her, she punched me in the nose. I doubled over in pain, struggling to make sense of what just happened. I looked up half a second later and she was gone. As I parked by the curbside on Randolf and Wacker, waiting for the police to arrive, I got a ticket for loitering. It was a day I wished to forget. I held an ice pack over my swollen nose as I narrated my ordeal to the girls.

"I'm so sorry, Mom," Amara said, tears streaming down her full cheeks. Her focus had now shifted from her school to my near broken nose.

"Did you call the police?" she asked.

"I did, but she was gone by the time they arrived."

In the course of my job, there had been a few times that the passengers ran off without paying the fare, but getting punched was a brand new experience.

"You have to stop driving mom," Ketandu said. "It's too dangerous. What if she had a gun? She would have shot you."

She was right about the shooting part. Cab drivers got shot sometimes. In the previous month, two cab drivers were robbed and killed on the south side. I knew it was a dangerous job. I planned to enroll in nursing school as soon as the girls got to senior year of high school and they didn't need me so much.

"I will be careful," I promised. "I won't ever try to stop anyone again who refuses to pay me. It's not worth the danger."

Amara began to find her niche at the beginning of her sophomore year. She joined the Black Student's Union, the Model UN and discovered her passion for slam poetry. She now had a group of friends with whom she sat in the lunchroom. I was relieved to see her high school experience take a turn for the better. Ketandu was a junior, totally dedicated to the math team, an extracurricular that birthed some of her closest friendships. They were a team of six girls who went by the name, Math Team Girl Gang. They got together every night after school to prepare for upcoming math competitions. They represented their high school in competitions across the city and state and won medals in their honor. Ketandu was selected to be the orator by the team of math coaches, a position she served with pride until she graduated high school. Being on the math team came with its share of challenges. The competitions ran late most nights. We lived on the Northside where finding street parking was a problem.

"Again, you know I can't pick you up at 11 p.m. When we get home, I will circle around looking for parking until 2 a.m. and that is just not obtainable," I said to Ketandu for the umpteenth time.

"It's okay, Mom. I will take an Uber home."

"That's not the point. Your friends have their parents waiting to pick them up. Don't you see how that makes me look bad?"

My complaints didn't hold her back. They made it to the State finals and Ketandu and the Math Team Girl Gang were excited. They looked forward to traveling to Springfield Illinois for the competition and sharing a hotel room.

Aside from the rigors of the math team, Ketandu was also the captain of the Science Olympiad team. She and one of her best friends from the math team partnered and built a hovercraft for one of the science Olympiad events. This hovercraft and the team earned a spot in the state finals. I waited with bated breath for her call. I hoped they won first place for that hovercraft. They had worked tirelessly. I remembered the delight on her face the day she got home and proudly announced, "Mom, Lauren and I got the hovercraft to move." I got the long-awaited call late in the evening. She sounded tired and a little disappointed.

"The hovercraft came in second place," she said.

"It's okay. Second place is still a really good result."

Her phone went dead as we spoke, and while I waited up for her, I fell asleep on the couch. Waking with a sudden jolt and glancing at the wall clock in front of me, I saw that it was past midnight and she wasn't home. I grabbed my phone, punching her number in frantic motion. It went straight to voicemail. My anxiety heightened with each voice mail response. She eventually called. "My phone died mom,"

"I know, but what is taking you guys so long?"

"We have to put stuff in the class."

"Put what stuff where? You will give me high BP with this whole thing. You will stop attending these competitions, if you keep coming home at ungodly hours," I ranted. But I knew she wouldn't ever give up those competitions. The math and science teams were her life. She had worked very hard for them. Besides, we knew that engaging in meaningful extracurricular activities made her

college-ready., If we wanted the good colleges to look at her, we had
to show them that she was busy in high school. While her AP classes
pulled her in one direction, and math and science teams pulled her
in another, their piano teacher, Irene, made demands of her own.

"You need to record this piece for your college applications," she
said. "You mastered *Prelude* and *Fugue*, at such a young age. Colleges
will be impressed when you send them in."

One Saturday morning, when she had no competitions to attend, we drove down to a piano studio and recorded her classical
pieces. It took many attempts before we finally got a perfect recording. We left the studio physically and mentally drained.

I worried sometimes that the girls were doing too much. It
bothered me that they might burn out. Every time I thought to slow
down, I remembered where we came from, and it made me push
even harder. My girls were going to utilize every opportunity that
came their way, seize every fine moment they encountered.

Ketandu had seized some fine moments when she made friends
with the girls from her math team.

One evening over dinner, she announced, "I want to invite the
Math Team Girl Gang over for lunch, mom."

"To which house? To this tiny apartment?" I asked.

"What are you talking about mom?"

"Didn't you tell me Lauren's Mom's walk-in closet is bigger than
our entire living room? Please, I don't want them to come and see
how poor we are."

Ketandu's eyes bulged in shock. "Mom, you really think I would
be friends with people who are superficial? If the girls were anything
like what you just described I want you to know that I would not be
friends with them. You raised me to do better, Mom."

I felt a pang of shame that it took my teenage daughter to

remind me of the things that truly mattered. The Nigerian culture was embedded in class consciousness. My mind flashed back to the girls' old school in Nigeria – the mothers with their Gucci purses and Mercedes cars and their snooty demeanor every time they drove past me in my weather-beaten car. I was grateful that it was all in my past.

The Math Team Girl Gang came over the following weekend. I watched with delight as each girl made for a second helping of the spicy Jollof rice and the savory puff-puff. They all sprawled on the floor of the small room, giggling without a care in the world. No one seemed to notice the size of the apartment or the fake Persian rug which I had spent hours scrubbing for their visit.

Ketandu slowly advanced to her senior year of high school and I was confident in her grades and extracurricular activities. She entered the Walgreens Writing Competition, although she had little time to prepare for it. I got a call one afternoon saying that she was a finalist for the Expressions Challenge. She wrote a compelling story about teen pregnancy. As I looked over the essay minutes before she turned it in, I knew in my heart that it would earn her a spot in the finals. I invited a few friends for the unveiling of the winner. There were three other finalists whose stories were just as good.

We walked into the venue of the event on a cool Saturday evening. I was holding on to Amara's hand, trying not to fall in my three-inch stiletto heels. I dressed for the occasion; the mother of the potential first-place winner. I was glad I took the time with my appearance as we walked through the fancy doors of the Museum Of Contemporary Arts on Michigan Avenue. A dashingly handsome man stood by the door in a black tuxedo, his long dark hair pulled back in a ponytail.

"Welcome to the Walgreens Expression Challenge," a young usher in a dazzling red evening dress said, handing us the program. We were seated at a table across from a man that looked familiar and just then I realized who he was.

"That's Stedman, Oprah's boyfriend," I whispered to Iyabo, who had walked in a few minutes after us with her daughter, Kanyinsola.

Guests nibbled on hors d'oeuvres. Soft music and laughter filled the room as we awaited the results. Seeing that it was such an elegant event, I was overcome with a sudden desire to see Ketandu win first place. As the evening drew to a close, the MC turned down the music, indicating it was time to announce the results. My chest rose and fell in rapid succession as he took the stage. The third-place winner was announced and I was relieved that it was not Ketandu. Next was the second place and it wasn't Ketandu.

"Ladies and Gentlemen, I present to you, the winner of the creative writing Walgreens Expression Challenge, Ketandu Chiedu."

The room exploded with applause and loud cheering as Ketandu walked up to the stage to receive her plaque and her check. Ketandu's English teacher, Ms. Batiste was present for the occasion. She walked to the stage with Ketandu, her face beaming with pride.

The girls climbed that ladder that would eventually lead to college, thriving in their respective classes and extracurriculars. I felt the time was right to steer my dreams to the front burner. Taxi driving had served its purpose, but I wanted more for myself. I still missed Greenhouse and went back to visit ever so often. I knew I had only scratched the surface of my romance with the health-care industry. So, the following fall, I enrolled in the community college, commencing the journey that would eventually lead to a nursing degree. Juggling the girls, taxi driving and school was no easy feat. I didn't dwell on the details of my new life or how difficult my first class was going to be as I walked into that English class on the first day.

"You don't spell flavor with a U," my English professor said, correcting me for the umpteenth time. I struggled with the American English and punctuations, appalled at how badly I fared in the class. It was both a humbling and frustrating experience, one that I learned to put behind me when I finally finished the class with an A. I went on to take classes in mathematics, microbiology, chemistry, biology and anatomy and physiology, all of which I needed for the nursing program.

As Ketandu rounded off her junior year, I was confident that she had enough in her portfolio to apply to any college of her choice. Having excelled in AP Math and AP physics with a five in both exit exams, she was in a good place in her college applications. She had won the Walter Payton Junior Book Award for Harvard University, but her heart was set on MIT.

Oblivious to the mundane routine of my personal life, I vicariously relished the fast-growing list of the girls' accomplishments. It was past noon and I cruised the streets of downtown Chicago scouting for a fare. Mondays were usually slow if there were no conventions in town. Business typically started to pick up on Tuesdays. I drove slowly, almost absentmindedly, worrying about money. I glanced at the thin wad of bills lying beside my phone, an indication that I was having a really slow day. Usually, I would have made my taxi lease and gas money by noon, and the hours left would be for my profit.

Days like this when I struggled to make money were becoming frequent, and the introduction of Uber was the main reason. Profit from the taxi business continued to plunge with the introduction of Uber and other car services. Many cab drivers abandoned the taxi business, crossing over to Uber. I asked myself a thousand times why I wouldn't give up taxi driving for Uber. I had a nice car that would fit the Uber X specification. But a part of me resented Uber for coming into the city and sweeping away the transportation business. More so, I resented that Uber drivers had a free pass: they didn't have to go to taxi school, didn't have to take the city license exam three times, and didn't have to memorize a thousand streets in Chicago like I had to.

I would snigger cynically every time someone got in my cab and said, "Thank God you know where you're going. These Uber drivers don't know their way around the city."

To which I would respond, "Exactly! Besides, they are not vetted by the city. You could be in the car with a serial killer." My response always worked like magic. They would nod in the affirmative, wide-eyed, and vow not to get into another Uber. Taxi drivers still had their faithful passengers who kept the business barely afloat and I was thankful for them.

I looked up and saw a hand in the air. It was an elderly lady who wanted a taxi. She was across from the traffic lights, and just as I was about to pick her up, the traffic light turned red and I screeched to a halt. There was a Blue Ribbon taxi in the left lane who also had his eye on the fare. Cab drivers were notorious for stealing each other's fares. It became a survival of the fittest on slow days. They stole my fares until I learned to be aggressive. My eyes were on the Blue Ribbon taxi. He was an older Middle Eastern gentleman with a full, grey beard. I predicted that as soon as the light turned green, he was going to try and swerve in front of me, and sweep up my passenger. He tried just that.

"Keep moving Papa!" I yelled, swerving to block him from getting ahead of me. "Go find your own. This is mine."

"Good for you," my passenger said, as she opened the door to get in. "I saw how he tried to bully you."

"They do that to me all the time, more so, because I'm a woman and they think they can walk all over me. But I never let them."

"Don't let them. I wouldn't ride with him anyway. I would ride with you. Girl power."

Yeah...girl power," I repeated, chuckling.

I knew instantly that it was going to be a fun ride. I now knew how to "dig into their pockets" for big tips and my methods never failed. I always got big tips from women on account of being female. Early on, I discovered that Americans are patriotic, so a story about how much I loved America and how much I longed to work hard and live the American dream, always earned me a big tip. Lastly, if I found a way to weave my girls into the conversation and let them know they attended Walter Payton, that sealed the deal. Walter Payton College Prep was a respected high school in the city. Being in Chicago and having two children in Payton was akin to having them in Harvard. On this very slow day, I was going to deploy all my methods.

As we cruised along Lasalle Street, deep in conversation, she said, "I hear a mild accent. Where is that from?"

"Nigeria, but I've lived here a long time. I feel American now. I love it here and I'm grateful for all the great things this wonderful country has offered me and my girls."

As we continued in conversation, I bestowed praises on the country and all the opportunities my girls had been exposed to. She began to sob. Puzzled by her tears, I said "I'm sorry. Did I say something to make you upset?"

'No," she said, wiping her tears with the sleeve of her grey jacket. "Don't be sorry. You didn't say anything wrong. My husband passed away five years ago and I still miss him very much. He was a true patriot and would have loved to hear all these beautiful stories you're telling me."

Guilt tugged at my heart. I was only trying to get a big tip and here I was, making an old lady cry.

"It sounds like he was a really great guy."

"He was wonderful. We were married for forty-eight years."

'I'm so sorry. His memories must be very dear to you."

We rode the rest of the way in silence. She did not tip as much as I wanted, but as she got out of the taxi, she scribbled on a piece of paper. Handing it to me she said, "Tell your daughter to apply here for a full scholarship. She mustn't tell her friends about it. They will be her competitors. Good luck to you and your daughters." I drove off knowing that the piece of paper was worth more than a thousand-dollar tip.

With the girls inching closer to college, I was slowly coming into my own. But there was one last hurdle left, one that could ruin everything. Our immigration status was pending. As Ketandu's college application approached, I could no longer bury my head in the sand. I had to confront Emeka's petitions against me with the U.S. immigration services. I had to fight for our legal stay if Ketandu was going to explore the success that awaited her in her college journey. My sojourn had not come to an end. There was more around the corner!

Chapter 11

DIAMOND OF BIAFRA

THE CYCLES OF LIFE REVOLVED LIKE THE SEASONS - FROM blistering summer afternoons to stormy winter nights, my life had transitioned at every turn. Gone was the carefree little girl who played barefoot in the dusty red sand of Obosi. Gone was the troubled teenager who vowed to find her father by any means necessary. It was in searching for my father that I inadvertently embarked on the path to unveiling joy, a journey that led me to all the wonderful strangers that fate placed in my path.

My self-worth was tied to my daughters' success. I took great pride in what I had been able to achieve with them. For an unwanted child who had no blueprint on how to love, I had come a long way.

There was still a lot of ground to cover.

College application was in full swing as Ketandu wrapped up her junior year. She had taken both the ACT and SAT and scored high on both tests.

"I didn't study Mom, and I had a 33 in my first attempt. Now, I know I can have a perfect 36 if I sit down and study for the next one."

"Ki, you know I can't afford a tutor like your friends' parents," I said. "We are just going to have to ride it out, so give it your very best shot."

"Don't worry about tutoring, Mom. I'll be fine."

I ordered ACT Prep by Kaplan, and she went through every practice question in the textbook.

As we prepared Ketandu for the most important exam of her life, the elephant in the room loomed large. It was time to petition immigration services for our residency. I could no longer hold it off as Ketandu needed it for her college applications. She had made the semi-final lists of both the Jack Kent Cooke and Bill Gates scholarships from a pool of over twenty thousand applicants. Being offered the scholarships rode on the back of her legal residency, so I had to act fast. I had hired an attorney in the past but that did not do much. In my desperation, I reached out to Francis who had an answer to most things.

"Why don't you contact the Ombudsman," he suggested. "They will help with your case."

I had never heard of the Ombudsman, but that evening I did my research and I was convinced that they could help us. I emailed them. Ten days later, I got a response notifying me that they would look into our case. I was elated. One Thursday evening in March, I opened my mailbox to an envelope with the Immigration logo.

I went up the stairs with the letter clutched tightly in my sweaty palm. The Ombudsman must have contacted them, and that must be the reason I was hearing from them. Barging into the apartment, I kicked off my shoes by the door. Ketandu and Amara were sprawled on the living room floor engrossed in homework.

"Are you okay, Mom?" Ketandu asked, sitting up.

"I got a letter from Immigration."

"Open it then."

I slumped on the brown leather couch, my fingers quivering as I ripped open the envelope.

"Notice of Intent to Deny..." Color drained from my face.

"What does the letter say, Mom?" Ketandu asked, searching my face. Swallowing the lump in my throat, I continued to stare at the letter.

"Are they denying us, Mom?" Ketandu asked again.

I nodded slowly.

Maybe writing the Ombudsman was not a good idea after all. But what was I to do? We had been in limbo for far too long. It was time to face my biggest fear; time to take this bull by its horns. I was up all night tossing and turning. It was a lengthy letter, one that disclosed all the reasons why we were being denied. I did not wish to disclose it to the girls, but the main reason for the denial was all the letters that their father had written in the past. It had come back to bite us.

Early the following morning, as I got dressed to go downtown to consult with the attorney, Ketandu walked into my room and said, "I'm not going to school today, Mom."

"Why?"

"What's the point? I won't focus. I'll go with you wherever you're going."

That morning it was Amara's turn to lead the Morning Prayer and she prayed like she never prayed before:

> *Lord Jesus, I think they're about to*
> *kick us out of the country.*
> *You can't let this happen to us.*
> *Send us help, please*
> *Send our Green card…*

We had prayed about this for many years. It was part of our daily morning confession. It was a beautiful spring morning. I drew in a deep breath as we trudged to the train station. Not even the sweet scent of daffodils could calm the deep fear that gripped my heart. Amara got off at Division and Clark, and Ketandu and I continued downtown. My lawyer's office was on the 24th floor of a fancy building in the Loop. We were ushered to the conference room as soon as we arrived. Twenty minutes later, Michael, my lawyer strolled into the room, holding a thin cream colored file. Pulling up a chair, he sat across from us, tugging at the collar of his frayed T-shirt. Micheal always had a listless look, something that made me think he hated his job.

"Hi, Michael. I got this really troubling letter and…"

"Yes, I got it," he interrupted, waving his copy at me. He glanced at the letter with indifference and said, "I still don't understand why your ex-husband was writing them."

He bent over the letter for another couple of minutes and looking up at me he said, "I don't think there's anything I can do for you."

"What do you mean?"

"The case against you is insurmountable," and looking at Ketandu, he asked, "Were you born here?"

"No."

"You will get deported too."

My head began to pound violently, and I was afraid I was going to pass out. I wanted to shout at him, to tell him to shut up and do his job for once, but my voice failed me. I pushed open the door and staggered out of his office, blinded by tears.

"How dare he say those things? He didn't even try. Didn't look like he was even interested in trying," Ketandu said.

I looked at her. My sixteen-year-old superstar who had worked so hard and accomplished so much; and this lawyer had just told her it was over. Her American dream was over. I punched the elevator button like I would hit a panic button, desperate to get away from his office as fast as possible. Lasalle Street buzzed with traffic and cars moved slowly in both directions. I walked briskly, going nowhere. I needed to walk, to clear my hurting head, and to make sense of the lawyer's words. "Mom, stop please," Ketandu pleaded as she ran to catch up with me. "It's going to be okay."

"How will it be okay? You heard the lawyer."

Tears cascaded down my sweaty face. I didn't try to stop them; I couldn't even if I wanted to. My dream was over. Maybe some-one was playing a cruel joke on me. Maybe it was a nightmare and I was going to wake up. I was shaking uncontrollably, oblivious to the nosey passers-by that stopped to glance at me. My world was spiraling and I had no idea how to make it stop.

"Mom, please stop," Ketandu pleaded, clutching my puffy face with both hands. "We will fight this. It's not over. We will get an-other lawyer, a woman this time. Women are more compassionate."

She pulled out her phone and started to browse the web. Time froze, it began to move in slow motion, and then it froze again as I stood watching Ketandu. I had always prided myself on being able to handle bad situations. I had been through a lot, and for each tribulation, I always knew what to do. For the first time in my life, I stared adversity in the face and I didn't have a clue about how to combat it.

"Look at this lawyer, Mom," Ketandu flipped her phone, showing me a picture. "She has kind eyes and she is pretty too. Let's call her. I like her."

We walked across the street to Thompson Centre and made our way to the basement, taking up an empty table in one of the cafes. Ketandu dialed the number and handed me the phone. The call was answered at the first ring.

"We can have you come in on Monday," a young paralegal said.

"No, I have to see the lawyer today. I'm not sure, I will be alive by Monday."

"I'm sorry, but she's fully booked for today."

She hung up. My hands shook violently as I called another lawyer. This lawyer asked me to send him pictures of the letter from immigration and he called back within minutes.

"I'm sorry but your case is complicated. I would advise you to try Canada. I will send you a link to Canadian immigration..."

"I'm not moving to Canada," I yelled. "This is where we belong. This is the only country my children have known for most of their lives."

I was delirious with grief. Was it truly over for us? The great schools, awards, piano lessons, and Mandarin practice? I watched as it all threatened to disintegrate and I was too helpless to stop it. I was slowly losing my mind. I tried to convince myself that it was a bad dream, that if I persevered long enough I would stop hallucinating.

Just as we began to search for another lawyer, my phone rang. It was the paralegal from the first call.

"Lisa can see you today at two."

"It's almost one o'clock, let's head out Mom," Ketandu suggested.

Two Dalmatians were stationed at the entrance of the law office, giving off an instant homely aura. Despite my morbid fear of dogs, I remained calm as they took turns sniffing me. For the first time, I wasn't scared of dogs. Having their sharp canines digging into my flesh seemed less torturous than my life that was fast crumbling before me. I almost willed them to bite me, to detract from the pain I was feeling in that moment. We were led down a short hallway to a conference room. Ketandu sat beside me, holding my right hand in a tight clasp. Apprehension grew with each tick of the silver clock above my head. Would she reject my case? Would she say there was nothing she could do for me, like the previous lawyers? My hand tightened around Ketandu's as these dark thoughts raced through my head. My eyes, swollen and fatigued with tears, roamed the tastefully furnished room. The mantelpiece in the corner held a photo of an elderly couple standing behind a German flag, a signal of an immigration story. Hope teased my soul for an instant, but I brushed it aside.

We waited for twenty minutes and a petite brunette dressed in a dark pantsuit walked in. She took the seat across from mine.

"Hello, my name is Lisa. How may I help you?" Her grey eyes, so warm and reassuring, bored into mine.

As I opened my mouth to speak, I burst into a loud sob. I heard a voice say to me, "Tell her about you. Tell her everything." So, I began from my childhood. I told her my story of rejection, isolation, despair, and loneliness. I told her about my failed marriage and having to flee to America to give my girls a better future. My tired body wracked with deep sobs as I exorcised my heart of the story of a lifetime. Every time I tried to stop, her kind eyes urged me to keep on speaking. Spent, the tears gradually subsided.

She looked down at the letter from Immigration on the polished table and said, "I will take your case." Hope teased me again.

"I grew up as a ward of the state. My life story is very similar to yours." Turning to Ketandu who was wiping my tears with her left hand, she said, "I can tell that not only do you love your mother, you like her too. What school do you attend?"

"Payton."

"And your sister?"

"We both go to Payton."

"That is a great school. The best in the city."

Turning back to me, Lisa said, "You've done well for yourself and your daughters. I will fight for you. I will give your case everything I have." As she got up to usher us out of the room she asked, "Do you have any questions?"

I had a question, one that plagued my mind since we walked in.

"How much would this cost me?" I asked, holding my breath as I waited on her answer. I knew it would cost several thousands, since the case was so complicated.

"It will cost you nothing."

I wasn't sure I heard her. Reaching for Ketandu's hand to steady my gait, I asked again.

"You heard me, Joy. I will represent you pro bono."

I started to sob again, this time wailing loudly.

"Stop crying. You have paid it forward. We have thirty days to submit a rebuttal. Now, go and find me all the documents I asked for."

I stumbled out of Lisa's office in as much shock as I was when I first got there, only this time, it was a different kind of shock. God had sent me an angel. I was not alone even if I felt otherwise. I saw a ray of light, a gleam of hope at the end of the long, winding gloomy tunnel.

We had a deadline of thirty days to come up with the rebuttal. The countdown began. First, I had to compile a list of thirty people who witnessed my abusive marriage and were willing to testify that Emeka's petition to immigration was born out of spite. I had to find documents and several pieces of evidence to buttress my case. It seemed like an impossible task to accomplish in thirty days. But I was going to try everything in my power to avoid deportation. My daughters' dreams were at stake. Everything I built in the past eleven years hung in this precarious balance.

As Ketandu and I headed north on the Red Line, the sky looked a little brighter. My shoulders felt a little lighter. I hugged my daughter and said, "I don't know what I would have done if you hadn't come with me."

"We will be okay, Mom. Everything will be fine."

I looked into the hopeful eyes of my 16-year-old, glad that I had listened when she said she would skip school and come with me.

The weekend was busy as I was preoccupied with contacting old friends. Regy, my neighbor from Nigeria was the first person I called. She had lived in the apartment above mine in Lagos.

"Gini? What?" she said over the phone. She had relocated to Texas from Nigeria and was now a U.S. citizen. "I was your neighbor. I saw everything you went through. If I have to fly down to Chicago to testify, I will. You and those precious girls are going nowhere."

Her warm voice vibrated through the phone, reassuring me that I had a fighting chance. I placed several calls to Nigeria asking people who knew Emeka and me as a couple to write affidavits for me. I called Cathcrine, another dear neighbor, and within the first weekend, I had harnessed a total of eleven witnesses. As my hope rose so did my worry about how the situation would impact the girls.

Ketandu was navigating college applications. She applied to intern in one of the prestigious government particle physics labs. She also had pending applications for the Bill Gates Scholarship, MOSTEC-a summer program at her dream school MIT; and the Jack Kent Cooke Scholarship, all of which required proof of residency. Amara was rounding off a successful sophomore year and coming up to junior year. I desperately prayed that they would keep focused. Every night, when I got home, I searched their eyes for signs of depression. I knew I had to present a hopeful demeanor for their sake. I didn't want them to give up. It would kill me to see that happen. They had come too far, and worked too hard.

We had scheduled a college tour for the upcoming spring break before all hell broke loose. As the break approached, we counted down to our road trip to the Ivy League Colleges and MIT. Our rental car and hotels across seven states on the east coast were fully booked.

"We have to cancel the tour," I announced.

"I guess we should," Amara said.

"We are not even sure of our fate here anymore," Ketandu added.

The following week, while I was at Lisa's office to drop off some documents, I mentioned that we canceled our college tour.

"Go on your tour."

"I don't even know. The girls and I decided to cancel."

"Nonsense. Go. It will help ease your mind. And when you get to New York, have a Pastrami."

I felt a rejuvenation with Lisa urging me not to cancel the trip. We had less than two weeks to submit our rebuttal to the Immigration services, but she was confident that I turned in most of what I needed for the case. And if she needed anything else, I was just a phone call and an email away. She had already interviewed most of my witnesses. I decided to heed Lisa's advice and embark on the trip.

One early spring morning just before the sun peeked through the clouds, we piled into a rented 2017 silver Camry and headed east. Ketandu sat beside me as I drove and Amara sat behind, her hand placed on the picnic bag filled with sandwiches and dried fruit. I glanced at the GPS as we hit the interstate, and it was a fifteen-hour drive to Massachusetts. We intended to visit the seven Ivy League colleges and MIT. Since MIT was Ketandu's top choice, we decided to start with Cambridge Massachusetts. We cruised down the quiet highway, stopping a couple of times for bathroom breaks and gas refills. Ten hours later, barely able to keep my exhausted eyes open, I handed the wheel to Ketandu. She had passed her road test and gotten her driver's license. We switched seats and she cruised down the busy New York state highway while I dozed beside her. As it got dark, I took over the driving, feeling energized enough to finish the last lap of the journey.

We arrived in Boston at 8 O'clock, bone-tired. I was grateful for the fifteen-hour hitch-free journey. We made straight for our hotel room, a nice suite with a double bed, falling into a deep slumber as our heads hit the pillow. It was a one-week journey and since we had seven states to visit, we intended to make the best use of our time. Early the next morning, we made our way to Harvard, wading past hundreds of tourists who looked and acted like pilgrims on holy land. We walked across the Harvard yard to take pictures with the statue of John Harvard, Ketandu holding on to the foot of the statue for good luck. MIT was down the road from Harvard, so we decided to leave the car and walk to MIT. Ketandu's eyes bulged out of their sockets as she gawked at the huge white pillars at the entrance of MIT. I thought about our immigration dilemma and my heart sank. Brushing the gloomy thought aside, I focused on the beauty of the school and how much it meant to my daughter. Thirty minutes later, we were on the road to Rhode Island to tour Brown University. Brown was a truly beautiful school situated in the small town of Providence. Time flew by as we went from Yale to Princeton, University of Pennsylvania, Columbia and Duke. Each school had a uniqueness that captured our hearts in different ways. I loved Harvard the most, not so much for its beauty but for its prestige. I grew up hearing about Harvard. Seeing how I gushed over Harvard, Ketandu reminded me again, "Mom, I will choose MIT over Harvard if I get accepted into both. You know that right?"

"We shall see my daughter. Let the will of God be done."

The beauty of Yale and the warmth of the tour guide blew me away. Ketandu was applying to all the schools, and I knew that even though she loved MIT, it was going to be a tough choice if she got into more than one.

We saved New York for last. Having been a Chicago taxi driver for many years, I was confident that I would find driving in New York easy. But nothing prepared me for the standstill traffic and the rude, impatient drivers. When we finally made it to the highway, I said to the girls, "Never again, will I try driving in this crazy city." Lisa's Pastrami had to wait. I would try it another time. If I knew what it looked like I would have lied and said that I tried it and loved it, but I didn't.

Rex Orange County's *Nothing* rattled the car speakers as we drove home to Chicago. It was a successful trip and one that took my mind away from the torture of the unknown. I was glad that Lisa convinced me to take the trip. The only school we could not visit was Cornell. It was one of Amara's top choices. We had to visit another time if we survived the immigration ordeal.

Dark clouds hovered over me as we approached the Indiana/ Chicago border. I dreaded returning home. I didn't want to face the battle that lay ahead. But I had no choice, face it I must. Lisa was putting the finishing touches to the rebuttal. Thankfully, she didn't need anything while we were gone, at least nothing that she couldn't access.

The morning after our return, I went to Lisa's office to sign the last documents. She was going to mail out the rebuttal that day. My heart pounded loudly as I stared at the wad of papers that lay on her desk. It was as thick as an encyclopedia. Were they really going to read all of this? I wondered. I watched Lisa as she placed the last paper on top of the pile. As I started to leave, Lisa approached me and held me in a tight hug. "We hope for the best, Joy."

"Yes," I whispered, holding back tears. "We hope for the best."

The only thing left to do was to wait and pray. Lisa didn't know how long it would take to hear back from Immigration Services. "It could take anything from four months to one year," she said.

We didn't have one year. Ketandu had all these applications that required proof of residency. The Bill Gates and Jack Kent Cooke scholarships were not due until later in the year. But her internship program at Fermilab and her summer program at MIT applications were due in a couple of weeks, and they both required her proof of residency. As the clock ticked, I hoped for a miracle. I didn't want her to miss out on some of the greatest opportunities of her lifetime. Working in Fermilab was a unique opportunity, one that didn't happen for most people. It was one of the biggest particle physics labs in the country and many students desired to intern with them. It was only a handful that was chosen each year. Ketandu was one of the lucky few.

Days flew by at the speed of light and the predicament that I feared most came upon me. The deadline for Ketandu's Green card submission to MIT arrived and the offer for the summer program was rescinded.

"This is the worst day of my life," Ketandu said, her voice heavy from crying.

She called MIT asking for an extension but it was declined.

"You can still apply to the school in October," said the woman on the phone, her kind voice assuring Ketandu that all hope was not lost. It was her seventeenth birthday and I silently chided the cruel fate that handed her such bad news on such a significant day.

"Dry your tears, Ki," I said to her. "You still have Fermilab for the summer."

"How, Mom? They need my green card or work permit. I have neither."

"Fermilab is not due for another two months. God will give us a miracle. He knows you deserve it."

"I don't want to raise my hopes, Mom."

I had never felt so helpless in my entire life. I was a grief-stricken mother, the one whose heart broke into a million tiny pieces as she watched her daughter's dreams crumble like a house of cards. In my desperation, I reached out to Lisa.

"Isn't there anything we can do to facilitate a work permit until we hear back from Immigration Services?' I pleaded. "My daughter has been dealt a devastating blow by the MIT program, I fear what the next one would do to her."

Lisa handed us a lifeline. She asked us to write the office of the Illinois Senator. She might be able to petition Immigration to expedite a work permit for Ketandu.

That weekend, Ketandu crafted an email to the office of the Illinois senator. She asked that the senator use her office to expedite her work permit from Immigration services. She wrote about her love for science and the rare opportunity to work as an intern at the prestigious government lab.

"It's a compelling letter," I said. "I believe with all my heart that she will write us back."

While I was at work a few days later, Ketandu called, her voice so animated that my passenger could hear her.

"Mom, she wrote back! The office of the senator wrote back! They said they will write Immigration for us."

I was thrilled with the good news. Even though it was a work permit, I was hopeful that she could at least have her dream summer job.

Ketandu and the office of the senator corresponded a few times and two weeks before the start of summer we received the work permit. It was truly a miracle. Normally, renewing work permits took anything between three and six months. But with the intervention of the senator's office, it took three weeks. It felt surreal to hear back from a senator, and most significantly to have her impact the desperate need of poor immigrants. This was more than I could ever imagine or expect of a Nigerian senator. I was once again filled with hope and love for this great country.

Weeks passed since Lisa turned in our rebuttal, and there was no word from Immigration. I tried to establish as much normalcy as I could muster for both me and the girls. Ketandu focused on her college applications and Amara found joy in her liberal arts classes. They continued to thrive in school despite the odds stacked against them. Watching them every day, and how hard they worked, fuelled my resolve to keep fighting. Every morning we woke up, was a day closer to the verdict from immigration.

It was a typically hot August evening, and the unrelenting sun scorched my face as I headed home on Lakeshore Drive. A large crowd littered North Avenue beach. Their tanned skins glistened under the blazing sun as they lay on huge beach towels soaking up the summer day. I suppressed the envy that knotted my insides as I watched them bask in the sun without a care in the world. I wondered if I would ever be this carefree again. The denial letter from Immigration had changed my life. I couldn't remember the last time I smiled. My apprehension intensified as Ketandu's application deadlines loomed closer. I pulled into the taxi parking lot and shutting my eyes for a brief second, I tried to think of what life would be like if we were denied the appeal to remain in the country. I refused to think of a plan B. An alternative plan meant I was accepting defeat. I hopped into my private car and drove slowly home, looking at the streets and the landmark buildings like I was seeing them for the last time. My heart ached.

"Dear Lord," I prayed. "This suspense is killing me. I don't know how much longer I can hold it together. If you're punishing me for something I did, let me bear this sorrow alone. Spare my children. Give them their green cards and withhold mine."

I found a good parking spot in front of my apartment building. This was a rare treat as Rogers Park was known for their parking space deficit. It felt like a ray of hope amid my many troubles. I walked to the mailbox, and yanking open the rusty squeaky box, my eyes fell on a white envelope with the Immigration Services emblem. My heart stopped and voluntarily restarted. Slowly, I retrieved the envelope from where it lay beneath a pile of bills and stared at it for a full minute. The future of my children lay in that envelope. Was it a yes or a no? I wondered. Leaving the rest of the envelopes behind, I locked the mailbox and raced upstairs, my heart racing in synchrony. I banged on the door of the apartment and Amara let me in, a confused frown creasing her thick eyebrows.

"Mom? Are you okay?" she asked, as she looked at my face dripping with sweat.

"I don't know if I'm fine. We have received the verdict from Immigration."

She took the envelope from my hand and passed it to her sister. Ketandu was always the strong one. But she had the most at stake with this letter and I wondered if it was wise to let her open it. My hands trembled violently and my heart raced wildly. I feared I would have a stroke.

"It's okay, Mom. I will open it," Ketandu said.

I walked over to Amara and held her tightly as Ketandu began the task of opening the letter that would change our lives forever. Time froze, catapulted, and froze again. Slowly, she ripped the envelope open and unfolded its contents. My eyes watched her expression. I would first know of the outcome from her demeanor. Her face remained blank as her eyes darted across the letter and all of a sudden she blurted out: "Notice of Approval."

I thought I didn't hear her the first time, so I asked, "What did you say?"

"Notice of approval, Mom. It says Notice of Approval."

We looked at one another and burst into tears. "Is it over? Is the storm truly over?" I asked no one in particular. I felt nothing in the beginning, I was numb. The tears flowed freely and there was no way to stop them. Ketandu held my face in her hands as she did on that Friday morning when the first lawyer practically threw us out of his office.

Wiping my tears and hers intermittently, she said, "It's over, Mom. I told you it was going to be okay."

"Let's call Lisa just to be sure," I said. We huddled over my phone as I dialed Lisa's cell phone number.

"Take a picture of the letter and send it to me immediately," Lisa instructed.

Grabbing my phone, Amara took a blurry picture of the letter. It didn't matter that it was not clear as long as Lisa could read it. We waited with bated breath for Lisa to interpret the words of the letter and call us back. Three minutes later my phone rang.

"That's it, Joy! We've overcome the Notice of Intent to Deny. Your green cards have been approved."

Delirious with jubilation, we screamed and cried and danced and sang. I was scared my neighbors would call the police but if they did, it would have been alright. We were no longer illegal immigrants; we had as much right as anyone else in America.

For the first time in ten years, my head hit the pillow and I didn't open my eyes until morning.

Three weeks later, on Emeka's birthday, my Green Card arrived – indeed, God has a sense of humor. It was also coincidentally the day we arrived in the United States of America, eleven years earlier. The girls and I huddled over the envelope as I ripped it open. This time I didn't need Ketandu. I held the green card in my hands watching with fascination at how my name glowed in the light.

"It's not even green, so why do they call it a green card?" Amara asked.

"I wonder," I replied, chuckling at her question.

Ketandu and Amara's green cards didn't come with mine. I was worried Ketandu might miss some of her college application deadlines. The application deadline for the Bill Gates scholarship was a few weeks away. We expressed our concerns to Lisa and she came up with a plan to have Ketandu's teachers write recommendation letters which Lisa forwarded to Immigration Services. Two weeks later they were called for interviews. It was an informal interview.

The interviewer was nice and assured them that it was just protocol. He asked them about school and how their names were pronounced.

Their green cards arrived ten days later, on the due date for the Bill Gates scholarship application. I got home, retrieved the green cards from the mailbox, handed Ketandu hers and she went straight to her laptop and completed the Bill Gates Scholarship application. It was due that night at 11:59 p.m.

The next on the queue was Questbridge- a foundation through which Ketandu had applied for some colleges. It was the information my taxi customer had given me many months earlier: the older lady that I had brought to tears with my stories of allegiance to the United States. Ketandu applied like the old lady told us to. She had made MIT her first choice and Princeton her second. One cold December afternoon, Ketandu called my phone, frantic. "Mom, Questbridge is out. Hurry! Let's open it."

It was a busy afternoon and I was getting ready to take my customers, Mr. and Mrs. Allen, home to the suburbs. They were old faithfuls who had retained my services for many months. Since it was an important moment for my daughter, one that I wouldn't miss for anything in the world, I asked my customers to give me about half an hour.

Ketandu and Amara got into the back seat of my taxi as I pulled up to their school entrance. Ketandu flipped open her laptop. We had become masters at opening tension-laden mail. The car fell silent as we nervously waited for the message to load.

"Are you ready?" Ketandu asked.

"Yes, take a deep breath," I said.

I watched her face intently as she hit the button on the laptop.

"I didn't match with MIT," she said. We groaned, disappointed. "But guys...wait," she said. "I matched with Princeton!"

"Oh my God! Princeton!" We screamed and jumped, the car bouncing up and down to the rhythm of our movement.

Later that evening, I asked her if she was disappointed that she didn't match with her dream school. "No, Mom. Princeton is a great school. Besides I'm still in the pool of MIT applications for the regular decision in March."

Whatever the outcome would be come March, she already got into a great Ivy League. We had to wait to find out how she fared with the other colleges.

Ivy Day as it's popularly called, rolled around quickly. It was a tension-filled day for many students across the world. That day sealed the fate of the hundreds of thousands of students who were vying for spots in Ivy League schools. I hurried home that evening, nervous for my daughter. I was still hoping she would land offers from Harvard and MIT. We huddled in front of Ketandu's computer as we always did. It was late March and less than a month to her 18th birthday.

"Can I video you opening your decision letters?" I asked, nervously.

"I guess," she said. I was even more nervous than she was. "So, which one should we open first?" she asked.

"I think you should open MIT last," Amara suggested.

"I will start with Yale."

She clicked the Yale decision button and an image of confetti and balloons exploded.

"Bulldogs, bulldogs, bow wow wow Eli Yale! Welcome to Yale class of 2023."

"Congratulations!" Amara and I chanted, applauding.

"Two down, two to go," I said.

Next was Harvard. I was particularly nervous about Harvard as it was my dream school for her. I clenched my fists and paced the floors of the small living room as she got ready to open the Harvard decision.

"Stop pacing, woman," she chided playfully. "Now you're making me nervous."

"Okay, okay." I readied myself.

Inhaling loudly, she turned her face from the screen and clicked the button. Time froze.. She looked at the screen out of the corner of her eyes. I held onto Amara's arm for support.

"I got into Harvard!"

"Oh my God! Oh my God! Oh my God!" Screams and laughter erupted throughout the room. She jumped up and leaped into my arms. We laughed and cried.

"*Harvardi Harvardi Harvardii*," I sang, dancing around in a circle.

Next was the most important – MIT. Her voice quivered a little as she gave herself a final pep talk.

"Whatever the decision, I want you to know that I'm extremely proud of you. And if it is a no, remember this does not define you." Amara said as she continued to film the event.

"Yes, I agree," I said. "You already got into Yale, Princeton, and Harvard so we have three great schools at this point." Still, I desperately hoped MIT would be a yes. She had worked very hard. She deserved the school of her choice.

"Take a deep breath and go for it," Amara said. She inhaled a generous amount of air and clicked the button, apprehension filling the air as we waited for the screen to respond.

"I got into MIT!"

"Yes, yes, yes!" Tears streamed down my face. At this point, I was already numb from the several cycles of apprehension and euphoria. Ketandu grabbed her phone and started to make a call.

"Who are you calling?" I asked.

"Irene."

"Hello, Irene. I got into MIT and Harvard and Princeton and Yale,"

"That's my girl… That's my girl…" Irene said over and over. She was more than a piano teacher. She was a second mother to them. I thought about the fact that we didn't have that many people to celebrate with. This was a huge moment in our lives, a time when we should be calling close family. But I couldn't think of one close family member who would genuinely or even be remotely interested in sharing this very special moment with us. I brushed aside the tinge of sadness and focused on the joyous event before us. It was coming together so beautifully. From being at risk of leaving the country, Ketandu had gotten into the top schools in the U.S. all on a full ride.

Exactly one week later, we crowded around Ketandu's laptop to open the Stanford decision.

"It's honestly okay if I don't get in."

"Yes. You shouldn't care too much.'

"Stanford is a great school."

"How many will you attend?"

She navigated to the Stanford website while her sister videoed her.

"Guys, I got in!"

"Of course, you got in! Five out of five. Thank you, Jesus," I cried. Celebration erupted in the room once again followed by hugs and high fives. The college admission process had come to a climax.

Three weeks later, she heard back from the Bill Gates Scholarship foundation - she had been offered the scholarship. This was followed by the scholarship award from the Jack Kent Cooke Foundation. The floodgates of success were wide open in our favor.

Ketandu spent the following weeks traveling to each of those schools. "I want to be sure that MIT is where I really want to go."

"But you know it's where you want to go. You refused to attend Harvard for me," I teased.

When she returned from the tour of the five schools, she began to talk more fondly about Stanford.

"I'm confused, Mom. I love MIT, but I really like Stanford too. The weather is great and it's really beautiful."

"MIT is your first love. Focus on it."

I watched as she struggled to decline the other schools and I said to Amara, "Who says no to Harvard, Princeton, Yale, and Stanford?" It broke her heart to turn down all those great schools that had all offered her a full ride and other equally wonderful perks. I decided that when it came to Amara's turn, we wouldn't apply to as many schools. Declining offers from all these great schools was excruciatingly painful.

Amara began her college admission process in her junior year. She knew she had big shoes to fill and the thought terrified her. Even though her interests were vastly different from Ketandu's, I could tell she was worried about underperforming in the wake of her overachieving big sister. In the second semester of her junior year, she was nominated by the faculty for the Junior Book Award. It was an award Ketandu had also won in her junior year. I was glad that she won this award as it gave her the much-needed bounce in her step. She was a gifted writer and was now the captain of the school's Slam Poetry group, Louder Than A Bomb. She performed in various competitions across the city. She was also the president of the Black Students' Union, a position she held with utmost pride. Over the years she had developed a strong interest in social justice. It was now clear that she was going to pursue an education in the liberal arts.

Anxiety overwhelmed her as deadlines approached for college essays and the American College Testing (ACT). She underperformed in her initial trial, and we both knew that she had to raise her scores if she was to stand a chance at getting into the top colleges of her choice.

"You can do this," I said. "All you need is three more points and you're all set." Sometimes when I felt the pleading wasn't doing the trick I yelled. "You better raise your ACT score if you don't want to find yourself in community college with me."

"You can do this. Don't worry about your sister's success. You have what it takes too. You got into Disney Gifted and Walter Payton. You are still the same person right?"

The distant look in her eyes was a reflection of the imposter syndrome that afflicted her. My heart broke for her, but still, I did not relent. She was just as smart as her sister, and I wasn't going to let anything intimidate her or stop her from being the best version of herself.

She needed to raise her science grade in the ACT. We bought additional ACT prep books and she focused on the science section. I could not afford a tutor, so we had to buckle down at home. One month later, she sat for the ACT again and raised her science score by the much-needed three points.

"Good job," I chimed. "You only had to believe in yourself."

We agreed that she would apply to two top liberal arts schools and two Ivy League schools. She applied to Williams College, Pomona, Cornell, and Columbia. There were tons of essays to be written and deadlines to be met. Ketandu called most nights to look through her essays and offer tips. One night, in the middle of writing an essay, she started to vomit. I heard the retching sound and rushed to the bathroom to find her doubled over the toilet bowl.

"I feel terrible, Mom. I don't think I can do this. My head hurts."

I felt her forehead and it was slightly warm. She had a history of vertigo. It happened sporadically. But I knew that this episode was triggered by the pressure she was under. I gave her Tylenol and sent her to bed. The next morning I had a heart-to-heart talk with her.

"It won't matter that much to me if you don't get into an Ivy League or top liberal arts college. I will always love you and will still be proud of you even if you end up at the University of Illinois."

Her face lit up. "I just want to make you proud, Mom."

"I'm proud of you already, you just don't know how much."

I resolved to stand back and not breathe down her neck anymore. She completed her essays in time for her deadlines. Her applications were completed. We only had to wait to hear back from the schools.

In February, barely three weeks after the completion of her application, she received a letter from Cornell. "Open it quickly," I said. "Let's see what they want."

"This is to inform you that you will be receiving an offer of admission into Cornell..."

She gasped in surprise. "Wow! A likely from Cornell? Oh, happy day."

I got on my phone and called Ketandu, "Your sister just got a likely from Cornell."

"This is great news, Mom!"

By the middle of March, we heard back from the other schools. She was accepted into Williams and Pomona both on a full ride. On Ivy day, we got the formal letter of acceptance from Cornell with a full-ride scholarship, and she was waitlisted for Columbia. Even though she loved both Williams and Pomona and they were the two topmost liberal arts colleges in the country, she knew Cornell was her home.

My work with the girls was done. I could put up my feet and pat myself on the back. Now, in my final semester of nursing school,

I sit in my living room listening to the crackle from the fireplace, and reflecting on the various twists and turns to my life. While I have accepted the fate that I will never have the love of my parents, I glory in the gift of my daughters and all the wonderful people that have graced my life. I celebrate my journey and the roadblocks I overcame at every juncture. And I raise my glass in honor of that Biafran bastard, rejected and scorned at every turn, who has evolved into a Biafran Diamond.

Blurb / About

Born on the denouement of the Nigerian Civil War, Joy Iweka was about 5 years old when she first realized she was different from other children. Growing up in Obosi, a small town in eastern Nigeria, her grandparents were the only parental figures she had, but their presence and love couldn't fill the deep void created by the absence of a mother and an unknown father.

Her quest to find happiness is punctuated by the series of harrowing events she encounters on her way to becoming a teenager and eventually an adult.

After the failed attempt to create the loving home she dreamed of as a child, Joy gets a break from the hardship in Nigeria to live the American Dream with her two children. This shift marks the beginning of another tumultuous experience that leaves her wondering if she would ever unveil that elusive joy.

About the Author

Joy Nnenne Iweka is a parent coach, child advocate, and a registered nurse. In this memoir, she chronicles the first fifty years of her life- the ups, the downs and everything in between.

She lives and works in Chicago, as she moves into a new phase of life as an empty nester. With both children in college, she is currently focused on her career as a nurse. She enjoys watching soccer, reading other memoirs and coaching parents of gifted children.

Joy Iweka can be contacted via the following ways:

Email:
unveilingjoy71@gmail.com

FB: https://www.facebook.com/joy.iwekachiedu
IG @jnnenne

Photos

At the Walgreens Expression Challenge

The girls with their Mandarin speech gold medals

At Harvard for the college tour

At Yale for the College tour

Ketandu's Junior book club award ceremony

AMARA'S JUNIOR BOOK CLUB AWARD

At age 1

Andrea and I at Federal School of Arts and
Sciences, Victoria Island, Lagos.

ME IN MY ROOM AT THE UNIVERSITY OF JOS

KETANDU BONDING WITH HER NEW BORN BABY SISTER
AFTER I BROUGHT HER HOME FROM THE HOSPITAL

277

THE GIRLS AT OUR APARTMENT IN DOLPHIN ESTATE

SUSAN AND I AT QUEENS

WHITE WEDDING AT LAGOS

Traditional wedding at Obosi

Traditional wedding at Obosi

Amara's classical music award

THE GIRLS AT THE STUDIO RECORDING SOME OF THEIR CLASSICAL PIECES

A CUSTOMER ASKED FOR A PICTURE AFTER I DROPPED
HER OFF AT A HOTEL DOWNTOWN CHICAGO

March 28, 2019

HARVARD COLLEGE
Admissions & Financial Aid

Dear Ketandu,

Congratulations! I am delighted to inform you that the Committee on Admissions has admitted you to the Harvard College Class of 2023.

Our admissions committee considers each application with great care, voting

IT Admissions

ar Ketandu,

behalf of the Admissions Committee, it is
· pleasure to offer you admission to the MIT
ass of 2023! You stood out as one of the
st talented and promising students in one
the most competitive applicant pools in the
tory of the Institute. Your commitment to
·sonal excellence and principled goals has
·vinced us you will both contribute to our
·erse community and thrive within our
idemic environment. We think that you and

March 29, 2019

Download PDF

Stanford University

Ketandu Deborah Chiedu
Stanford ID: 06377528

Dear Ketandu,

Congratulations! You have
been admitted to the
Stanford Class of 2023!

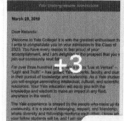

KETANDU'S ADMISSION TO HARVARD

COLLEGE TIME

COLLEGE TIME

SUPERVISING KETANDU DOING HER HOMEWORK

GRADUATION FROM NURSING SCHOOL

Made in the USA
Middletown, DE
23 October 2022

13327670R00182